NATURAL RESOURCES AND SOCIAL CONFLICTS IN THE SAHEL

Proceedings of the 5th Sahel Workshop

4-6 January 1993

EDITORS

LEON BRIMER, LARS KROGH AND MARLENE MEYER

Natural Resources and Social Conflicts in the Sahel
Proceedings of the 5th Sahel Workshop 4-6 January 1993
Edited by L. Brimer, L. Krogh and M. Meyer

Editorial address and exchange request:
Leon Brimer
Institute of Pharmacology and Pathobiology
Bülowsvej 13
DK- 1870 Frederikberg C
Denmark

Distributed and sold by
Aarhus University Press
Aarhus University
DK- 8000 Aahus C
Denmark

Montage and layout: Kjell Erik Hansen
English proof-reading: Louise Tyler
French proof-reading: Dominique Otoul
Printed in 250 copies
Printed at Aarhus University Centre

Cover photo: Leon Brimer; inserted photos: Jacques Vassal

Copying of articles is permitted for educational use, if reference is made for the origin.

ISBN 87-984671-0-7

Contents

Editors

Leon Brimer, M. Sc., Ph.D. Born in 1949, he obtained his M.Sc. in pharmacy 1978 from the Royal Danish School of Pharmacy, Copenhagen, the study period including a one year scholarship at the Department of Biochemistry. He received his Ph.D. pharm. (in phytochemistry/pharmacognosy) in 1986 from the same institution. From 1981-84 he was an Assistant Professor at Department of Pharmacognosy, Royal Danish School of Pharmacy, and from 1984-88 Associate Prof. at the same department. Invited guest lecturer at the Danish Bilharziasis Laboratory (WHO Collaborating Centre) 1988-89. Associate Prof. at the Department of Pharmacology and Pathobiology, Section of Pharmacology and Toxicology, the Royal Veterinary & Agricultural University, Copenhagen, from 1989. Research within medicinal and toxic constituents in plants, with special emphasis on cyanogenic toxins in cassava (*Manihot esculenta*) and Acacia species.

Marlene Meyer; M.Sc. (Geography). Born in 1963, she studied Agricultural Geography and Remote Sensing at the Institute of Geography, University of Copenhagen where she obtained her M.Sc. in 1990. She worked as a research assistant at the Institute of Plant Ecology, University of Copenhagen until 1991, and returned then to the Institute of Geography as research fellow. Presently she is working on her Ph.D. project, which is funded by the Danish Counsil of Development Research (DANIDA).

Lars Krogh, M.Sc. Born in 1961, he studied Soil Science at the Institute of Geography, University of Copenhagen where he graduated in 1990. He obtained a Ph.D. research grant from Danish Council of Development Research, studying nutrient cycling and soil degradation in northern Burkina Faso.

Introduction

This volume presents papers and abstracts read at the 5th Sahel Workshop held at Sandbjerg Manor, Denmark, 4-6 January 1993.

Topics discussed at the workshop were divided into three major groups: social conflicts, management of natural resources and food-and cashcrop production.

The opinions expressed in the proceedings are those of the authors. The workshop and informal sessions provided an opportunity for participants to exchange ideas and experiences, and set a stage for future dialogue and cooperation.

The organisers wish to express their thanks to the Danish Ministry of Foreign Affairs, Department af International Development Cooperation (DANIDA), who financed the workshop (Journal no. 104. Sahel 5), to Danish Red Cross Society who provided facilities for our secretary and was helpful with fax and mailing etc., and further to acknowledge the most valuable help received from Kristine Juul, Tove Degnbol and Christian Lund, all from Roskilde University Centre, Denmark.

Copenhagen, April 1993

Leon Brimer, Lars Krogh and Marlene Meyer

The Tuareg conflict in Mali

Gunnvor Berge
Centre for Environment and Development
University of Oslo, Norway

Introduction

The Tuareg rebellion in Mali, or "le probleme du nord" as it is euphemistically called in the country itself, is one of the less known of the conflicts on the African continent. The level of conflict and the scale of human misery are undoubtedly greater in countries like Liberia, Somalia or Sudan. One should note, however, that those conflicts were once small and limited. The fear of an escalation and a resulting "Libanisation, Liberianisation ou Somalisation" (Les Echos no. 208, 9. Nov. 1992:1) is keenly felt in Mali.

The Tuareg rebellion is not limited to Mali. For one thing, the fighting has led many Malian Tuaregs to flee to neighbouring countries, mainly to Mauritania, Algeria and Burkina Faso. The official Malian number of Tuareg refugees is now 100.000 (Les Echos no. 209, 13.11.92:6), whereas unofficial numbers are more than the double of this. Second, Tuaregs in Niger are also rebelling against the Nigerien government. These two rebellions are closely related, but as my work experience with Tuaregs is tied to Mali, my knowledge of the conflict in Mali is much more profound than is the case concerning Niger.

There are four points, or issues, that I am going to elaborate upon in this presentation.

1. The causes of the rebellion are to be found partly in events and processes that date far back in time, and in part more recent and current events. Which causes do I see as the central ones? How do these explain aspects of the rebellion itself?

2. The development of the rebellion has taken different courses in different areas. My contention is that these different courses in part may

be understood taking the resource base and the ways of life tied to the use of resources into consideration.

3. The Tuareg rebellion does not occur in a vacuum. Though many of the causes of the rebellion are local, it is necessary to stress the importance of such processes as the democratization process in Mali and Niger, the breakdown of established borders and the reunion of peoples who have been divided by such borders, and scores of violent conflicts. Such processes, at present, take place in other countries of the Sahel belt as well as in Europe.

4. A peace treaty was signed between the Tuareg rebels and the Malian government in April 1992. The peace treaty opens for some sort of particular status for Mali's 3 northern regions, an area the Tuaregs refer to as Azawad. To what extent can the Declaration on the Rights of Indigenous Peoples suggest solutions to problems faced by other minorities within the framework of a modern nation-state?

The presentation will elaborate on each of these four issues in turn.

Central developements to take into consideration when understanding the rebellion

Different processes caused the Tuareg rebellion to break out in May/June 1990. Some of these processes have roots that date far back in time, to before colonization. Other processes are related to the changes that have taken place in this century, whereas others again are related to current developments. In this first point I address the following questions; Why do the Tuaregs rebel against the central governments of Mali and Niger? Who are the rebels? Why did the rebellion break out in 1990? And finally; why did Tuaregs from the Adrar des Ifoghas play such a central role in the first phase of the rebellion?

a) Why do the Tuaregs rebel against the central government of Mali?

The Tuaregs, or the Kel Tamasheq as they call themselves, are a berber speaking population, of red as well as black skin colour. It is extremely difficult to assess the actual number of Tuaregs. Whereas my estimate would be somewhere between 1- 2 millions, I have seen figures as high as 3 millions (Attayoub 1992). For a number of centuries the Tuaregs have adapted to desert life, living concentrated mainly in mountainous massifs on both sides of the Sahara, as well as in certain areas around the Niger river. Most, maybe 1 million, live in Niger, whereas about half a million live in Mali[1].

At the time of colonization, the Tuaregs had a strong identity tied to being pastoral nomads. They kept a diversity of animals. If the different kinds of animals were to be optimally herded, quite a lot of labour was needed. The Tuaregs achieved this through rather large camps, where families with different occupations were living together. The families living together in a camp were also hierarchically divided; a main division went between nobles and others of free status, such as vassals and artisans, and slaves. Free families belonged to *tiwsatin (sing. tawsit)* or descent groups, that were made up of families from many different camps. The free were mostly red-skinned, the slaves mostly black. The slaves did most of the heavy manual work such as watering and herding animals, moving camps, and gathering wild plants. The slaves' movements were, like those of women, more geographically restricted than those of noble men. Besides taking decisions concerning the movements of the camp, noble men travelled over long distances, took part in caravans, and protected or plundered trading parties crossing the Sahara. They also raided neighbouring groups, Tuaregs as well as others, in order to get animals or slaves, and equally protected their camps against the raids of other Tuareg groups. Thus, the Tuaregs traditionally exploited resources both close and distant in space, through a socially stratified and occupationally divided social organization. They also acquired resources they did not produce themselves by trading with, at times through dominating, Songhay agriculturalists living along the Niger river and the big lakes to the west.

The Tuareg find that their traditional way of life has been profoundly changed with the developments of this last century. When the French defeated the Tuareg around 1917, the vast Tuareg home area, because of internal strife within the French camp, became attached to different French administrative units. The borders drawn then are still in force. At independence around 1960, the Tuareg found themselves divided between five different countries; Niger, Mali, Burkina Faso, Algeria and Libya. For one thing, the borders have limited the free movements of

---

1) *From the last Malian census of 1987 (BCR 1990), we have calculated that there are 398 000 Tuaregs in Mali today, if we suppose that Tuaregs have the same fertility rate as other ethnic groups, given a population growth of 2% annually. It is clear that this number is an underestimation of the actual number of Tuaregs in Mali. But it is also difficult to believe that the actual number is much higher than around 500,000.*

Tuaregs and their camps in their search for water and pasture. Another result of the borders is that trade, another important activity for Tuaregs, and in particular for another nomadic group in the area, the Arabs, easily becomes smuggling in the eyes of the governments.

Yet another important change is the abolishment of slavery by the French in 1905. Even though the slaves of Northern Mali were slow to take advantage of their freedom, most had left their former masters between the 2. world war and independence (Winter 1984).

Also, throughout the century, the important trans-saharan trade controlled by Tuaregs has dwindled away. Boats following the coast, airplanes and lorries have taken the place of camels. Animal raiding has become illegal, and the state has been strong enough to enforce the prohibition. Whereas nomads and agriculturalists have had complex relationships with alternating domination and subordination around the Niger river, the nomads were the strongest at the time of colonization. Colonization blunted the nomads ability to exercise power over agriculturalists.

Looking at this list of changes — difficulties with pastoral nomadism related to borders, trade becoming smuggling, the downfall of caravans, raids prohibited, slavery prohibited, no right to dominate agriculturalists through force — it is easy to see that the group who has lost most of its obligations, as well as its prestige and power, is the former free nobles, the *imoushar* warriors. The rapid changes have left many nobles in a void.

Then Mali became independent from France in 1960. Many Tuaregs never saw independence as anything but a new colonization ("Nous, Touaregs", printed i.e. in IWGIA Newsletter no. 62 1990:135), this time by black sedentary peoples from the south instead of whites from the north. Tuaregs now found themselves subordinate to people they had formerly fought and raided. Some had hoped for an independent saharan Tuareg state, and steps to this effect were taken by the French in 1957 (the creation of OCRS (l'Organisation Commune des Regions Sahariennes), but de Gaulle went against the plan in 1958 (Dayak 1992:62).

In 1962-64, Tuaregs rebelled against the new Malian government. The rebellion was led by a noble from the Ifoghas *tawsit* in Adrar des Ifoghas, and the rebellion never spread outside this area. Mali's government reacted by a vigorous repression of the civil population. Central Tuareg leaders who fled to Algeria, were subsequently extradited to Mali. In Mali some were executed, others imprisoned.

The years prior to and right after independence were years with high rainfall and abundant pasture. Even with all the changes that had taken place since colonization, the nomads did not at that time experience the full effect of having their resource base basically reduced to pastoral nomadism. It is difficult to argue that questions related to resources played any important role in the 1962-64 uprising in Adrar.

Then the droughts hit the Sahel. The first serious drought since independence lasted from 1967-1973, the second from 1984-1986. Whereas I see most of the changes that have affected the Tuaregs' possibilities to survive in Azawad as related to general developments and processes instigated by colonization, many Tuaregs, however, now feel that the Malian government, rather than France, is the main cause of their troubles. In part this feeling can be explained by the good years when the French ended their rule, and the terrible years brought by the droughts. The feeling may also be understood in light of how the Malian government handled the droughts. It is a fact that even during some of the worst crisis years, Mali was a net exporter of grain. Such a fact can be understood in national economic terms, but not by those starving. Also, much of the international help destined for the nomads never reached them. Whereas corruption is a serious problem also in the south, the Tuaregs interpret misappropriation of funds within an ethnic paradigm. It is not uncommon to hear Tuaregs accuse the Malian government of having used the drought to try to fulfill a wish; the eradication of nomads altogether. Whether the government actually did so or not is irrelevant here; the point is that Tuaregs think so.

The droughts led to massive migration to neighbouring countries. Through this labour migration Tuaregs were again adding resources from outside Azawad to their livelihood. Economic support by the migrants seems to have allowed some nomads to keep on being pastoralists (Bernus 1991).

To sum up. Colonization, a strong geographic reduction in the resource base upon which the Tuaregs based their living, a breakdown of their traditional social hierarchy and traditional way to exploit resources, a change in the power imbalance between nomads and agriculturalists in favour of the agriculturalists, an independence that most Tuaregs felt was not for them, a new government issued from black southern agriculturalists, serious droughts, corruption and misappropriation of funds during the droughts, Tuaregs seeing the Malian government as the cause of their misfortune, and mass migration caused by the droughts draw the contours of the Tuareg situation around 1990.

b) Who are the Tuareg rebels?

Many of those who migrated never found work, and became the socalled *ishomar* — or unemployed — in Algeria and Libya. A central point in relation to the *ishomar* is that they base their identity on being victims of ecological, political and economic circumstances over which they have no influence, and that they have no higher education. In exile they are marginal. In the Tuareg society, however, they are central, in the sense that they are men from central noble *tiwsatin*, the leaders of tomorrow. Many young *ishomar* recruited themselves or were forced into Kadhafi's Islamic Legion in Libya. As far as I know, an overwhelming majority of Tuaregs that received military training belong to the traditional free groups of society, whereas only very few former slaves went through military training and later joined the rebellion. To become warriors was also an identity more easily combined with their origins than heavy manual work. In the legion they received excellent training in desert war, as well as actual practice in places like Chad, Lebanon and Iraq.

Thus, with their violent oppression of the first rebellion and their careless handling of the droughts, the Malian government laid the foundation for today's rebellion. In Libya, in the beginning of the 1980s, young exile Tuaregs started an illegal organization with three slogans; *"one country, one religion, one people/one identity"* (Bourgeot 1990:147). Their ultimate goal was to create a free Tuareg state. This embryo developed into today's rebel movement.

In the western part of the Tuareg territory, it appears that many Tuaregs left for Western Sahara where they trained and fought with Polisario.

I mentioned that the Tuaregs, in addition to having a social hierarchy tied to occupations, were organized in *tiwsatin*. Whereas the camps belonging to a *tawsit* is usually spread over quite a big area, Tuaregs are still able to localize a *tawsit's* home range. The official rhetoric of the rebels is that the *tiwsatin* belong in history. They see but disadvantages in the divisions between Tuaregs that tiwsatin draw, and try to create new and common identity markers for all Tuaregs. However, as the rebellion has developed, different groups of rebels have created different rebel organizations. These coincide to a large extent with *tiwsatin, both*

in the recruitment of members, and as to where they operate. (See also
Dayak 1992:40 on this point.)

To repeat, those who started the rebellion were nobles forced into exile,
young men central in terms of Tuareg identity but marginal in the
context of exile. Moreover, they had little other schooling, and were
skeptical to those that did. The schism that has been ever present in the
Tuareg rebellion between "les combattants" — rebels with weapons —
and the intellectuals — rebels without weapons — originated before the
rebellion even broke out.

Acronym	Name	Leader	Fraction	Place
MPA*	Mouvement Populaire de l'Azawad	Iyad Ag Ghali	Ifoghas	Boughessa in Kidal
ARLA*	Armée Révolutionnaire pour la Libération de l'Azawad	Abderhamen Gala		Tegargart in Kidal
FPLA	Front Populaire de Libération de l'Azawad	1. Rhissa Ag Sidi Mohamed 2. Moussa Jikode (Blaise Compaoré)	Chamenamas	Taïkarène, Tawarde in Menaka
FIAA*	Front Islamique Arabe de l'Azawad	Boubacar Sadeck Ould Mouhamoud	Maure	Tinidimane in Timbuctu
	Le groupe armé de Zigui	Zigui	Kel Antessar	Near Mauriania
	Le groupe armé de Timitré	Timitré	Idnan	Near Mauritania
	Le groupe armé de Halbaboti	Halbaboti		Tidamene near Niger
	Le groupe armé de Izilili	Izilili		Azawak Valley in Menaka

Source: Les Echos special no. 208, 9.11.1992:6-7

Organizations marked with * have united in MFUA (Movements et Fronts Unifies
de l'Azawad), the rebel movements that have signed the peace treaty.

c) Why did the rebellion break out in 1990?

A group of *ishomar* made its first attack as early as in 1985, but found that the time was not ripe to start a rebellion. The expulsion of many thousand drought refugees from Algeria and Libya in the following years changed this.

The armed rebellion started in Niger. In January 1990, Algeria decided to expel between 20,000 and 25 000 Tuaregs who had arrived as refugees during the droughts. Whether they were Malians or Nigeriens was unclear, but in the spring of 1990 about 18 000 Tuaregs were returned to Niger (Africa Research Bulletin 15. June 1990, L'Express 29. June 1990). They found little to accommodate them. Tents and other equipment given by UN and other international donors to ease their return were instead sold at markets, for instance in the capital Niamey.

The stories around the incident at the prison in Tchin Tibaraden 7. May 1990, where some Tuaregs were imprisoned, are many and diverse. Tuaregs attacked, or were provoked into attacking, some guards. It seems, however, not at all to have been a well planned attack if an attack at all, and the Tuaregs were without modern weapons. Nevertheless, the government of Niger reacted by sending elite troops armed with heavy machine guns and armoured vehicles to the area. Officially, between 31 and 70 Tuaregs were killed at Tchin Tibaraden, in the first of several massacres. Some Nigerien Tuaregs escaped to Mali, where they were imprisoned at Menaka. This lead to the first Tuareg attack in Mali 28-29. June 1990.

This attack was well planned, and was led by a young noble *ashamor* of the leading (Ifoghas) *tawsit* from Adrar des Ifoghas, with years of military training in Libya behind him. The attack closely resembles almost all attacks by rebels to this day. The attacks have mostly been directed against administrative or military units, in order to kill or scare southern representatives of the Malian state to the south, and to acquire weapons, cars, food and other necessary equipment. The rebels attack when the enemy is least expecting it, they do not to take unnecessary risks, and see no point in losing or spending lives for no reason. While some people disagree on this point (see Dayak 1992), I see the form and structure of the rebel attacks to resemble Tuareg animal raids, as well as modern guerilla warfare.

The Malian army's answer to the rebel strategy has been to retaliate by spreading terror among and killing civilians. There has been no real battles between the Malian army and the rebels.

The distribution of Tuaregs

Source: Aghali-Zakara 1986:15

d) Finally; why did nobles from Adrar des Ifoghas play such a leading role in the first phase of the rebellion?

From the first attack on, Tuaregs from Adrar des Ifoghas have played a leading role in the rebellion. The reasons for this are manifold. For one thing, the first Tuareg rebellion took place in this area. Ever since, the Adrar des Ifoghas area has been under military rule. The brutal way the uprising was quelled, as well as the strong military presence in Adrar des Ifoghas ever since, has kept a hatred towards military southerners particularly alive here. Geographically the area lies close to Algeria and Libya. Almost all trade, as well as labour migration, goes to the north. This has, of course, led to strong colonies of *ishumar* from Adrar in these two countries. It has also lead to a strong resentment towards the fact that people from the south, with whom the Kel Adrar has no positive ties, rule them.

Another reason may be the present marginality of Adrar, even within the Malian Tuareg home area. In former centuries, the caravan route through Adrar des Ifoghas made this desert area central, and a major market town was formerly situated here. Besides the fact that caravans are scarce nowadays, Adrar des Ifoghas has also been marginalized through the almost total lack of any development efforts by the Malian government as well as by NGOs, and by the fact that the area for long periods of time has been closed for foreigners.

Geographically the Adrar des Ifoghas, being mountainous, is more suited for guerilla warfare than the sandy areas further west and south.

Yet another factor might be that many Tuareg *tiwsatin* fought against the French and were heavily decimated resisting the French colonization. The noble *tiwsatin* of Kidal, however, never fought the French. In the years prior to independence, they were thus not as reduced as those further south.

Also, probably due to the fact that the Adrar des Ifoghas is quite poor in resources in relation to, for instance, Gourma, the proportion of slaves had always been lower than in the south. The abolition of slavery seems to have led to fewer difficulties of adaption for the nobles here than further south. The independence of noble Tuaregs from the services of slaves, combined with the fact that population of the Adrar des Ifoghas is almost exclusively Tuareg, gives a more homogenous population than in any other area included in Azawad. A fight for a Tuareg state may thus seem more feasible here than in the southern part of Azawad, where only about half the population is Tuareg. The homogeneity of the population also gave the rebels a civil support that they couldn't have expected elsewhere.

To sum up; the droughts and the way in which the Malian government handled the ecological refugees had laid a foundation for a militant Tuareg rebel movement. Life in exile led a big number of disinherited, disillusioned, marginalized *ishomar* to accept the possibilities for military training that Libya and Western Sahara offered. The involuntary repatriation of many thousand drought refugees to Niger and Mali, combined with the poor reception they received, was the direct cause of the rebellion to break out in 1990. *Ishomar* from Adrar des Ifoghas were particularly central in the early phase of the rebellion, because of the

Locations mentioned in the text

The shaded area shows the approximate size of the Azawad as
understood by the rebels (i.e. the 6th, 7th and 8th region of Mali)

marginality into which the developments of the 20. century had left the
area, in part a result of the Adrar Tuareg rebellion in 1962-64 and the
subsequent military oppression of this particular Tuareg area. But the
situation of the Tuareg was such that the rebellion would have broken
out sooner or later anyhow.

The conflict has taken different courses in different areas

The rebellion has taken different courses in different areas, of which I will concentrate on two here; the one represented by the Adrar des Ifoghas region, and the other by the area southwest of the Niger river. In both areas the rebels, until recently, have operated in very similar ways, with surprise hit and run attacks against administrative and military posts. The terror against civilians by which the army has retaliated is also the same, and has led about ¼ of the Malian Tuareg population to flee to neighbouring countries.

All the first attacks by rebels were carried out at the north and east side of the river Niger, with the mountainous Adrar des Ifoghas and the border areas between Mali, Algeria and Libya as a centre. For once the borders helped Tuaregs. The rebels could withdraw into Libya and Algeria without being persecuted by the Malian army.

Contrary to the relative homogeneity of the population of Adrar des Ifoghas, the area west and south of the Niger river is populated by different ethnic groups, as well as by a more socially diverse Tuareg population. The heterogeneity is related to a more diverse resource base; rainfall is more abundant, there is more pasture, more animals per km^2. Partly because of more rain, partly because of the Niger river, the area also opens for agriculture. The most important ethnic groups besides the Tuareg and Arab nomads are the Songhay agriculturalists living and cultivating along the Niger river, and the Fulani cattle herders and millet growers in the very south. About half the population is non-Tuareg, and among the Tuareg, the former slaves outnumber the Tuaregs of free status.

The Songhay mainly live in villages along the Niger valley. Here, Tuaregs and Songhays have a longstanding conflict related, in particular, to the rich bourgoutieres (mainly *Echinochloa stagnina*) in the river that both Tuareg and Songhay animals feed upon, and which can also be turned into human food, if need arises. This forage is central to the well being of Tuareg animals and thus to the Tuareg during parts of the year, whereas the nomads move to the interior with their animals when pasture and water permits. The conflict has been accentuated lately through the government's and certain NGO's support to farmers to transform bourgou-forage lands to fields for the cultivation of floating rice. Also, the government has made settlements for nomads along the river, in order to make them sedentary. By the people involved, the conflict around the use of the river is experienced in part, as a conflict between ways of life, in part in ethnic and racial terms.

For a long time, the area south-west of the Niger seemed little affected by the rebellion. When the rebellion spread to this area, its dynamics changed. South-west of the river the rebellion got an ethnic twist. In almost all the towns, where large populations of sedentary Songhays and black Tuaregs greatly outnumber the Tuaregs, the black population, in understanding with the army, plundered shops belonging to Tuaregs or Arabs, and broke into and destroyed homes and other things belonging to those with red skin. The Tuareg slaves seem to take an undecided position, sometimes protecting other Tuareg and their property, sometimes taking part in the looting.

In the south-west sedentary Songhay have created a militant movement with the explicit aim to spread terror amongst and to exterminate all nomads. They strongly oppose the peace treaty signed between Tuareg and Arab rebels and the Malian government, as they were not given the opportunity to take part in the discussions leading to the peace treaty. Whereas the situation in the Adrar des Ifoghas region now (dec. 1992) is relatively calm, Tuaregs who are against the peace treaty carry out their attacks in the south-west, and the Malian government has recently stationed 150 elite troops in the area. Reports that Tuaregs are found killed for no reason, and that Tuareg women are violated by the soldiers, are common.

To sum up. In the Adrar des Ifoghas, where the population is almost uniformly Tuareg, the rebellion is related to problems experienced by Tuaregs in relation to the Malian state. In the south-west, the rebellion has made another covert and historical conflict, that between sedentary Songhay and nomadic Tuareg. This conflict is strongly related to rights to scarce resources, in particular as to how, when and who gets to use the Niger river. Whereas the conflict between the Malian government and the Tuareg rebels are dealt with in the peace treaty, the conflict between different ethnic groups in the 6. region is not related to. Ethnic groups other than Tuareg and Arabs were not represented during the peace negotiations, and do not seem to accept the solutions presented in the peace treaty.

The rebellion does not take place in a vacuum

Having touched upon many of the local factors that played a role in the development of the Tuareg rebellion in Mali, I find it important to stress that this rebellion does not take place in a vacuum. For one thing, big changes have taken place in Mali and in Niger since the rebellion broke out. Second, there are currently violent conflicts in almost all Sahelian countries. Third, Europe, an important point of reference for the Tuareg, is experiencing changes that few had predicted some years back. Some countries, like Yugoslavia, are splitting up, others, like East and West Germany, are reunited, and the Common Market seems to make federations out of what were independent states. These processes also influence the course of the Tuareg rebellion. Here, I will elaborate upon the changes having taken place in Mali, as those are probably the least known.

Both in Niger and in Mali, a struggle to topple totalitarian regimes, followed by free elections and the creation of new constitutions have taken place since the Tuareg revolt started. These processes have been running parallel to the Tuareg rebellion, but not independent of it. Geographically, their focal point has been the south, whereas the Tuareg rebellion is taking place in the north.

In Mali, the rebellion, together with the struggle for democracy and liberty of the press, weakened the powers of the state. In the autumn of 1990 student demonstrations and common unrest threatened to topple General Moussa Traoré, who had been in power leading a military dictatorship since the coup d'etat in 1968. The Malian government seems to have realized that it was not able to take the Tuaregs by force, as it was in 1962-1964. The Tuareg rebels numbered maybe a couple of thousand armed, well trained, motivated men, who knew the desert and had chosen death rather than a continued life in exile. The Malian army counts but about 7000 men, and it had to cope with the rebellion as well as the growing resentment against the regime in the south. Malian soldiers are mostly from the south, they are badly equipped, and not trained for desert war. In the whole of Mali rumours about the supernatural forces of the rebel enemy added to demoralize the Malian army.

During the Tuareg uprising, right after independence, the world did not, or did not want to care. Hardly anything can be found about the first rebellion neither in Mali nor in the international media. The Malian government was able to use very oppressive measures against the rebels. The worldwide optimism related to the possibilities of the newly independent African states made a rebellion at that point insupportable. The fact that the noble Tuaregs are red rather than black also made it difficult to support their struggle in the first optimistic years of a newly independent African state.

It is still difficult for Tuaregs to get much attention in the international press, but the difference from the beginning of the 1960s is still tremendous. Several articles have appeared in the international press, Amnesty International, IWGIA and other human organizations have protested against massacres and the breaches of human rights carried out by the Malian army. Even books have appeared. Tuaregs have presented their case for the United Nations. NGOs and researchers working in Tuareg areas have protested against massacres. In different countries, organizations in support of human rights in Mali and Niger have been created. This rebellion is thus taking place also at the international scene.

Thus; the military strength of the rebellion, the timing, the international caring about what is going on, and the struggle democracy in the south of Mali, were factors that, when combined, led the Malian government to sign a peace treaty with the rebels.

The peace treaty and indigenous rights

The Malian government signed the first peace treaty in January 1991, only two months before Moussa Traoré lost power. This peace treaty was soon broken by both parties involved. It served, however, to lay the foundations for a second peace treaty, signed on 11. April 1992, that has now been ratified by the first democratically elected president in Mali since the independence, Alpha Omar Konaré, as well as by the majority of Tuareg movements. The Malian government has done little to implement the treaty, however, and it has also been broken by a group of rebels fighting for full freedom for Azawad. The situation today is unstable and precarious. In Niger, more than 200 intellectual Tuaregs and Tuareg leaders are now (Jan. 1993) imprisoned on the mere suspicion of them being "rebels without arms", arrests that have destabilized the situation even further.

The aim of the peace treaty between the Malian government and the rebels is to create peace in Mali's three northern regions and at the same time save Mali as a state. This is accomplished through the Malian government accepting some sort of particular status for Northern Mali. The treaty includes ideas about the final result of the peace process, such as a demilitarized democratic semi-sovereign North Mali, where democratically elected northerners are in power, and where North-Mali is equal to the rest of the country when it comes to central human goods. It also includes ways to get there, such as withdrawal of Malian troops, democratic elections, increased development efforts in the region both internationally and by increasing the percentage of Mali's GNP to the area, and finally by creating joint commissions where rebels, Malian authorities and mediators are represented, to see to that the treaty is carried through.

1993 is United Nation's International Year of Indigenous Peoples. A proposition for a Declaration on the Rights of Indigenous Peoples is now being elaborated by the Working Group on Indigenous Peoples in the UN: The concept of indigenous peoples may easily lead the discussion astray when it comes to Africa. My point in introducing this Declaration now, is to underline the *structural* similarity in the problems facing indigenous peoples and Tuareg nomads. To mention but a few parallels; in the first paragraph it is stated that indigenous peoples have a right to self-determination, autonomy and self-government. Paragraph 27 states rights to self-determination in matters dealing with internal social and cultural factors, as well as administration and the use of land and resources. In paragraph 5 it is stated that indigenous peoples have a collective right to live in peace and to be protected against genocide. Finally, paragraph 16 states their individual and collective rights to own, control and use territories that they have traditionally exploited. The Declaration also addresses the difficult issue of the rights of other than indigenous groups living in and being dependent upon exploiting the same areas.

The similarities between the peace treaty and the Declaration on the Rights of Indigenous Peoples — both concerned with autonomy, self-government, control over vital resources, protection of the civil population against abuse from a country's army — should be clear enough that we might ask whether certain African peoples structurally can be said to be indigenous peoples. It has never been easy for nation/ states, not in the least democratic ones, to open for different legal treatment for particular groups within its borders. Norway, my own country, has a long history of oppressing the in part nomadic Sami population in the north through democratic procedures, obligatory schooling in Norwegian, being but one case in point.

Will Sahelian governments and different ethnic groups find legally acceptable solutions to their conflicts that take social and cultural diversity into consideration, as well as the right to land and resources, within a state context? Will the Declaration, if not strictly applicable, still be a tool for thought in this process? Without such solutions I fear that Africa will develop into new Yugoslavias and Liberias. I think it

extremely important to reflect upon peaceful solution efforts, and I am
grateful to DANIDA for having agreed to finance a seminar in May,
where questions relating to the relevance of the Declaration on the
Rights of Indigenous Peoples in Africa will be discussed.

References

Africa Research Bulletin no. 9701, 15. June 1990

Aghali-Zakara, Mohamed 1986: Essai de psycholinguistique touarégue.
Bulletin des Etudes Africanines de l'INALCO, Vol. VI, no 12:5-96

Attayoub, Abdoulahi 1992: Touaregs, un peuple ménacé. Déclaration, Nations-
Unies, le 29 juillet 1992.

BCR (BUREAU CENTRAL DE RECENCEMENT) 1990: RECENCEMENT
GENERAL DE LA POPULATION ET DE 'HABITAT 1987. Bamako:
Ministére du Plan.

Bernus, Edmond 1991: Continuité et rupture chez les Illabakan du Niger.
TOUAREGS exil et résistance. Revue du Monde Musulman et de la
Méditerranée. 57. Aix-en Provence: Edisud.

Bourgeot, André 1990: Identité Touarégue: de l'aristocratie á la révolution
Etudes Rurales no. 120, Oct.-déc. 1990:129-162

Dayak, Mano 1992: Touareg, la tragedie. Editions Jean-Claude Lattès.

Les Echos no. 208, 9. Nov. 1992

Les Echos no. 209, 13. Nov. 1992

L'Express no. 2033, 29. June 1990

We, the Tuaregs. 1990: IWGIA NEWSLETTER no. 62: 135-147.

Winter, Michael 1984: A study of family and kinship relations in a pastoral
Twareg group of Northern Mali. Dissertation submitted for the degree of
Doctor of Philosophy, University of Cambridge 222.

HAPEX-Sahel

Eva Bøgh

Institute of Geography, University of Copenhagen

Denmark

The HAPEX-Sahel-experiment (Hydrological Atmospheric Pilot Experiment in the Sahel) is an extensive landsurface-atmosphere experiment taking place in Niger. The programme is mainly financed by the EEC and is being conducted on recommendation from the World Climatic Research Programme. Similar programmes have been implemented in the past — such as HAPEX-MOBILHY in France in 1986, FIFE in 1987 and 1989 in the United States, and EFEDA in Spain in 1991. These studies have permitted the development and verification of experimental strategies, which are now being investigated in the extremely climatically sensitive region of Sahel.

Objectives

The programme has two related objectives: the first is to study the process of evaporation and the energy-, water- and carboncycles of the region to improve parameterization of landsurface processes. The other is to use the same data in the development and application of methods for monitoring the surface processes on a large scale by using remote sensing techniques. The programme is multi-disciplinary and is aimed at improving our understanding of the bio-physiological and metereological processes which govern the exchanges of energy, water and carbon, as well as the process of biomass production and desertification in the Sahel.

Strategy

The experiment is being carried out near Niamey. This area is regarded as representative for a large part of the Sahel. It is furthermore interesting because of a strong North-South precipitation gradient.

The strategy consists of a low intensity monitoring over 2 years (1991-92) to allow a study of seasonal variation, and a high intensive data collection period in August-October 1992. This time of year is most interesting due to the transition from wet to dry conditions and the successive strong modifications of energy-balance, surface hydrology and vegetation.

To study the interactions between the surface and the atmosphere three spatial scales for data collection have been defined. The large-scale (100 × 100 km^2) is defined to allow remote sensing studies to be related to ground-based measurements. NOAA, METEOSAT, LANDSAT, SPOT and SAR-images have been derived for the full period, — although principally for August-October 1992, when groundmeasurements were intensified. Within this large domain 3 super-sites were selected. The isohyets are extremely dense in the large-scale area, and the super-sites were located along a N-S-transect to represent different levels of rainfall regimes. In this way the variability of surface conditions and climate of the large-scale area is reflected. On the super-site-scale, data is collected from aircraft operations and balloons (measurements by radioprobe of heat, vapour, windspeed and CO_2), thus supplying information on surface characteristics and the state of the upper atmospheric layers. The most comprehensive data sets have, however, been collected on the third scale, which is the traditionel scale of micrometerology. Within the super-sites 3 or 4 meterological stations were established during the high intensive data collection period. The stations were located over representative surface-types — such as millet-fields, bush-fallow, degraded bush-land and tiger-bush (laterite plateau). An intensive measurement campaign was organised around these stations (200 × 200 m^2) during two consecutive months by more than 80 scientists of hydrology, soil science, vegetation & ecology, metereology and radiometry (remote sensing).

The long-term monitoring is continously carried out throughout the study area by national institutions in collaboration with ORSTOM. Metereological observations are routinely collected from 3 upgraded weather stations; an intensive study on precipitation distribution over an area of 16,000 km^2 is still running; hydrological observations of runoff, infiltration and aquifer-recharging are made; biometric measurements and the dynamics of vegetation are studied — and maps of pedological, geological and ecological properties are assembled and analyzed.

Analysis of data

The flux measurements of energy and mass (H_2O and CO_2) over the different surface-types will be related to parameters associated with the state of vegetation, the soil condition, the water-budget and the atmosphere. The objective is to develop models describing the interactions between the quite complex heterogenous surfaces, and the atmosphere on the microscale basis.

Techniques will be developed to extrapolate the models to a large-scale by using remote sensing data from aircrafts and satellites. The objective is to produce physiologically based models to understand and quantify the dynamic surface-states (state of vegetation, soil condition, hydrology).

The various collected spatial data (incl. maps) will be used as an input to a meso-scale modelling program. Previous numerical experiments of the general atmospheric circulation have shown that a reduced vegetation cover in the Sahel may contribute to a reduction in rainfall. Sensitivity studies will be performed with the model.

All data collected during the experiment will be stored in a joint database located in Toulouse.

Danish contribution

Within the overall framework, the group of Copenhagen University has been responsible for operating two stations for ground observations of water, energy and CO_2-fluxes above millet. The present author has been responsible for the biometric measurements such as Leaf Area Index, Sapflow and biomass at the two sites and, in cooperation with RUC, for the mapping of soil and vegetation types around the sites.

Applications of results

The comprehensive data materiel collected during the experiment will, hopefully, prove to be an important basis for an improvement of integrated environmental models with perspectives ranging from climate change and desertification to environmental management. Within this range the present author will be focusing on integration of data with physical models in a Geographical Information System, for generation of dynamic information on water-balance, plant production and land-use. Proper understanding of the spatial inter-action in time and space of these components is necessary to provide the foundation of an efficient assessment of sustainable development in the Sahel.

Participatinq institutions of HAPEX-Sahel:

Denmark: Roskilde University Centre.
University of Copenhagen, Inst. of Geography.

France: Centre National de Recherches Metereologiques, Toulouse.
CNRM, Toulouse.
INRA, Montfavet.
Institute de Mecanique de Grenoble, Lab.Etude des Transferts en Hydrolgie et Environnement.
LERTS, Toulouse.
LSIT-GSTS, Strasbourg.
Universite Paul Sabatier, Laboratoire d'Aerologie, Toulouse.

Germany: Frei Universitat, Institut für Meterologie, Institut für Atmospha-riche Wissenschaffen.

The Netherlands: Agricultural University of Wageningen, Dept. of Metereo-logy. Dept. of Soil Science & Geology, Dept. of Waterressources.
Winand Staring Centre, Wageningen.

Niger: Direction de la Meterologie Nationale, Niamey.
Direction de la Topographie, Niamey.
Direction des Ressources en Eau, Niamey.
DRE/INRAN, Niamey.
ICRISAT Sahelian Center, Sadore.
IRI, Niamey.
ORSTOM, Niamey.
Universite de Niamey, Dept. de Physique.

UK: Institute of Ecology & Resource Management, Edinburgh.
Institute of Hydrology, Wallingford.
University College London, Dept. of Geography, Dept. of Photo-grammetry and Survying.
University of Reading, Dept. of Metereology.

USA: Agricultural Research Center, Hydrology Lab.
The Florida State University, Dept. of Metereology. Dept. of Met. and Supercomps.Res.Inst.
Jet Propulsion Laboratory, California.
NASA Ames Research Center, Earth Systems Science Division.
NASA GSFC.
Oregon State University, Dept. of BioResources Engineering.
San Diego State University, Dept.of Geography.
University of Arizona, Dept.of Hydrology and Water Resources.
University of Maryland, Dept.of Geography, Laboratory for Global Remote Sensing.

Etude expérimentale des modalités de la production gommière d'*Acasia Senegal* rétrospective des programmes de développement gommier au Sahel Sénégalais

M. Dione[1] et J. Vassal[2]

1. Institut Sénégalais de Recherches Agricoles, Direction des
Recherches sur les Productions Forestières, Dakar, Sénégal.

2. Institut de la Carte Internationale de la Végétation,
Université Paul Sabatier, Toulouse cedex, France.

Summary

This paper partly accounts for an experimental programme of research carried out from 1989 to 1991 in the experimental plantation of Mbiddi, northern Senegal. 7 populations of gum Acacias have been studied in 3 distinct dune sites. Differences in the biological behaviour of trees are described in these situations. From the bottom to the top of dunes were observed...

1. a decreasing of the rates of growth and of survival
2. an acceleration of the rhythm of defoliation
3. an increasing of the mean gum yield per tree.

In parallel there was noted a decrease of the water storage from hollows to dune tops. These results can help to choose the optimal sites for plantation as well as appropriate periods for tapping.

In the second part ot this note a historical approach is made concerning gum acacia from the colonial period. Lessons learned from the different projects carried out in the senegalese gum belt are particularly stressed in special recommendations.

Introduction

Ce document fait, pour une part, le point sur l'avancée récente des recherches expérimentales menées en vue de l'amélioration de la production gommière d'*Acacia senegal*. Nous résumons ainsi les principaux résultats obtenus à la station expérimentale de Mbiddi (nord-Sénégal) dans le cadre d'un programme francosénégalais (Université P. Sabatier, Toulouse — Université de Rouen — Institut Sénégalais de Recherches Agricoles/DRPF, Dakar — 1989/1991) portant sur la modélisation du comportement de populations artificielles de gommiers dans différentes situations édapho-topographiques.

Dans une deuxième partie, nous faisons un historique et un bilan des programmes de développement, fondés sur les gommiers, qui ont été mis en place au Sénégal depuis l'époque coloniale. Nous insistons particulièrement sur les problèmes actuels que pose la production gommière en liaison avec les variations climatiques de ces vingt dernières années et des contraintes socio-économiques.

Caractérisation de la zone gommière Sénégalaise

Situation géographique
La zone gommière sénégalaise se confond presque avec la région agroécologique appelée zone sylvo-pastorale. Celle-ci est une calotte d'environ 40,000 km^2 occupant pour l'essentiel les parties nord-ouest à nord-est du pays, entre les latitudes 13° et 16° Nord et les longitudes 12° et 16° Ouest.

Climat
La pluviométrie est l'élément climatique déterminant. Elle varie de 600 mm en bordure sud de la zone à 200 mm au nord (Carte 1). Dans cette »fourchette« pluviométrique on distingue communément les sous-zones éco-climatiques 1/ sahélienne *sensu stricto* (200-400 mm de pluviosité moyenne annuelle) et 2/ soudano-sahélienne (400-600 mm de pluviosité moyenne annuelle) - (Le Houérou 1988).

Il y a un contraste marqué entre la saison pluvieuse ou hivernage (de juillet à septembre) et la saison sèche (d'octobre à juin).

La saison des pluies est dominée par l'arrivée de masses d'air très humides d'origine océanique (les moussons), porteuses de l'essentiel des précipitations. Durant cette saison, les vents sont de secteur sud-ouest et sud. L'humidité de l'air varie entre 34 et 87% (moyenne 60% environ); les températures oscillent entre 25° et 35°C (moyenne de 29°C). Du Sud au Nord on note un gradient décroissant d'humidité de l'air et un gradient croissant de température.

La saison sèche est dominée, d'octobre à février, par l'arrivée de masses d'air fraîches et humides (vents dits »alizés maritimes«) de secteur nord et nord-ouest. Ils laissent la place, entre mars et mai, à des masses d'air chaud et sec portées par un vent de secteur nord-est et est, l'harmattan.

Le mois de juin est souvent une période de transition marquée par l'arrivée de la mousson alors que les précipitations sont encore peu significatives.

Géomorphologie et sol

Les formations dunaires du Ferlo sableux sont d'ancienneté variable (7.500 à 60.000 ans), de faible dénivelé et plus ou moins érodées selon leur âge. Ces reliefs sont séparés par des dépressions où s'accumule une eau de ruissellement issu des sommets et versants et où la tendance à l'hydromorphie est forte.

Les sols d'origine éolienne sont peu évolués et plus fréquents dans la partie nord du Ferlo. Ils sont de type »isohumiques brun-rouge subarides« et »isohumiques bruns calcaires«. Ce sont des sols sableux profonds, pauvres en matière organique. Le phénomène d'hydromorphie se traduit par l'existence de sols intermédiaires avec présence, dans les horizons profonds (à »pseudogley«), de proportions d'argile plus importantes.

Les sols ferrugineux tropicaux (sols »dior«), plus ou moins lessivés et de texture sableuse à sablo-argileuse, sont très fréquents dans le sud-est du Ferlo. Ils sont pauvres en matière organique et de couleur rouge.

Les sols cuirassés n'occupent que 5% de la zone Sud-Est du Ferlo.

Végétation

Dans le sud du Ferlo on rencontre des savanes arborées, arbustives ou herbeuses, tandis qu'au nord s'observent des steppes arborées, arbustives ou herbeuses. Dans les deux cas la strate ligneuse est constituée en majorité d'épineux où abondent les Acacias gommiers.

Dans la partie nord de la zone gommière (carte 1) *Acacia senegal*, autrefois espèce principale, se trouve aujourd'hui associé à de nombreuses espèces compagnes telles que *Acacia tortilis* subsp. *raddiana, A. seyal, Zizyphus mauritiana* (jujubier) et *Balanites aegyptiaca* (»dattier« du Sénégal). On y note aussi des espèces non épineuses comme *Boscia senegalensis* (à fruits comestibles très exploités en période de disette), *Calotropis procera, Anogeissus leiocarpus*...

La transition vers le Sud est marquée par l'abondance d'espèces comme *Sclerocarya birrea* et *Combretum glutinosum*. *Sclerocarya birrea* fournit un fourrage recherché durant les mois de mai et de juin, période de soudure. Le sud de la zone gommière est caractérisé par un cortège légèrement différent d'espèces qui s'associent aux gommiers et par une plus grande abondance relative d'*Acacia senegal*. On note l'apparition de *Faidherbia albida* et d'espèces non épineuses comme *Sterculia seti-*

gera (»platane« du Sénégal) qui donne une gomme proche de la gomme »Karaya« indienne et *Pterocarpus lucens* (palissandre du Sénégal) qui fournit du bois de chauffe et un excellent fourrage.

Vocation économique de la zone gommière

La zone gommière a pour principale activité économique l'élevage de type pastoral (près de 40% du cheptel en bovins, ovins et capris du Ferlo). En plus de la gomme arabique, les savanes et steppes de cette région offrent un appoint fourrager indispensable en saison sèche ainsi que d'autres« produits de cueillette comme le »sump« (fruit de *Balanites aegyptiaca*), le »bouye« (fruit d'*Adansonia digitata* ou baobab), le jujube ou »siddeem« (fruit de *Zizyphus mauritiana*) et diverses feuilles et écorces servant à la confection de tisanes (*Combretum glutinosum, Combretum micranthum*) ou à divers usages en pharmacopée.

Plusieurs essences servent à la fabrication d'ustensiles et de divers meubles domestiques. Une bonne partie est exploitée pour le bois de chauffe et le charbon de bois (*A. nilotica* notamment) surtout dans le secteur sud de la zone gommière.

Station de recherches forestières de Mbiddi

La station de Mbiddi se situe à l'extrémité nord de la zone gommière sénégalaise. Fondée en 1974 par El Hadj Sène, ancien directeur national des Eaux et Forêts du Sénégal, avec l'aide du Centre de Recherche pour le Développement International (CRSDI), ce centre a été d'emblée voué aux recherches expérimentales sur les Acacias gommiers. La station comprend 5 bâtiments administratifs; elle possède un parc météorologique et une pépinière. L'ensemble de la plantation a une superficie de 500 hectares environ. Les différents placeaux sont disposés en 5 massifs principaux autour du forage profond du village de Mbiddi. Les plantations ont été effectuées au rythme de 25 à 75 hectares jusqu'en 1980.

Cette station a surtout permis jusqu'ici de mettre au point des techniques de culture et d'exploitation du gommier *Acacia senegal*. L'amélioration génétique et la recherche d'autres espèces gommières, qui figuraient parmi les objectifs initiaux, n'ont pas connu de développement très substantiel. Nos travaux sur les relations entre production gommière, biologie de l'arbre et milieu marquent un infléchissement nouveau des recherches dans la station.

Le secteur de Mbiddi est peuplé de 1500 habitants environ appartenant aux éthnies peulh et maure dispersées dans un terroir de 630 km² essentiellement voué à l'élevage pastoral. C'est dans ce contexte géographique, bioclimatique et socioéconomique qu'ont été menées les recherches qui font l'objet des paragraphes suivants.

Recherches expérimentales sur les modalités de la production gommière d'Acacia Senegal

Matériel et méthode

Les arbres faisant l'objet de cette étude sont issus de semis effectués à partir de semences récoltées autour de Mbiddi ou dans le nord-Ferlo.

7 placeaux de 30 à 40 individus ont été délimités dans 3 parcelles d'arbres âgés de 10 à 14 ans. Les placeaux retenus sont situés dans trois sites dunaires (sommet, replat et dépression) afin de rendre compte des variations de comportements biologiques dans ces situations distinctes (Vassal *et al.* 1992). Les observations et relevés concernent la phénologie, la croissance, le rendement en gomme, la survie, l'humidité du sol et les paramètres climatiques (tableau ci-dessous).

année de plantation et n° de code dans la station	site dunaire et code	nombre de sujets étudiés
1975 (PGA 74)	Sommet (1 S)	30
	Replat[1] (2 R)	30
1975 (PRP 75)	Sommet (3 S)	2 x 30
	Dépression (4 D)	2 x 30
1978 (PRP 78)	Sommet (5 S)	40
	Replat (6 R)	30
	Dépression (7 D)	30

Nombre de sujets: 280

Relevés journaliers: température, humidité relative, précipitations

Relevés par quinzaine: rendement en gomme par arbre[2]

Relevés mensuels: phénologie (défoliation), survie, humidité du sol pour la tranche 0 à 3 m de profondeur (sonde Campbell 503DR)

Relevés annuels: dendrométrie (hauteur totale et circonférence des principales branches, diamètre du houppier).

D'autres observations ont été faites parallèlement mais ne sont pas exploitées ici (floraison, fructification — relevés mensuels; hauteur du houppier — observation annuelle).

---

1) *Parties subhorizontales intermédiaires entre les sommets/versants et les dépressions interdunaires.*

2) *Des échantillons de gommes ont été régulièrement prélevés sur des arbres référenciés et envoyés pour analyse physico-chimique à l'Université de Rouen (Dr J.C. Fenyo).*

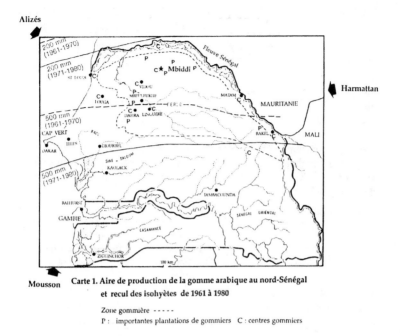

Mousson   Carte 1. Aire de production de la gomme arabique au nord-Sénégal
et recul des isohyètes de 1961 à 1980

Zone gommière - - - - -
P : importantes plantations de gommiers   C : centres gommiers

Chaque arbre a été saigné au moins une fois durant la saison sèche, en octobre, novembre, décembre, mars ou avril. Tous les arbres étudiés (280) ont été référenciés. L'étude, entreprise en 1988, se poursuit encore aujourd'hui. Les résultats exposés ici concernent la période d'octobre 1989 à mai 1991.

Principaux résultats (Vassal *et al.* 1992)

Comportement des arbres après la saignée: Les saignées jouent un rôle important dans l'induction du processus de gommose (Mouret 1988; Dione 1989b; Vassal et Mouret 1992).

Si l'on compare par exemple le comportement des arbres des différents placeaux 1S, 3S, 5S (en sommet dunaire), après saignées partielles (1S) ou quasi totales (3S, 5S) en octobre-novembre 1989, on constate de meilleurs rendements dans les lots en majorité écorcés.

	% arbres producteurs (1989/90)	production moyenne/arbre (g) (1989/90)
1S	22	7,2
3S	93	256,0
5S	87	461,8

Une comparaison entre deux fractions du placeau 3S, après saignées en octobre-novembre 1989 et mars-avril 1990, montre par ailleurs que les saignées tardives sont nettement moins productives que celles du début de saison sèche:

	% arbres producteurs (1989/90)	production moyenne/arbre (g) (1989/90)
saignée oct./nov. 1989	93	256,0
saignée mars-avril 1990	10	10,6

Notons que cette différence de comportement selon la date de saignée est moins sensible dans les dépressions interdunaires.

Influence du site dunaire sur le comportement des gommiers:

Croissance: En comparant les données dendrométriques dans des placeaux de même âge (mesures de mi-1990) on constate que les dimensions moyennes des sujets croissent globalement du sommet dunaire vers la dépression interdunaire.

Cette différence de vigueur des arbres, selon les sites, a déjà été notée par Sène (1988) et Sylla Gaye (1989).

Degré et rythme de défoliation: Les observations effectuées d'octobre 1989 à mai 1991 montrent un asynchronisme de la défoliation selon le site.

Voici le classement des différents placeaux selon le mois où se manifeste le degré maximum de défoliation:

		hauteur moyenne (cm)	diamètre du houppier (cm)
plantations 1975	1S	381	358
	3S	278	356
	2R	402	423
	4D	556	633
plantations 1978	5S	277	426
	6R	353	493
	7D	422	543

1989/90	1991/91
3S: novembre	3S: novembre
6R: janvier	6R: janvier
5S: janvier	5S: janvier
1S : mars	1S: janvier
7D: avril	2R: janvier
4D: avril	4D: février
2R: avril	7D: mars

Les arbres des sommets dunaires se défolient donc plus tôt que ceux des dépressions: entre ces deux situations, le maximum de défoliation passe ainsi de novembre à avril. Ce comportement phénologique distinct a déjà été signalé par Sène (1988) et Sylla Gaye (1989), mais non clairement décrit.

Rendement gommier et rythme de production gommière: Le rendement en gomme et le rythme de production varient selon les sujets en fonction du site.

Si l'on considère par exemple les placeaux totalement saignés (en octobre-novembre), au cours de la saison de production 1989-90, les lots s'ordonnent ainsi dans l'ordre de rendement moyen croissant des sujets: 4D (88,3 g), 7D (100,2 g), 6R (167,2 g), 3S (274,3 g), 5S (461,8 g).

Le rendement gommier est donc nettement plus élevé sur les sommets dunaires. Dans ces sites, on note un pic très net de production en décembre. Dans les dépressions, la production est faible, étalée de décembre à avril-mai et sans pic marqué.

Durant la campagne 1990-1991, la production gommière n'a pas été très différenciée dans les trois sites dunaires. Celle-ci semble avoir été perturbée par l'important déficit pluviométrique enregistré (224,5 mm en 1990 contre 387,5 mm en 1989): le rythme de production du placeau 7D (dépression) en 1990-91 est ainsi similaire de celui des sommets dunaires en 1989-90.

Ces résultats concordent partiellement avec les observations de Sène (1988) effectuées dans la même station de 1985 à 1987: cet auteur note en effet de très bons rendements en sommets et replats dunaires. N'ayant observé qu'un nombre réduit d'arbres dans dépressions, il n'a pu apprécier totalement les variations des rendements selon les sites. Sylla Gaye (1989), entre 1983 et 1985, a observé une augmentation inverse du rendement gommier, du sommet dunaire vers la dépression, ceci dans une période marquée par un déficit pluviométrique accentué.

Ainsi, le comportement gommier des arbres dans les différents sites dunaires apparaît-il très variable selon la pluviométrie de l'année (Vassal et Dione, vol.) ou selon la recharge hydrique du sol.

Taux de survie: Les taux de survie, entre 1988 et 1991, ont varié selon les sites dunaires. Il ont été dans l'ensemble, nettement plus élevés dans les dépressions interdunaires (4D: 97%; 7D: 80%) que sur les sommets dunaires (1S: 55%; 3S: 94%; 5S: 43%). Ceci corrobore les observations de Sène (1988) et Sylla Gaye (1989).

Relations entre degré de vigueur de l'arbre et rendement gommier

Les relations entre degré de vigueur et production gommière n'ont pas été clairement mises en évidence jusqu'ici. Les résultats sont en effet contradictoires: Dione note une corrélation positive entre diamètre des troncs et rendement (1989ab) alors que Sylla Gaye (1989) ne décèle, de 1983 à 1984, aucune relation significative entre ces paramètres et interprète cela comme une résultante de la sécheresse qui a précédé la période de production.

Si l'on considère plus particulièrement les observations relatives à la saison de production 1989-90 (dans les lots totalement saignés en octobre-novembre), il apparaît nettement une *corrélation négative* entre degré de vigueur des arbres (illustré par les hauteurs et circonférences des branches maîtresses) et la production moyenne par arbre (coefficients de corrélation égaux à -0,78 pour les hauteurs et -0,67 pour les circonférences). Un résultat analogue a été obtenu en tenant compte des réponses aux saignées: les écorçages apparaissent d'autant moins efficaces que les arbres sont plus vigoureux (coefficients de corrélations égaux à -0,81 pour les hauteurs et -0,93 pour les circonférences). Ces résultats s'accordent bien avec les observations traditionnelles des récoltants de gomme dans les gommeraies naturelles. Notons que les relations entre production et degré de vigueur sont moins significatives pour la saison 1990-91 compte tenu des faibles productions générales de gomme enregistrées durant cette saison.

Relations entre rythme phénologique foliaire et rendement gommier

Dans les 3 sites dunaires, on note un net parallélisme entre les rythmes de défoliation et le rendement gommier. Si l'on prend l'exemple de la parcelle PRP 78, durant la campagne de production 1989-1990, on s'aperçoit ainsi que:

- sur les sommets et les replats, le maximum de rendement mensuel est atteint en décembre, juste avant le maximum de défoliation de janvier;
- dans les dépressions, le maximum de rendement est décalé en février-mars et précède le maximum de défoliation ici différé en avril.

Le lien entre maximum de défoliation et pic de production est également net dans les autres placeaux. Ceci conforte les observations traditionnelles des récoltants ainsi que les remarques générales de Dione (1986) et Sène (1988).

Relations entre les réserves hydriques du sol et le comportement biologique des gommiers

Pour tenter de rendre compte des différences de comportement des sujets dans les 3 sites topographiques dunaires, nous avons effectué des mesures mensuelles de stocks hydriques dans chaque placeau dans une tranche de sol de 0 à 3 m.

- Sur les sommets dunaires, le stock hydrique moyen mensuel est faible et relativement constant (moyenne annuelle comprise entre 38,5 et 52,8 mm, période: décembre 1989-mars 1991), sans pic marqué au cours de la saison des pluies (40 à 58 mm en septembre).
- Dans les dépressions interdunaires et sur les replats, le régime hydrique du sol est marqué par un pic très net en septembre (77 à 106 mm). La moyenne annuelle oscille entre 47 et 73 mm.

Les comportements biologiques observés (§ 2.2.2.) peuvent être interprétés à la lumière de ces nouvelles données.

Rythmes de défoliation: La défoliation précoce des gommiers, en sommets dunaires, est liée aux conditions sèches relativement constantes de ces sites et à l'établissement, dès octobre, d'un pallier hydrique.

La défoliation tardive des sujets, dans les dépressions, ne s'affirme nettement que lorsque le stock hydrique, après une diminution brutale (à partir de septembre) atteint un certain palier au mois de décembre.

Le comportement phénologique des arbres de replats est intermédiaire.

Croissance: Les différences de régime hydrique, dans les divers sites, ont une incidence sur la croissance des gommiers, fait déjà souligné (mais non clairement quantifié) par Sylla Gaye (1989). L'amplitude des stocks hydriques, au cours de l'année, semble jouer plus particulièrement un rôle. Elle est importante dans les dépressions (60 mm entre septembre et mars dans le placeau 7D) et favorise une bonne croissance dans ces sites. Elle est faible sur les sommets (8 mm entre septembre et mars dans le placeau 1S) et induit une croissance limitée. Ceci peut signifier que le stock hydrique du sol durant l'hivernage, notamment en septembre, influe plus ou moins positivement, selon son importance, sur le rythme de croissance. L'hivernage correspond en effet à une période d'intense activité physiologique.

Production gommière: D'une manière générale, la production gommière moyenne par arbre et le % de sujets producteurs augmentent tandis que la moyenne et l'amplitude des stocks hydriques diminuent. Cette relation est très nette lorsque l'on considère plus particulièrement l'amplitude des réserves en eau du sol, comme en témoignent les coefficients de corrélation:

C = -0,82 (production moyenne par arbre/amplitude des stocks hydriques)
C = -0,95 (% d'arbres producteurs/amplitude des stocks hydriques).

Ceci explique les bons rendements observés sur les sommets dunaires, niveaux où les stocks hydriques sont peu importants et relativement constants.

Conclusion:

Il apparaît que les stocks hydriques, aux différents niveaux de la toposéquence dunaire, influencent nettement le comportement biologique du gommier *Acacia senegal.*

Sur les sommets, la croissance est ralentie; les pourcentages de survie y sont plus faibles que dans les dépressions et replats. Ces situations de haut de pente, du fait de la pauvreté des sols en eau, favorisent une bonne exsudation de gomme (conséquence vraisemblable d'un stress hydrique, cf. Vassal et Dione, ce vol.) parallèlement à une défoliation plus précoce. Les saignées d'octobre-novembre sont plus favorables à l'exsudation sur les sommets, plus secs, que dans les dépressions plus longtemps pourvues en réserves hydriques.

Les programmes de développement gommier au Sénégal

L'histoire des programmes gommiers au Sénégal s'identifie en fait à celle des actions menées en vue de la protection et de la valorisation d'*Acacia senegal* (Freudenberger 1988). Déjà, à l'époque coloniale (1890-1960), plusieurs types de mesures ont été prises pour la sauvegarde et l'extension des gommeraies.

Après plus d'un demi-siècle d'efforts en faveur des gommiers, marqué notamment par l'adoption du Code Forestier (intégrant le gommier dans la catégorie des arbres dont l'exploitation est soumise à réglementation) et de l'institutionalisation de l'appartenance à l'Etat de certaines gommeraies (entre 1900 et 1940), un vaste potentiel gommier d'environ 7.000 km^2 était disponible, en 1956, sous la forme de Réserves Domaniales (forêts classées et réserves sylvo-pastorales). Celles-ci furent source d'une production soutenue jusque vers les années 1970.

De 1974 à 1984, le Sénégal, avec l'appui de nombreux donateurs, entreprit la plantation de gommiers à travers la zone sylvo-pastorale. On pouvait ainsi recenser en 1983 plus de 13.000 hectares de gommeraies artificielles. Nous allons voir comment, au cours de la période coloniale et après l'indépendance, les problèmes gommiers et leurs solutions ont évolué tant sur le plan institutionnel que sur le plan de la technique ou de la recherche.

Période coloniale
Cette période fut surtout marquée par des *mesures institutionnelles* visant à une meilleure protection et régénération des gommeraies. Une illustration en est l'application du Code Forestier qui, à partir de 1900, règlementa notamment la saignée des gommiers. Elle fut complétée, en 1935, par l'adoption du Régime Forestier d'Afrique Occidentale qui accorda à l'Etat la possibilité d'acquérir la propriété de certains espaces naturels. Cela se traduisit, à partir de 1946, par la création de Forêts Classées et de Réserves sylvo-pastorales englobant la majorité des gommeraies.

A partir de ce moment, les saignées furent contrôlées. La présence, dans les gommeraies, des pasteurs et de leurs troupeaux fut seulement tolérée compte tenu des dégâts causés par le piétinement des semis et rejets et des ébranchages abusifs pratiqués en saison sèche pour fournir du fourrage vert au bétail.

Cette période institutionnelle fut aussi caractérisée par l'extension vers le sud de la zone de récolte de la gomme (Freudenberger 1988). Ainsi fut développé le premier plan d'ensemble destiné à l'amélioration de la production de gomme avec pour axes prioritaires:

* l'extension de la zone de récolte,
* la protection des peuplements,
* l'application des normes de saignée et de conditionnement.

On assista ainsi, à partir de 1950 à l'ouverture d'un réseau de pare-feux réduisant sensiblement la dévastation des peuplements par l'incendie et facilitant l'accès aux gommeraies. L'installation de plusieurs forages, dès 1952, acheva la levée des contraintes logistiques à l'extension de l'exploitation gommière. La récolte impliquait en effet, auparavant, de longues et pénibles campagnes de trois à quatre mois nécessitant d'importantes réserves d'eau et de nourriture. La zone gommière était alors inhabitée en saison sèche.

Après ces aménagements, la production gommière resta cependant limitée du fait de contraintes techniques et sociales diverses. On tenta alors d'intensifier la production, notamment par la mise en place, entre 1948 et 1954, de plantations gommières expérimentales »á sec« et »irriguées« autour des forages. On tenta aussi l'implantation de gommeraies communales où les populations devaient s'investir dans les travaux culturaux de plantation afin de bénéficier ensuite du droit d'exploitation des gommiers parvenus à mâturité. Mais la divagation animale empêcha le développement de ces gommeraies communales et des plantations »à sec«, tandis que les coûts en main d'oeuvre et moyens financiers rendaient irréalistes les gommeraies »irriguées«.

Durant cette même période, des recherches sur *Acacia senegal* furent entreprises en station expérimentale (Linguère - 40 hectares) sans donner les résultats escomptés sur le plan multiplication végétative (par recépage) et résistance aux insectes ravageurs.

Après l'Indépendance

La sécheresse de 1968-72 remit à l'ordre du jour la problématique gommière gelée après 1954 car elle entraîna la mort de plus de 60% des gommiers et une chute drastique des exportations de gomme dure du Sénégal (passant de 5.400 tonnes en 1970 à 292 t en 1975). L'Etat ainsi que les donateurs et négociants internationaux de la gomme se mirent ainsi d'accord sur la nécessité de plantations gommières à grande échelle.

La réalisation de plantations d'Etat, qui était alors prévue dans le plan quadriennal de développement économique et social (1969-1973), commença à voir le jour avec la création, en 1974, de la station de recherches forestières de Mbiddi dans le nord du Ferlo. Par ailleurs, du fait de sa nature relativement rustique, le gommier *Acacia senegal* constituait une essence de reboisement particulièrement privilégiée dans le contexte nouveau de désertification.

A partir de 1979, vu le coût élevé de telles plantations et les difficultés rencontrées par l'Etat pour en assurer le suivi, on s'orienta vers la création de gommeraies communautaires subventionnées pour les paysans. Dans ces plantations les arbres sont associés, durant les premières années, aux cultures agricoles traditionnelles (mil, haricot, pastèques). Grâce aux récoltes annuelles ainsi obtenues le problème du délai des retombées financières des plantations gommières trouva une solution. Ces plantations sont d'autant plus appréciées que les agriculteurs bénéficient de hausses substantielles des rendements dues aux travaux culturaux mécanisés (sous-solages profonds, labours) avant plantation. La clôture subventionnée assure une protection déterminante contre la divagation animale. De plus, le propriétaire de la parcelle a désormais la possibilité de récupérer, de laisser ou d'exploiter sur place les sous-produits restants au moment opportun.

La plupart des gommeraies communautaires ont été installées dans le sud de la zone gommière. Freudenberger (1988) a recensé 4.700 hectares de peuplements de ce type dans le département administratif de Linguère qui occupe près de la moitié de la zone gommière. Il faut souligner, avec Freudenberger, que l'urgence de planter pour résoudre la crise gommière a relégué au second plan les questions foncières et de gestion à long terme des plantations.

Compte tenu du Code Forestier en vigueur, les villageois ont généralement été peu associés à la conception des reboisements en gommiers. De ce fait, ne se considérant pas comme propriétaires, ils ont fortement négligé ces plantations dès le retrait des forestiers. D'autre part, ni l'Etat, ni les pasteurs (peu intéressés par la délimitation des propriétés privées dans les zones de parcours) ne se sont préoccupés de ces gommeraies qui ont rapidement périclité.

Tirant les leçons de ces difficultés, la politique des reboisements en gommiers se réorienta de nouveau, à partir de 1984, grâce à l'adoption du principe des parcelles agroforestières. Dans ce sytème, l'Etat assure une assistance matérielle et financière aux paysans qui en font la demande. La subvention consiste en la fourniture de plants et de clôtures ainsi que d'un appui technique pour la mise en place de parcelles de 4 à 30 hectares. Pour des parcelles de 10 à 30 hectares, une contribution à l'amortissement des frais de clôture et de façons culturales est demandée, soit 150.000 à 250.000 FCFA (3.000 à 5.000 FF).

Malgré cet effort notoire de plantation, les gommeraies artificielles demeurent encore aujourd'hui largement inexploitées alors qu'elles sont arrivées à mâturité. Ceci est dû, pour une part, à un vide institutionnel car, dans les réserves sylvo-pastorales et forêts classées, la loi n'autorise pas de propriété aux usagers. La recrudescence des vols de gomme après saignée accentue le manque d'intérêt des villageois vis à vis des gommiers. Par ailleurs, dans les zones des terroirs villageois, le Conseil Rural, responsable civil de la mise en place des gommeraies communautaires, ne bénéficie pas d'attributions légales pour pratiquer l'exploitation forestière des gommiers et encaisser les revenus.

Les incertitudes sur la viabilité économique des plantations persistent quand celles-ci se présentent comme des alternatives aux autres cultures de rente. La forte mortalité enregistrée dans les gommeraies du secteur nord de la zone a aussi assombri les perspectives. C'est ce contexte qui a favorisé, depuis 1987, l'émergence de liaisons plus systématiques et plus formelles entre les services de recherche et ceux du développement gommier. C'est ainsi que la station de Mbiddi a été sollicitée (voir ci-après) pour conduire des tests de saignée et préciser les capacités gommières des plantations. Les services de développement gommier espéraient ainsi mieux évaluer la rentabilité des plantations et l'intérêt de la poursuite de l'élan de plantations.

Liaison recherche-développement

Durant la période des plantations massives, le transfert des résultats de l'expérience de la station de Mbiddi, dans le domaine de la sylviculture des gommiers, s'est fait sur la base de visites et de stages plus ou moins prolongés de responsables des projets gommiers et de leurs collaborateurs. Ce fut ainsi le cas pour les initiateurs du Projet sénégalo-allemand de Reboisement et d'Aménagement Sylvo-Pastoral de la Zone Nord (PRAZN), promoteur des importantes gommeraies communautaires et des parcelles agroforestières dans le sud de la zone gommière (Vindou, Mbeuleukhé, Kamb, Dahra, Linguère). Il en fut de même pour les responsables du projet Boisement Vlllageois de Louga et Bakel qui ont vulgarisé la mise en place de vergers à gommiers dans le sud (Dahra, Louga, Déali).

Tous ces projets illustrent l'attention accordée à l'espèce *Acacia senegal* ainsi qu' à une meilleure maîtrise des techniques de régénération des gommiers en liaison avec les recherches conduites à la station de Mbiddi (Dione 1986; Dione et Sall 1992).

En ce qui concerne la production de gomme des plantations, un premier protocole de recherche fut mis au point en 1987 dans le cadre du PROBOVIL, à Louga et à Déali, c'est-à-dire dans les parties sud-ouest et centre-sud de la zone gommière. Le but était d'identifier la période optimale des saignées et d'évaluer les rendements potentiels. Les saignées furent négatives à Louga durant la période d'octobre 1987 à mai 1988; à Déali, une campagne de saignée sur trois, entre 1987 et 1990, fut positive. Si l'on se réfère aux résultats obtenus à Mbiddi (voir plus haut), il est probable que c'est l'abondance relative de la pluviométrie combinée à des températures moins élevées (Dione 1989b) qui a limité la productivité des gommeraies. A Déali, où le régime thermique est cependant moins influencé par la proximité de la mer qu'à Louga, on peut s'attendre à des productions substantielles si l'hivernage est déficitaire sur le plan pluviométrique. Suite à ces résultats, l'exploitation d'*Acacia senegal* a été réorientée, dans le secteur de Louga, vers la production de fourrage d'appoint, la réalisation de brise-vent et l'amélioration des sols dégradés par la monoculture arachidière.

Un deuxième protocole de recherche, conduit avec la PRAZN à Mbeuleukhé, a permis entre autres de déterminer la période optimale de saignée et d'évaluer les rendements en gomme. La meilleure production des placeaux non cultivés durant l'hivernage précédant les saignées a illustré la nécessité de séparer les phases d'activité agricole et gommière dans les parcelles agroforestières.

Choix des types de gommeraies

Du fait de la sécheresse, l'intérêt porté aux gommeraies naturelles (autrefois fierté du Sénégal, car productrices de »crus« notamment connus sous le nom de »Ferlo«) s'est considérablement affaibli. Cependant, comme le fait remarquer Freudenberger (1988, 1992), ces peuplements sont toujours la source principale de production, notamment dans le département administratif de Linguère.

Il est évident que, vu les prix de revient, la gestion des gommeraies naturelles est plus rentable que celle des plantations dont les capacités gommières demandent encore à être mieux précisées. Les missions de reconnaissance, effectuées dans ces plantations, confirment cependant l'existence d'une productivité potentielle réelle. L'explosion fréquente de conflits sociaux relatifs aux droits d'exploitation constitue toutefois une contrainte sérieuse. C'est ainsi que les concepteurs et »praticiens« se scindent en deux groupes:

• Les uns pronent la réalisation de plantations monospécifiques et industrielles sans prise en compte des autres intérêts des gommiers (rôle écologique, apport de fourrage complémentaire, amélioration de la fertilité des sols, rôle de brise-vent, apport de bois de feu et de service, etc...).
• Les autres préconisent un aménagement des gommeraies naturelles et leur gestion en concertation avec les récoltants, quitte à prévoir le réaménagement des dispositions institutionnelles en ce qui concerne la propriété et les droits d'usage.

Au niveau recherche, les préoccupations relatives aux gommeraies naturelles et artificielles ont été associées dans un même programme scientifique de »recherche sur la gestion des ressources naturelles en zone sylvopastorale«. Ce programme est pluridisciplinaire et utilise une approche »participatoire« pour le diagnostic des problèmes et la recherche de solutions pratiques aux contraintes liées à la gestion des ressources gommières. Basées à Dahra-Djoloff, ces recherches s'inscrivent dans le cadre plus global du programme »Zootechnie et Aménagement de l'espace agro-sylvo-pastoral« qui prend en compte la vocation pastorale dominante de la zone gommière. D'autres programmes de l'Institut Sénégalais de Recherches Agricoles (ISRA) concernent aussi le gommier:

- *Programme »Microbiologie, Ecologie et Physiologie des ligneux«*: études thématiques sur les gommiers en vue de la réhabilitation des terres agricoles et pastorales dégradées — essais de modélisation du comportement des gommiers et de la productivité gommière;
- *Programme »Sylviculture et Aménagement des Forêts Naturelles«* dynamique des gommeraies naturelles et aménagement;
- *Programme »Agroforesterie«:* mise au point des technologies agroforestières basées sur les usages multiples d'Acacia senegal dans le contexte agro-sylvo-pastoral (haies vives, banques fourragères, restauration de la fertilité des sols, etc...).

Sur le plan développement de la production, les mutations nécessaires pour appréhender la situation gommière actuelle et introduire de nouvelles approches sont encore très timides. Cela se traduit par l'absence de projets abordant les questions gommières. Un certain *statu quo* s'est installé (malgré quelques velléités positives) du fait de l'insuffisance des liaisons entre recherche pluridisciplinaire et développement rural.

Conclusion
Le développement des programmes à base de gommiers, au Sénégal, est caractérisé par une extension progressive de la zone de production vers le Sud. Aujourd'hui, cela se traduit par une augmentation du potentiel gommier, notamment grâce à la régénération artificielle, sans que l'on observe pour autant d'avancées significatives dans le domaine de l'exploitation elle-même. L'application des résultats expérimentaux obtenus à la station de Mbiddi permettrait d'améliorer la production grâce à un choix plus rationnel des sites de plantation et à un meilleur pilotage des périodes d'exploitation.

La zone gommière a désormais une composante naturelle et une autre artificielle. La spécificité de chacune d'elles découle beaucoup de leur localisation géographique. Dans les grandes plantations monospécifiques du Nord-Ferlo les taux de survie sont faibles et les capacités gommières plus réduites à cause des déficits pluviométriques accentués. L'élevage prédominant et la nature relativement nomade des pasteurs rendent l'exploitation gommière aléatoire, faute de récoltants professionnels. La forte mortalité prévalant dans ces gommeraies impose le maintien d'un effort de reboisement permanent pour regarnir les plantations car cette région est la plus marquée par la désertification. C'est l'intégration de l'exploitation gommière au système pastoral traditionnel qui permettrait sans doute une gestion optimale de ces gommeraies: c'est le cas à Vindou où ont été créés des groupements d'intérêt économique de pasteurs qui passent un contrat de cession ou d'exploitation des plantations et des autres ressources comme l'eau des forages, les pâturages des réserves sylvo-pastorales et des forêts classées. Au Sud, les potentialités gommières sont plus importantes du fait d'une pluviométrie plus stable et plus abondante mais ici ce sont les contraintes institutionnelles et foncières qui limitent l'exploitation. Dans les deux grands secteurs de production, l'absence de prise en compte des différentes utilisations d'*Acacia senegal*, dans l'évaluation économique potentielle des systèmes de production agro-sylvo-pastoraux, ferait considérablement sous-estimer l'intérêt réel de cette espèce. Compte tenu de la vulnérabilité de l'élevage et de l'agriculture, liée aux sècheresses épisodiques et aux ravages des insectes, la production gommière, en tant que revenu d'appoint, peut sécuriser l'économie rurale si elle s'intègre à un aménagement global des terroirs.

Perpectives et recommandations

Programmes de développement
Ces programmes devraient se fonder sur une relocalisation progressive de la zone gommière tenant compte du recul des isohyètes vers le Sud, ceci dans les limites pluviométriques 300-500 mm considérées comme optimales pour la production de gomme. Ils serait bon par ailleurs que ces programmes 1/ soient de nature polyvalente et s'intègrent aux autres systèmes de production existant dans la zone gommière, 2/ associent les populations bénéficiaires ainsi que les institutions en charge des problèmes gommiers, 3/ prennent en compte un aménagement des dispositions foncières et d'usage ainsi que de cogestion.

Programmes de recherche
Ces programmes devraient inclure:

• la poursuite des expérimentations à la station de Mbiddi et l'extension des observations à des localités plus méridionales du sud-Ferlo afin de mieux préciser le comportement des gommiers dans des régions correspondant mieux aujourd'hui à la zone de pluviométrie optimale;

- des études sur le fonctionnement hydrique des arbres (bilan hydrique, potentiels de sève et transpiration) aux étapes successives du processus de gommose;
- des travaux complémentaires sur les modalités histologiques de la gommose en relation avec différents états de stress hydrique;
- une approche approfondie de la variabilité génétique des populations d'*Acacia senegal* étudiées ainsi que du comportement des deux phénotypes à écorce gris clair et gris foncé;
- une évaluation de l'influence des insectes (après perturbation du rythme phénologique) et de l'impact des défoliants chimiques sur l'exsudation gommière.

REFERENCES BIBLIOGRAPHIQUES

Dione, M. (1983a) — La survie des jeunes plantations dans la réserve sylvopastorale du Nord Sénégal en relation avec les problèmes hydriques. Thèse M. Sc., Université de Laval, Québec, 186 pp.

Dione, M. (1983b) — Rapport d'activité 1982 du Programme 304-02 — Projet Gomme Arabique et Reboisements pastoraux ISRA/DRPF. Centre National de Recherches Forestières, Dakar, 71 pp.

Dione, M. (1986) — Actions de recherche et de développement sur le gommier et la gomme arabique au Sénégal. Bilan, contraintes, perspectives. Mémoire de confirmation ISRA/DRPF, Centre National de Recherches Forestières, Dakar, 93 pp.

Dione, M. (1989a) — Quelques résultats sylvicoles préliminaires concernant les deux phénotypes de *Acacia senegal*. 3ème Symposium sous-régional sur le gommier et la gomme arabique (SYGGA III), Saint-Louis, Sénégal, 25-28 octobre 1988, publ. ISRA/DRPF, vol. 1:105-109.

Dione, M. (1989b) — Période de saignée et potentialités en gomme arabique de quelques localités de la zone gommière du Sénégal. 3ème Symposium sous-régional sur le gommier et la gomme arabique (SYGGA III), Saint-Louis, Sénégal, 25-28 octobre 1988, publ. ISRA/DRPF, vol. 1:117-126.

Dione, M. (1989c) — Rapport sur les tests de saignée effectués à Mbeuleukhé dans le cadre du protocole d'appui scientifique au Projet Zone Nord. Campagne 1988/1989 — ISRA/DRPF, Dakar.

Dione, M. & Sall, P.N. (1992) — Les recherches forestières dans la zone sylvopastorale: bilan succinct et perspectives. Rapport de la composante nationale/RCS au séminaire/bilan sur les recherches relatives au sylvo-pastoralisme au Sahel. Dakar, 7-12 mai 1992 — Publ. ISRA/DRPF, 16 pp.

Freudenberger, M. (1988) — Contradictions of gum afforestation projects. Observations from the Linguere Department of Northern Senegal. Bull. Int. Group for the Study of Mimosoideae, 16 :87-122.

Freudenberger, M. (1992) — The great gum gamble: a planning perspective on environmental change in northern Senegal. Ph.D., University of California, Los Angeles, U.M.I. ed., 469 pp.

Le Houerou, H.N. (1988) — Introduction au projet Ecosystèmes Pastoraux Sahéliens — Sénégal — Rapport P.N.U.E./FAO, Rome, 146 pp.

Michon, P. (1968) — Les gommiers au Tchad. Bois et Forêts des Tropiques, 117: 27-30, publ. CTFT, Nogent-sur-Marne, France.

Mouret, M. (1987) — Les acacias gommiers. Essais expérimentaux. Recherches histologiques sur la gommose. Thèse de doctorat 3ème cycle, Université P. Sabatier, Toulouse, 184 pp.

Sene, A. (1988) — Recherches sur la productivité gommière d'*Acacia senegal* dans le Nord-Ferlo (Sénégal) — Thèse de doctorat 3ème cycle, Université P. Sabatier, Toulouse, 243 pp.

Sylla Gaye, C. (1984) — Phyto-écologie et problèmes sylvo-pastoraux dans la savane sahélienne de Mbiddi, Nord-Sénégal. Thèse M.Sc., Université de Laval, Québec, 2 vol., 269 pp.

Sylla Gaye, C. (1989) — Comportement de *Acacia senegal* en plantation et dans la nature du Sahel sénégalais. Perspectives d'avenir des reboisements gommiers. 3ème Symposium sous-régional sur le gommier et la gomme arabique (SYGGA III), Saint-Louis, Sénégal, 25-28 octobre 1988, publ. ISRA/DRPF: 139-169.

Vassal, J., Sall, P., Dione, M., Fenyo, J.C., Vandevelde, M.C., Servant-Duvallet, S. & Chappuis, A. (1992) — Modélisation du comportement de populations artificielles d'acacias gommiers (*Acacia senegal*) dans le Ferlo sénégalais. Compte rendu de fin d'étude d'une recherche financée par le MRT, France, 74 pp.

Vassal, J. (1992 — sous presse) — Etat des connaissances sur l'induction de gommose chez *Acacia senegal*. In Physiologie des arbres et arbustes en zone aride et semiaride, publ. Groupe d'Etude de l'Arbre, Paris, 5 pp.

Vassal, J. & Mouret, M. (1992 — sous presse) — Etapes histologiques du processus de gommose chez *Acacia senegal*. In Physiologie des arbres et arbustes en zone aride et semi-aride, publ. Groupe d'Etude de l'Arbre, Paris, 6 pp.

The Project "Right to education" in Burkina Faso

Ingrid Fries
Upplands Väsby
Sweden

"Everyone has the right to education. The education shall be free, at least in the primary schools"...
(Article nr. 26 UN:s Declaration of the HUMAN RIGHTS, 10.th of December 1948)

The project was initiated in 1985, when Ingrid Fries was living in Burkina Faso, with her husband Jöran, between 1983-1985. In the beginning of 1985, Ingrid Fries was working as a consultant for UNICEF, Ouagadougou, in a Kindergarten-program, which was a part of the global UNICEF-program 1985-1990, called GOBI-FFF. During that period Ingrid Fries met Antoine and Franceline Bazie', directors of the school in the village Dazankie'ma, about 20 km's from Ouaga.

They told her about the problems they had to get money so they could construct another classroom at the school, which only consisted of one, single classroom for the whole village!

When the job at UNICEF brought Ingrid Pries to Dazankie'ma, she understood the urgent need of a new classroom.

Before leaving Burkina for Sweden, permanently, she went to the village again to say goodbye and on that occasion she also gave a small personal gift to Mr. and Madame Bazie', a gift, which was meant for their two, little daughters.

This small gift, however, Mr. and Mme. Bazie', used instead to buy some concrete in order to begin the construction of a new classroom!

On that hot afternoon, in June 1985, it was, therefore, the very first start of the project, which two years later was called "Right to education in Burkina Faso". When Ingrid Fries had returned to Sweden in 1985, she started to raise money from LIONS and others in order to help the school in Dazankie'ma to build a new classroom. But soon she realised, that they needed much more money to be able to complete the school. In september, 1986, she took the initiative to form the local association of United Nations Upplands Väsby, which is one of the 120 local Associations belonging to UNA, United Nations Association of Sweden.

The pupils at the high-school Vilunda, in Upplands Väsby, decided, when they heard from Ingrid Fries about the schools in Burkina, to have their amateur-theatre on the 24th. of October, the UN:s Day and taking an entrance-fee of 10 SEK. to support the school in Dazankie'ma.

The Association of UN in Upplands Väsby, received 10,000 SEK from the pupils at Vilunda High-school, to send to the school in Dazankie'ma! Next year, in 1987, the Association could send an application of support from SIDA to the project "Right to education" in Burkina Faso. In July 1987, our application was accepted by SIDA and the Association of UN in Upplands Väsby, could send about 110,000 SEK to the school in Dazankie'ma, to construct two new classrooms with equipment.

In 1988 we sent a new application to SIDA and we received about 60,000 SEK to build one new classroom in Dazankie'ma. This time we had also integrated the Gouronsi-village Tenado, 20 km's from Koudougou. Tenado is the birth-place for both Franceline and Antoine Bazie'. In Tenado we helped a cooperative for the women to get a mill to grind millet, but they also got support to build two new classrooms and two houses for the teachers at the school in Tenado, where there only was one single classroom.

The same year, in July 1988, came a letter of despair from M. and Mme. Bazie', who told us about the damage to the school in Dazankie'ma, caused by the heavy rains during the rainy season. Some of the classrooms, made of clay-brick , were completely ruined and most of the animals, belonging to the school, had drowned, during the 24 hours of constant rain.

The Association of UN in Upplands Väsby, decided then to send a new application, the third one, to SIDA to help the village to rebuild, but in concrete this time, all the buildings which were ruined by the rain and to buy new animals.

This time SIDA had also accepted our application for a trip to follow-up the project "Right to education" in the two villages Dazankie'ma and Tenado.

In 1990, we sent our forth application to SIDA, to build two more classrooms and two more houses for the teachers in Dazankie'ma. In 1992, our fifth application to SIDA was accepted and this time a trip to follow-up the project also was included. After four years we came to Burkina for about 15 days, at the end of October and the beginning of November, 1992. We went to Tenado and to Dazankie'ma, to look at the new buildings, the equipment and the school-garden.

We had a short conference with the teachers of the school in Dazankie'ma and we decided to develop the school in Dazankie'ma to a Pioneer-school, by introducing Environmental Education into the curriculum.

The local Association of UN in Upplands Väsby, will try to continue the cooperation with Mr. and Mme. Bazie, and the population in the two villages. The next time we send an application to SIDA, the sixth, we will try to follow-up the results from Rio, Brazil, where UNCED, UN'S conference about Environment and Development took place in June, 1992. All Nations, who participated, agreed to accept Agenda 21, a program of Action, with 5 Declarations, in order to Save the Earth.

The Rio-declaration implied also a commitment for the Rich countries to help the Developing countries to get enough financial support to make this possible.

Education and teaching about Environmental problems in Kindergarten, Primary schools, High-schools and Universities is, therefore, very important, perhaps the most important, if our children are to have a Future in this world!

Application nr.	1	2	3	4	5
Own cash SEK	11050	2000	10500	4000	10000
Own work	7500	-	2500	3000	10000
Contribution from SIDA	106700	58000	52000	26000	80000
Totally	125250	60000	65000	33000	100000

THE PROBLEMS WITH THE CFA-ZONE
Exchange Rate Policy in
Sub-saharan Africa

Peter Ellehøj[1]
Danida, Copenhagen
Denmark

Introduction

During the last decade, most African countries have been faced with persistent and unsustainable balance of payment deficits, low GDP growth, negative real growth rate of, per capita, income and huge debt service obligations relative to export earnings. In addressing these issues, a great deal of policy conditionality in programmes of stabilization and structural adjustment have focused on one aspect of macroeconomic policies: the exchange rate. The Bretton Woods institutions have argued that the overall poor economic performance of African countries is due, inter alia, to the absence of an enabling environment to encourage economic agents to invest and produce efficiently. The incentive structure does not promote efficiency in the utilisation of resources. In particular, it is argued that the macro-economic policy mix in many African countries has led to the overvaluation of real exchange rates, which has in turn discouraged export production and diversification and made imports artificially cheap. Furthermore, the balance of payment crisis can, to a large extent, be explained by the overvaluation of the domestic currency and the quantitative restrictions that are used in managing balance of payments.

Exchange rates do thus have a vital — if often overlooked — position in the evolution of developing countries. Exchange rates have this particular ability, being relative prices, that they are not as obvious as more direct, say fiscal, initiatives and one can get more uniform and less socially stirring effects through the use of monetary policy and exchange

---

1) *The opinions expressed in this paper are those of the author and does not necessary reflect the views of any institution to which he is affilated.*

rates as a policy instrument. Changing the exchange rates is, therefore, immediately attractive to policymakers, when facing internal economic difficulties. By doing this, however, a plethora of derived effects will occur: the terms of trade of the developing countries will change, thereby determining the prices producers can reap from producing cash crops; the size of the imports will be altered, influencing the production of local substitutes; the size of the external debt in local currency will be arithmetically adjusted; the willingness of foreign investors to invest in the economy of developing countries will be affected; internal distribution of wealth will be skewed; etc.

The quest of this paper is to examine the exchange rate system used by thirteen countries in Sub-saharan Africa — many of which are in the Sahel region. These countries — the CFA countries[1] using CFA as their currency (the, often used, term 'franc zone' encompasses all countries who uses the french franc or pegs their currency to it. Besides France and the CFA countries, the franc zone includes the DOM/TOMs, the Comores and Monaco) — have conventionally been associated with economic stability attributed to a fixed exchange rate with France and guaranteed convertibility of the currency, the CFA franc. But the CFA zone economies have experienced economic decline in recent years, and most countries have had to adopt economic austerity programmes. Farmers have protested against lowered crop purchase prices, while public sector workers have been antagonized by wage cuts and freezes. Most of the thirteen countries are thus becoming more unstable, both politically and economically, and are now widely being identified as prone for an imminent devaluation.

In this eclectic presentation, the scope is not as much to give an exhaustive picture of all the problems facing the CFA zone, but rather to expose some of the intricacies facing the decisionmakers in assessing the implications of a devaluation.

As can be seen from the table below, the countries in question are far from uniform. Wide disparities can be found not only in economic terms but also in human development terms. It is, however, telling that most of these countries are among the twenty less endowed in the world, when one uses the human development index. All the CFA zone countries are small — none have a population above 12 million inhabitants — and most are poor, particularly the Sahel countries of Chad, Mali, Niger and Burkina Faso. Most of them rely heavily on exports of a variety of agricultural products for their foreign earnings needed for imports of necessities, and the highest income countries are heavily reliant upon

---

1) *Throughout the text, the term CFA zone is used to characterize the thirteen countries in Sub-saharan Africa (listed in the figure).*

Country	Institution	Currency	Money Stock (1)	M in % (2)	GNP per capita (3)	Human Development Index
France	Banque de France	FF	4.970.000	97,50%	20.600	8
Benin	Banque	FCFA	2,66		380	149
Burkina Faso	Centrale	(0,02 FF)	3,20		350	157
Côte d'Ivoire	d'des Etats		16,91		690	123
Niger	Afrique		2,53		300	156
Senegal	de l'Ouest		7,04		720	137
Togo	(B.C.E.A.O)		3,20		410	132
Mali			2,72		280	155
TOTAL Union Monetaire Ouest Africain			38,30	0,75%		
Cameroon	Banque	FCFA	15,13		940	118
Central	des Etats	(0,02 FF)	1,24		390	144
African Rep.	d'Afrique					
Congo	Centrale		3,36		1120	113
Gabon	(B.E.A.C)		5,75		3780	91
Eq. Guinea			0,07		330	143
Chad			1,40		220	150
TOTAL CENTRAL AFRICA			26,95	0,53 %		

1) Billion of French francs (FF) in 1990
2) Repartition of the monetary base in percentage — the residual 1,22 % are composed of the DOM and Monaco (which uses FF), the TOM (who uses FCFP = 0,055 FF) and the Comores (which uses the franc comorien = 0,02 FF).
3) US$ per capita in 1991.

Sources: *Comites monetaires de la zone-franc/OFCE; World Bank Atlas 1992; Human Development Report 1992*

oil exports (Gabon, Congo and Cameroon). Most are also heavily dependent on official transfers and concessional lending.

The mechanism of the CFA zone

The existence, in West Africa, of a monetary union as the CFA-zone is rather interesting. With the debate in Europe of the emergence of a

The CFA zone

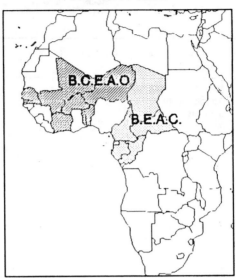

single European currency within the EMU, it is a surprise for some to learn that such a concept has existed within the CFA-zone since 1948. One should, however, stop the comparison here. The CFA-case is exceptional, if only by its longevity. Through its soon fifty years of existence, it has survived the collapse of the Bretton Woods system and is one of the oldest fixed exchange (or parity) system existing.

Exchange rates can be set in a variety of fashions. Often one talks of floating exchange rates or of fixed exchange systems. In between there is an abundance of variations. For the former, the exchange is left wholly to the market forces i.e. the price setting of the currency on the international markets is determined by the selling and purchasing of currency, in connection with exports, imports and investments. The fixed exchange rate is a given ratio of the exchange rates between several countries, which is maintained through central bank operations at a given par in disrespect of the fluctuations of the exchange market operations. The CFA-zone is, thus, a fixed exchange rate system where the convertibility, as well as the level of the CFA, is guaranteed by the Banque de France.

The CFA zone is composed of two separate unions: the West African

Monetary Union (BCEAO.) and the Bank of the Central African States (BEAC). A good part of the former French colonies in Sub-saharan Africa joined one or other of the two unions, albeit with some defections. Joining in 1985, Equatorial Guinea became not only the smallest member of the zone, but also the first not to have been a former French colony. Each of these central banks issue their own currencies, which are both known as CFA franc.

Currencies of the CFA zone are freely convertible into the French franc at the fixed rate of 50 CFA to 1 FF (a parity maintained since 1948), through 'operations accounts' established by agreements concluded between the French Treasury, and the individual issuing banks. It is backed fully by the French Treasury which also provides the issuing banks with overdraft facilities. The monetary mechanisms are characterized by: an annual monetary programming exercise which determines the planned growth in domestic credit in each member country; implementation of this monetary program through credit ceilings to each government and, in some cases, to the private sector, or through ceilings on central bank refinancing of private sector credit; and administered interest rates, including preferential rates for priority sectors. The monetary reserves of the CFA countries are normally held in French francs in the French Treasury. However, the BCEAO and the BOAC are authorized to hold up to 35% of their foreign exchange holdings in currencies other than the franc, when the reserves are positive. When the reserves are negative, convertibility is supported through the use of overdraft facilities on the same account. This implies, in principle, that the French Treasury will cover any balance of payment deficit these countries develop. Exchange is effected on the Paris market. Part of the reserves earned by richer countries can be used to offset the deficits incurred by poorer countries. Regulation drawn up in 1967, provided for the free convertibility of currency with that of countries outside the zone. Restrictions were removed on the import and export of CFA banknotes, although some capital transfers are subject to approval by the governments concerned.

The economic performance of the CFA zone

Although exchange rate policy is just one policy measure governments can use, it can be quite powerful in determining the relations to the outer world, indeed in protecting poorer countries from externalities. How has this zone then performed over time? Several studies have compared the members of the CFA zone with comparable countries in the region (see e.g. Lane C. & Page S. 1990) and found many compelling features, but also a number of caveats as to its viability.

On average the record is positive. The advantages of having a stable monetary union were evident up to the mid 80's. Until then, the CFA zone members benefited from a higher growth than other countries in Sub-saharan Africa. Another beneficial factor was a rather low evolution of the inflation rate. By 1986-88, the franc zone inflation was negative at -1% pro annum compared with 31% for the average of Sub-saharan countries[1].

The combination of a fixed exchange rate and a low inflation could have been indices for competitiveness in the international markets. The 1980's saw, however, the exchange rate being generally more overvalued. There are several reasons for this.

First, the introduction of floating regimes in neighbouring and competing African countries (Nigeria, Ghana, Sierra Leone, Gambia, and Zaire) aggravating the incentives to smuggling, which has developed into a big problem (especially from Nigeria and Ghana). The CFA countries have, thus, become less competitive, as the real manufacturing costs are higher than comparable others.

Secondly, the pegging to a relatively strong country. While the French franc was weak in the 60's and 70's, its inclusion in the European Monetary System has stabilised and strengthened it. As there has been a change in trade patterns away from France (which, at one time, stood for 80% of some countries' exportations), this has aggravated the terms of trade for the zone.

The zone stands now in a larger economic crisis. While record until the mid 80's was good, if not overwhelming, since then it has soared. The decline in output and economic activity can be seen as the result of both adverse international environment and poor domestic economic management.

Adverse externalities like the shifting terms of trade which has manifested itself, especially, through soaring commodity prices (coffee, cocoa etc.) are obviously one of the foremost reasons. While this was a general phenomenon, it hit the CFA zone the harder since its currency was pegged to a strong currency (the French franc), while their commodities were set in terms of a currency in relative decline (the dollar). Exports became less attractive while imports cheapened — with all the structural consequences this entailed. Most of the zone members have also seen themselves faced with severe payments arrears and classified as "severely indebted" by the World Bank.

---

1) *Inflation has, however, been partly suppressed by the accumulation of public sector arrears to the private sector — which amount to several percentage points of GDP in Côte d'Ivoire, Benin, Chad and Senegal.*

To this comes that a widespread poor quality government intervention in the functioning of the economy has created some long term damage. A striking example would be the financial sector, where great damage to the credit system has occurred. Centralized allocation of credit — particularly to public cooperations — allowed a high proportion of non-performing loans. This, and politically influenced lending, led to severe curtailing of the banking sectors in Benin, Côte d'Ivoire, Cameroon and Senegal.

As was noted at the outset, the overvalued exchange rate has been seen as one linchpin to these difficulties. It might be worth-while to recapitulate briefly some of the elements characterizing overvaluation of currencies.

Overvaluation of currencies and devaluation

That a Third World currency is overvalued is not an exceptional phenomenon. Most developing countries have, in fact, opted for an overvalued official exchange rate. Basically, the governments have done this as part of widespread programmes of rapid industrialization and import-substitution. Overvalued exchange rates reduce the domestic currency price of imports below that which would exist in a free market of foreign exchange. Imported capital and intermediate products are, thus, cheaper and should help fuelling the industrialization process. But overvalued exchange rates also make imported consumer goods, especially luxury products, cheaper — this can, however, be managed through import controls or dual exchange rates. The other side of overvaluation is that it reduces the returns to local exporters and to those import-competing industries, which are not protected by heavy tariffs or physical quotas. Exporters receive less domestic currencies for their products than would be forthcoming if the free market exchange rate prevailed. Moreover, exporters, mostly farmers, become less competitive in the world markets since the price of their products has been artificially elevated by the overvalued exchange rate.

If accompanying measures are not taken, an overvalued currency, thus, has a tendency to exacerbate balance of payment problems, simply because they make imports cheaper and exports more costly.

Besides the problems of balance of trade, it goes without saying that an overvalued currency creates internal structural distortions as the consumption is twisted, in what economists will denote rational behaviour, towards cheaper foreign imported products rather than locally produced. Moreover, consumption patterns are created, not only in basic commodities, but also in so-called luxury items, that may be difficultly reversible. In the consumption adjustment, as well as in the structural shift in production, one can thus find several repercussions on the social dimension.

A further problem arises when one considers the case where there is free convertibility and free movement of financial assets. In this case there is an incentive towards capital outflow from the country as the holders expect a devaluation. We shall return to this point later.

One can, thus, see that the overvalued currency, while in theory promoting the industrialization process, has some important side-effects. Where the economic red lights begin to flash is when the balance of payment has turned into chronic deficit, resulting from current account transactions (i.e. imports and exports). The standard way to handle this problem would be to devaluate the currency i.e. basically reduce the value of the currency in terms of other countries' currencies. This should, in theory, stimulate the demand for its exports by making them cheaper and discourage imports as foreign goods become dearer.

The textbook scenario is that of South Korea, which experienced rapid growth of manufactured exports due to the government's willingness and ability to adjust the exchange rate, tariffs, and subsidies.

Experiences with devaluations are, however, more mitigated than this experience. While devaluation is still widely proposed as a remedy for developing country problems, in the industrialized countries one has seen that governments are more and more reluctant to use this measure. The reason for this is that there is the so-called 'J-curve' effect. This effect, basically, says that the windfall in balance of payments take some time to occur, as the expected import downfall is lingered by the fact that there is a rather large part of imports that have already been ordered, and the shift in consumption and production takes some time to occur. It can also not be taken for granted that the exports will grow as much as expected, as this relates to the production structure of the economy and willingness of the outside world to make additional imports. Another feature is the shaken confidence in the currency: will there be another devaluation?

The most important feature of a devaluation, as seen by economists, is its inflationary effects. Experience from developing countries (especially in Latin America) have proved that this is not a point to be discarded. As mentioned before, the effect of a devaluation is to raise the price in local currency of imported goods. If, as a result of these higher prices, domestic workers seek to preserve the 'real' value of their purchasing power (be able to continue consuming as before), they are likely to initiate increased wage and salary demands. Such increases, if granted, will raise production costs and tend to push local prices up even higher. A wage-price spiral of domestic inflation is thereby set in motion. In fact, a vicious circle of devaluation — domestic wage and price increases — higher export prices — worsened balance of trade — devaluation could result. In effect, the decision to devaluate could simply exacerbate the balance of payment problem, while generating galloping inflation domestically. The experience of Latin American countries during the 50's and 60's, and many other LDCs in the 70's, have made policymakers in developing countries reluctant to use devaluation as a tool.

As for the distributional effect of a devaluation, it goes without saying that by altering the domestic price and return of 'tradable' goods (exports and imports) and creating incentives for the production of exports, as opposed to domestic goods, devaluation will benefit certain groups at the expense of others. In general, urban wage earners, those with fixed incomes, the unemployed and those small farmers and rural and urban small-scale producers and suppliers of services who do not participate in the export sector, stand to be financially hurt by the domestic inflation that typically follows a devaluation. On the other hand, large exporters (usually large land-owners and foreign-owned corporations) as well as the medium-sized local businessmen engaged in foreign trade, stand to benefit the most.

Nevertheless, devaluation is still a tool the policy-maker can use to correct problems that have proved too cumbersome. Recent experience in Sweden and Finland have shown, that this policy measure is not out of the agenda, even in the industrialized world. As so many other developing countries, the CFA zone is now — once again — under heavy pressure to devaluate its currency.

Mounting pressure for a devaluation

Several observers have called for a reform of the CFA, giving as reason that if the mechanisms of a single fixed exchange rate cannot ensure reasonably tight domestic macroeconomic policies and at least approximate uniformity across member countries, then the arguments for a single fixed rate at the given ratio fall away. This pressure for a devaluation stems especially from third party i.e. influential external donor countries (e.g. USA and Japan) who do question, to a far greater extent than before, the viability of the system when considering the overall situation. From "inside", that is France and the CFA member countries, this criticism has been publicly repudiated in strong terms. For the governments of the member states, talk of a devaluation is taboo, a non-issue. And rightly so. Obviously one can, and should, never admit that devaluation is being envisaged. This will only ruin the effects of the devaluation. Even so, the recurrent statements as to the maintenance of the present system cover, to a lesser extent, a belief in the qualities of the present system, but rather a realization of the complexities of changing the system, and a fear of the uncertain prospects of a new one.

The problem with this taboo is that it has become something of a ritual. Every time the heads of governments or the ministers of finance of the member countries meet, it has become almost an inevitable feature that rumours of an imminent devaluation roam around, large amounts of currency are fleeing from the CFA countries and investors are holding their breath (and money). At the meeting, somebody will seriously proclaim that there will be no change whatsoever, and the circus goes on until the next gathering.

At the time of writing, the CFA community and actors interested in this zone are again holding their breath, this time as to the outcome of the French parliamentary elections in March 1993. It is widely held that the new 'cohabitation' that would occur, might favour a reform of the CFA monetary arrangement. Let there, however, be no doubts that the CFA question is not a party political issue in France: a recent survey from Marchés Tropicaux has, once again, confirmed that the major political parties to a large extent, share the same views of France's relation to it former colonies. Although France is confronted with internal business pressure, the importance of the CFA zone to them is not economic, but rather political. The combined GNP of the CFA zone in 1991 constitutes only 4,1% of that of France, and the share of the zone in France's total exports in 1991, was only 1,37%. The CFA countries must be seen in the context of 'La Francophonie' and as allies in the construction of France's international political status. Nevertheless, there is a slight shift in the French position towards reforms.

The foreign pressure has been increasingly open-mouthed the last years, and several donors are raising the issue in bilateral and multilateral negotiations. The IMF and the World Bank have become more assertive on the issue and new loans to members of the zone, especially larger ones that would benefit most from a devaluation (Côte d'Ivoire and Cameroon), have to a great extent been stopped. Even in the CFA countries, government officials are increasingly sceptical about the costs of the present arrangement and are publicly stating this, something, hitherto, unheard of. There seems to be a consensus among African CFA zone members as to the need for a devaluation (unanimity is required by the governing treaties).

The needs of the individual countries are, however, quite different: Burkina Faso and Gabon, for example, would seek a far smaller devaluation than, say, Côte d'Ivoire and Cameroon. There has, thus, been considerations as to a two-tier system with differentiated devaluations with, for example, 10% devaluation for Burkina Faso and 40% for Côte d'Ivoire. Such a solution, while in many ways attractive, may hamper the much sought regional integration which assumes one exchange rate.

On the other hand, some are rather sceptical of the immediate tangibility of such an integration: of the total (official) external trade of the BCEAO countries in 1991, only 11% was within the union, for the BEAC countries the share was just 3%. The reason for this can be found in the fact that the member countries tend to produce rather comparable consumer and light industrial goods and grow the same crops. With such small domestic markets the potential for greater integration is rather limited.

While it is true that there are serious problems facing the CFA zone countries and an obvious target would be the exchange rate, the problem is more intricate than just changing the parity of the CFA, i.e. devaluating.

The problem with devaluation

The textbook case for — and against — devaluation was outlined because it underlies a lot of the current debate on the problems involved here. The problem with the CFA is, however, that it is not just an economic entity, but rather a political reality. Whilst the standard devaluation arguments concern individual countries, the analysis becomes intricate when examining a group of thirteen countries which, although sharing a large common political background, are faced with a quite variegated economic and sociological reality. One could say that there are the Sahelian countries and the "Forest countries". Each of them will have different production structures, prices to the producers, distribution circuits, institutional arrangements etc.

When examining the consequences of a possible devaluation, one does — given its far-reaching consequences — have a vast menu to look at: What will be the likely repercussions on the rural population and small peasants who, after all, constitute around 70% of the population of these countries? In general, what social repercussions will be generated? Given that the production structure will be altered as well as the resource exploitation, how will the environment be affected? What will be the modalities and size of a devaluation: will it be a one for all or several smaller devaluations? What will be the accompanying measures, macro- and microeconomic as well as social, following a devaluation? The list could go on, encompassing more points than are usually considered when economists assess the impact of devaluation. And this is precisely the point, devaluation will have a far-reaching effect and must, thus, be assessed as part of the quest towards sustainable development in its widest sense.

Devaluation is such a radical change in a country's relations to the outside world, as well as an important switching in the internal relative prices, that high caution must be observed when using this instrument. It has often been part of the "packages" dealt with by the IMF in the restructuring of developing countries, but the track record has been, to put it mildly, mitigated. The inherent problem seems to be that too often, the answer to the need and likely consequences of a devaluation has been based on narrow (macro-) economic analysis. The sociological, political, and even environmental aspects linked to the problem have been down-played.

It would be going too far to examine all these complexities here. Just looking at a few of the cases, where the standard economic arguments go that a devaluation will benefit the countries, reveals some of the problems with a devaluation.

First, let us look at the *exportable agricultural production*. The common argument in favour of devaluation is that it is the only way to increase the price to producers (to increase production), given that a budgetary deficit increase is not possible. The costs of production should, in theory, be lowered and the outlet for exports should be enhanced. However, several features impinge on this argument and blur the picture.

First, nothing proves the producers will reap the devaluation benefit as the state may pocket it[1], or the intermediaries may take it. Even though the state buys the production, it rarely pays it in cash, and there is, thus, a temptation to sell to private salesmen, who give less than the state guaranteed price.

Secondly, there is a problem with the production price elasticity (i.e. how the price will react to change). Nothing proves that the benefit will be invested in additional production and extension of cultivated area. The microeconomic "truth" that higher prices will lead to higher production should be amended. Economic-man functions in a social and ecological network with high risk-averseness, and there is a high specialization within the family that inhibits substitution and expansion. To this comes that, as it is difficult to see any enhanced effectiveness, an expansion of area will thus be the consequence. While agricultural production in the standard argument is often assumed to be based on financial restrictions, there are other factors which impede (production techniques, climate...) and shape the outcome. Finally, the sensitivity of the producers to the ratio production cost/factor costs, is also not unequivalent[2].

---

1) i.e. through 'equalization fund' as happened in Côte d'Ivoire in 1974 and more recently in Madagascar.

Thirdly, the devaluation benefit would be eaten up by rise in production factors, as imported production factors (fertilizers, etc) will automatically grow to higher levels. As these factors constitute around 40% of the selling price, one can see how this will affect the ultimate price. This is not to say that a substitution towards local factors could not be happening (more linkages between cattle and cultures could be wished to substitute fertilizers with fumures), but the experience of this has been that it is disappointingly slow. The reaped benefit is also only valid if there is a stable general price level. However, the experience shows that inflationary effects most often occur and circumvent this. Of course, to hamper this effect one could make accompanying measures of subsidy to imported production factors, but this will go against the general credo of the Bretton Woods institutions.

Lastly, to devalue presupposes a sufficient external demand elasticity (a great willingness to absorb an increase in exports). What is often overlooked in the argument, is that certain products are, in fact, price-makers (coffee and cocoa) and will, thus, lower world prices, leaving the exporters with less revenues than expected. Experience has, in fact, shown that if balance of payment has been reached, it has been at the price of falling imports, rather than rise in exports.

These arguments should reveal that it is far from certain that the effects on the exportable agricultural production will be positive. Recall then that the CFA countries are endowed with variegated production techniques, assortment, and capacities, and one can see the problem entailed in a one for all uniform devaluation.

Whilst the exportable agricultural production is the linchpin in the favourable analyses of an devaluation, several economists have pointed out that the *subsistence production* would benefit from a devaluation, as it will be protected from the external competition due to the fact that imports will have become more expensive.

Several points do, however, lead one to be sceptical as to whether a decrease of food imports will lead to increase in local production: the elasticity of production is rather small (agricultural production has only risen by 0,7% p.a. the last 20 years in Sahel, against a demographic increase of 2,5% p.a.); there is a problem with the distribution circuits, which already have difficulties in spreading the existing production; as for the exportable sector, there is still the fact that the price of the factors of production will rise and this may again, however, at a smaller scale, lead to increases in prices; there will be the need for a change in the consumption structure (rice to millet, for example) and one has seen

---

Page 56: 2) The case of Senegal in the period 1961-78 proved this for groundnuts but experience with cotton in Togo between 80-85 didn't.

the difficulties involved in achieving such a shift; the rise of the food price will penalize the small peasants; the urban poor will have difficulties in matching their revenue with the higher prices; the taxation of imported goods constitute an important part of the states' taxation base.

We have here concentrated on the repercussions of the productive, agricultural sector. This is also the most prominent reasons for a devaluation stemming from its advocates. It may, however, be worth considering the effects on a different sector: industry. Recall that overvaluation was initially advanced as an argument for promoting the take off of local industry. The record has been painfully disappointing. High real wages, falling competitivity, and a less than satisfying industrial policy have circumvented any real evolution of this sector. Furthermore, industrial control is characterized by foreign ownership (estimated at 70-90% according to countries) or state-owned (10 to 40%). There is a great lack of local entrepreneurs in the formal sector, but the informal sector seems to be as buoyant as ever. There is no doubt, however, that the present situation is detrimental to the industrial sector in the CFA countries. One could reflect that it has as much to do with the industrial policies, or lack thereof, and the self-enforcing negative perceptions among the industrial decision makers, as with the actual overvaluation of the currency. As to the latter point, the net foreign investments have been rather disappointing. It seems that investors fall in two parts: those firms who are well established (for example Bouygues, Crédit Lyonnais, Electricité de France, Société Nationale Elf-Aquitaine and Shell) have created themselves a secure market and have committed substantial new funds since the mid 80's and will stay whatever may happen, and the others, who regard the possibility of an imminent devaluation so risky that they are either keeping their investment tight until the situation clarifies or, as some argue, have totally given up on these countries. Recent surveys among industrialists in France reveal, that these firms refuse a devaluation of the CFA by 86%, largely because of the first group. This may seem a paradox when considering that the textbook case identified large exporters as benefiting from a devaluation. This did, however, linger on the assumption that governments' demonstrated willingness to maintain the incentive, in favour of exporting over long periods despite domestic inflation. Foreign banks and companies are not too confident as to the governments' ability to ensure this. This factor, combined with the fact that they would indeed suffer immediate large losses on the value of their present investments if a devaluation occurred, has consequently led business lobbies such as the "Conseil des Investisseurs Francais en Afrique", to strenuously support the status quo.

It is, thus, noteworthy that the present situation tends to hold the zone in a deadlock situation, impeding further — and much needed —

dynamic in the industrial sector.

In this little roundtrip of some of the consequences of devaluation, let us finally consider two additional points:

First, the CFA has become almost a sort of 'Euro-FrancCFA' i.e. in banking terms, a currency used by agents outside the zone to satisfy their international payments. Devaluation or not, there will still be a need for hard currency from adjunctant inconvertible countries (for example, 75% of the buying of CFA comes from the local exchange with Nigeria, which is ready to sell whatever products to get hard currency). The parallel markets have, thus, become a great provider of convertible currency, which is principally traded in London. This has obviously become a big liability for France which sees its own currency position committed to, in fact, give subsidies to non-zone countries.

Secondly, consider the figure that customs revenue constitute 30-40% of state budgetary income. When a devaluation occurs the revenue attained through taxation of imports will fall. Can the devaluation benefits compensate for this?

Devaluation is, thus, not such an easy concept to play around with, and the preceding reflections should have revealed that, if one does not play the devaluation card prudently and take well thought accompagning measures, it can very well be a Pandora's box that has been opened.

Conclusion

Where does all this leave us: Will there be a devaluation? Will it be for the better? It should clear by now that both questions are equally hard to answer.

Whereas the formal position on fixed parity remains unchanged, it seems that the official opinion in both France and Africa is moving strongly towards devaluation and reform of the CFA zone. While the older generation of politicians still have some objections of principle, it seems that what postpones a devaluation is rather vivid controversy over the extent and timing.

If the result of the reform is a devaluation, the preceding reflections should have shown that it is less than clear whether the result will be positive. While, on the one hand, aggregate indicators like the balance of payment could impede positive effects, it has, on the other hand, been shown that several factors will heavily hamper this result. It may even digress into a situation far worse than the one known today, with inflationary spirals and even more social degradation.

It is by no means an enviable situation facing the decision-makers of the concerned countries. While having insecure and contradictory

macroeconomic advice as to the likely consequences of a devaluation and
— hopefully — considerations as to the social consequences of such a
reform, they are still tangled up in a variegated web of politico-economic
interests. Each country has so many particularities that it will reap
different benefits — and costs — of a reform of the status quo.

For the moment the decisionmakers have opted for the way up, as the
way out: with the European Community as an example, they attempt to
create the synergia for pulling the region out of the crisis. In 1990, the
CFA zone governments agreed to develop an economic union, with integrated public finances and common commercial legislation. In 1991,
ministers of the zone approved the creation of a regional body responsible for compiling statistics and economic studies, which was to be called
'Afristat'. In Yaoundé in April 1992, a treaty was signed on the insurance industry, whereby a regulatory body for the industry was to be
established (Conférence Interafricaine des Marchés d'Assurances). It
was also agreed that a council of ministers were to be created, with the
task of monitoring the social security systems in the CFA countries.

How commendable these initiatives are, they come as too little too
late. More radical and immediate reforms are needed and, at the end of
the day, it would seem that devaluation may well become a self-fulfilling
prophecy. The system could eventually succumb under the pressure for
a devaluation, simply because it will prove too costly not to, whether one
believes in the concept of devaluation or not. The important capital flig-
hts — depriving the countries of valuable internal resources — and
investment inertia — not putting those remaining in productive use —
are costs that have built up over far too long. We may, thus, soon see a
reform of the system.

What will be of importance, is whether the governments of the CFA
countries realize that a devaluation is not the fulfilment of a long craved
need, but rather the beginning of a new era of innovative policymaking.
The important feature will not as much be the devaluation itself, but
rather the accompanying measures. These latter, must reflect the realization that a devaluation only remedies part of a problem and that
balance of payment imbalances is just one manifestation of a variegated
set of structural and systemic problems. To circumvent the adversities
that will inevitably follow a devaluation, policy measures must be taken
to make the best of the new situation. This challenge should also be the
foremost concern of their partners in development, the donors, who
must have the flexibility in their support to remedy for the social costs,
which a devaluation inevitably will have.

The exchange rate system of the CFA zone is flawed in detail, rather
than as a concept. The salient features of the system, guaranteed
convertibility and fixed exchange rates, are of high value for these devel-

oping countries and are valuable building-stones on their way to sustainable development. Whatever reform occurs, they should safeguard these features and refine the system to encompass the lessons taught by recent development history.

References

Bhagwati J.N. 1988. Anatomy and consequences of exchange control regimes. Cambridge, Mass.

Bhatia R.J. 1985. The West African monetary Union — an analytical review. IMF occasional paper 35.

Boughton J.M. 1991. The CFA franc zone: Currency union and monetary standard. IMF working paper WP/91/133

Coquet B. & Daniel J.M. 1992. Quel avenir pour la zone franc?. Revue de l'OFCE, august 1992.

Crockett A.B. & Nsoulu S.M. 1977. Exchange rate policies for developing countries. in Coats W.L. & Khatkhate D.R. (Eds.) Money and monetary policy in less developed countries, Pergamon Press, Oxford, pp.643-660

de Macedo J.B. 1985. Collective pegging to a single currency: the west african monetary union. In Edwards S. & Ahamed L. Economic adjustment and exchange rates in developing countries. NBER, University of Chicago Press.

de Macedo J.B. 1987. Small countries in monetary unions: the choice of Senegal. In Waterbury J. & Gersovitz M. (Eds.) The political economy of risk & choice in Senegal. Frank Cass & Co., London.

de Macedo J.B. 1985. Small countries in monetary unions: a two-tier model. NBER working paper no. 1634.

Devarajan S. & de Melo J. 1987. Adjustment with a fixed exchange rate: Cameroon, Côte d'Ivoire, and Senegal. The World Bank Economic Review, Vol. 1-3, pp. 447-487.

Duruflé G. 1988. L'ajustement structurel en Afrique. Editions Karthala, Paris.

Ellehøj P. 1991. Ved en korsvej. Udvikling no. 3, pp.37-39.

Engelhard P. & Ben Abdallah T. 1989. Faut-il dévaluer le franc CFA? Enda Tiers Monde, Dakar. Unpublished

Flickenschild H.M et al. 1992. Developments in international exchange and payments systems. IMF World Economic and Financial Surveys.

Gauvreau G. 1992. Le Franc CFA — Device ou monnaie? Institution ou prix? unpublished.

Guillaumont P. & S. 1989. Monnaie européene et monnaies africaines. Revue Française d'Economie, Vol. IV-1. pp. 97-116.

Honohan, P. 1990. Monetary cooperation in the CFA zone. The World Bank. Working Papers WPS 389

Lane C. & Page S. 1990. The difference in economic performances between franc zone and other Sub-saharan African countries. ODI, London.

Martin, G. 1986. The franc zone, underdevelopment and dependency in francophone Africa. Third World Quarterly Vol 8-1, pp. 205-235

Sy S.D. Impact prévu de l'évolution du système monétaire europeen sur le régime monétaire et financier des pays Africains membres de la zone franc. United Nations AEC, unpublished.

Vallée O. 1989. Le prix de l'argent CFA — Heurs et malheurs de la zone franc. Editions Karthala, Paris.

World Bank and UNDP 1989. Africa's adjustment and growth in the 1980s. Washington, D.C.

Various issues of: Marchés Tropicaux, Africa Confidential, Jeune Afrique, Le Soleil, Jeune Afrique Economie.

Local natural resources management in Burkina Faso: Constrains and Opportunities

Lars Engberg-Pedersen
Centre for Development Research
Copenhagen, Denmark

The natural resources in Burkina Faso are in a terrible condition. This is a debatable, but commonly held view and the assumption underlying the national programme for land management (*Programme National de Gestion des Terroirs*). Since 1986, the programme has been tested in different parts of the country, and today it is increasingly applied nationwide. Yet, no more than approximately 150 villages of the perhaps 7000 villages in Burkina Faso, are touched by the programme.

The programme is characterized by the following features:
- Natural resource management is decentralized to the village level. Through the participation of villagers, it is expected that the management of natural resources will be more successful, than the one carried out by the state alone.
- Village lands should be demarcated, in order to clarify the area of which each village is in charge. Moreover, the area should be divided into different zones according to their use. E.g., grazing grounds should be separated from cultivated lands and areas lying fallow.
- A council in charge of the management of natural resources should be established in each village. Representatives for all social and economic groups in the village, should participate in this council.
- The village councils should elaborate resource management plans with the support of technicians from the relevant ministries.

While the programme is regarded as successful, on the whole, a number of problems could undermine the efforts. These problems will be outlined below.

Natural resource use and management

There is a basic discrepancy between the levels of natural resource use and natural resource management. The management is confined to the village level, but some natural resources are used either at a household level or at a regional level. In both cases, interference by village councils may be regarded as illegitimate.

Stock breeding is a widespread occupation in Burkina Faso and an example of a regional use of natural resources. However, stock breeders differ in certain respects. Some have a few goats besides cultivating the land, while others do nothing but breed cattle. Some have settled in a village exploiting the pastures nearby, while others practice transhumance or migrate permanently with their animals. No matter how stock breeding is organized, it is seldom restricted to the grazing grounds of a single village. Herdsmen look for good pastures without considering the villages they belong to. Thus, stock breeding is organized at a regional level rather than at a village level.

This has caused problems e.g. when village councils prohibit cattle in parts of their territory without regard to the tracks along which herdsmen seasonally bring their animals. In such cases, the potential for conflict is great. Furthermore, stock breeders are represented in a village council only if they settle down in the village. This means that they can only influence natural resource management when they live permanently in a village, and their influence is, then, restricted to the territory of that particular village.

In a few areas, ten to fifteen village councils have formed an area council to cope with inter-village matters and stock breeding. While this is a step towards regional management of regional natural resource use, there is still a need for a more overall management of pastures and animal tracks.

Contrary to stock breeding, agriculture is organized within a geographically much more restricted area. Each household or family controls its own land. Land is not very often tilled in common. Thus, it is normally the family head who makes the decisions as to how the farming activities should be organized. When conflicts over natural resource use occur between families, village leaders ("chef de terre", "chef de village" etc.) are responsible for solving them. Likewise, newcomers should approach the village leaders when they wish to acquire land. Village leaders, therefore, are legitimate decision-makers in relation to certain well-defined issues, but not in relation to everything.

Daily decisions regarding the use of natural resources, are taken by the family heads. Natural resource management at a village level may, accordingly, run into problems of legitimacy.

Figure 1, illustrates these inconsistencies of the management with the use of natural resources. The figure outlines some of those levels and activities that should be considered in organizing natural resource management. The point is, that management and use of natural resources at different levels should conform to each other and to levels of legitimate decision-making. Consistency between the levels, as well as

Figure 1.	Natural resource use	Natural resource management	Existing legitimate decision-making
The region	stock breeding		
The village	village council	traditional leaders	
The family	agriculture		family heads

between the activities at each level should be a major preoccupation. The tentative nature of the figure should, however, be emphasized. There are more factors such as water usage and wood cutting that should be put into the figure, and an activity like stock breeding is sometimes organized within the village. Likewise, it should not be read from the figure that village councils are illegitimate or that stock breeding and agriculture are not managed. To a large, but varying extent, they are. Finally, prefects and forestry agents have a role to play at more levels, in relation to both management and legitimate decision-making. Reality is, therefore, much more complex than the figure.

The village and outside authorities

One major drawback is that village councils are not recognized as legally responsible bodies, within the state hierarchy. If their decisions are disputed, they have to go to the local prefect to get his support. Thus, the village councils cannot enforce their decisions when e.g. the prefect or the forestry agent disagree on the matter. There are examples of forestry agents authorizing outsiders to cut wood, despite local rules prohibiting it.

Furthermore, the land management programme has to tackle the scepticism existing between villagers and civil servants. Villagers often fear that the delimitation of village lands is the first step in a process towards greater state control of their activities. Thus, they sometimes vigorously oppose this part of the programme. Civil servants, on the other hand, are not accustomed to receiving orders or requests from below. Many years of centrally controlled decision-making have turned attention away from the citizens and upwards within the state hierarchy. Typically, civil servants find it awkward to respond to locally expressed needs.

Financial resources are another important problem. Within the village, finances are scarce and insufficient for conducting management activities, such as building rock lines and terraces, planting trees and digging wells. As the state is short of funds, donor agencies and NGOs are the only possible sources. However, donor agencies tend to prefer short "in-and-out" projects, meaning that village councils can count on necessary financial support only for a limited period. It is, accordingly, very important to find ways in which councils could become more or less financially autonomous during the period they have access to outside resources.

Processes of decision-making

The constitution of village councils for the management of natural resources departs from existing ways of organizing local affairs in two respects. First, village organizations are not normally composed of representatives from different social groups. In Burkina Faso, there is a strong tradition for groups carrying out activities at the village level, but these village groups ("groupements villageois") generally consist of, or are totally dominated by a single social group. By bringing e.g. women and stock breeders together with farmers, the perspective on natural resource management is potentially enlarged.

Second, solving conflicts over natural resource use has, hitherto, been the exclusive concern of village chiefs. Such matters have not been discussed in public. It is, however, the idea that village councils should establish rules for the use of natural resources and intervene in disputes, and this is actually taking place in some cases. This is important in relation to natural resource management. Local norms and practices almost forbid village leaders to deny newcomers land. It seems that village councils have much fewer scruples in this respect. They are more concerned about the conditions of the natural resources and the possibilities for people to make a living from village lands.

Another characteristic of the village councils is that they do not only discuss resource management, but also issues such as education and health. Villagers regard the council as a body for the overall development of the village. Yet, donor agencies tend to refrain from supporting any other activities than those related to resource management. Officially, the land management programme deals with natural resources and not with development in general. However, it is very unlikely that the efforts will be fruitful, if the donor agencies insist on this form of one-sector democracy. Villagers may withdraw their support for village councils if they believe that the councils cannot play a leading role in a broad development process.

Conclusion

There are evident constraints for a successful implementation of the land management programme. The programme does not deal with the different levels at which natural resource use takes place. Especially the stock breeders, sedentary as well as migratory, are being marginalized by the programme. Village councils are in a insecure situation, financially and legally. Scepticism prevails between villagers and civil servants. Village councils represent a considerable challenge to existing local institutions (rules and norms) for policy-making. The one-sector democracy approach is dubious.

However, there are also opportunities for initiating locally driven development efforts through the programme. One such opportunity is to take advantage of the strong tradition in the villages for working together in groups. Villagers are eager to better their living conditions, so with a relatively minor support, mainly of a financial character, it should be possible to create substantial change. Another feature is that through the work of the village councils, a democratization of local political life may take place. It seems that in some villages, women and young farmers increasingly participate in decision-making. Finally, the basic premise behind the land management programme apparently holds true. Villagers are in a much better position to carry out effective and appropriate natural resource management, than are technicians from the state bureaucracy. Compared to other villages, there are generally many more resource management activities in the villages in which the land management approach has been applied.

Management of natural forrests in semi-arid areas of west Africa — needs and possibilities

Jöran Fries
Swedish University of Agricultural Sciences
International Rural Development Centre
Uppsala, Sweden

Background

Important areas of natural savanna forests still exist in West Africa. In the whole of West Africa (Burkina Faso, Mali, Niger, Senegal and Tchad) they cover 43.4 million hectares, and in Burkina Faso, 7.2 million hectares (1). These forests are, however, disappearing rapidly, mainly because of the farmers hunger for new land for cultivation, but also because of overgrazing, fire and woodcutting.

The efforts to save these forests have mainly been restricted to their declaration as reserved forests, forêts classées, whereby the population living in and around them have been deprived of their rights to fell living trees. These reserves were effected already during colonial times in the 30's and 40's. In Burkina Faso, these forests comprise around 700,000 hectares, amounting to one tenth of the total forest area.

The fact that some forests were reserved for Government use has, however, not meant any safe protection against devastation. The demarcation has often been incomplete and the surveillance erratic. Forests along water coarses have had a certain protection, by the fact that these forests have been infested by river blindness (Onchocercose) which is spread by Simulium blackflies hatching in clear, running water. Thus, the sickness has been concentrated to areas within flying distance of the Simuleum. Now that this disease has been eradicated by a successful project covering several countries in West Africa, the pressure from the population to invade these forests has increased in recent years, very much enforced by the population growth and the rapid degradation of already cultivated land.

As the reserved forests, up until now, have had little value to the Government, it has been hard to mobilize resources for their protection and management. Few efforts have, therefore, been made to establish organized management. The increasing need for fuel wood has, however, in the 80's inspired two successful trials to cooperate with the population in creating economic management systems. The first of these was done in the 5000 ha Guesselbodi forest, 25 km east of Niamey, the capital of Niger and the other in a large forestry complex around the Nazinon River, 90-120 km South of Ouagadougou, the capital of Burkina Faso. The Nazinon-project, as it is called, now comprises 100,000 hectares. A third successful attempt has been made to manage natural forests, is the Nazinga project covering a total area of 96.000 hectares, situated around 200 km south of Ouagadougou. Here it is, however, not the harvesting of fuel wood that is the backbone, but instead ranching of wildlife for cropping and safari-hunting.

Below, short descriptions are given of these three success stories.

Three success stories in forest management

Guesselbodi, Niger
The Guesselbodi forest is situated about 25 km east of Niamey in Niger, where annual rainfall is around 700 mm. In 1981, a start was made in an attempt to manage 5000 ha of bushland, which in the previous years had been degraded due to wood cutting, overgrazing, fires and subsequent erosion. In fact, 40 to 60% of the vegetative cover had disappeared in the 30 years between 1950 and 1979.

According to the management plan, which was being applied from 1983, the forest was divided into ten parcels, approximately 500 ha each. One parcel was to be harvested and treated each year, giving a rotation of ten years, which was supposed to correspond to the time needed for the dominant species, mainly of the genus *Combretum,* to regenerate after a coppice cut.

The annual measures taken in one parcel at the time, are the following: All trees down to a given minimum diameter are felled and the commercial fuelwood is stacked at the roadside for sale, while the smaller branches are spread out on barren areas to improve soil conditions. By means of termites, this debris is decomposed and partly transported downwards, thus increasing water infiltration and content of organic matter in the soil. These measures are combined with others to further improve the soil on barren areas like stone or earth mounds, half moon ditches combined with tree planting, etc.

The clear-felled areas have to be protected from grazing for the first three years, but may then be used for organized grazing. The harvesting of grass for fodder may, however, be permitted all the time.

The main principles of this management is that it will lead to sustained and, possibly, increased production, which is economically feasible for the surrounding population. Income from the sale of firewood, grazing rights and other benefits, e.g. harvesting of fodder for stall feeding, cultivation and hunting, should cover the costs involved like cutting, anti-erosive measures, guarding etc.

Nazinon, Burkina Faso

Nazinon forest is situated 90-120 km south of Ouagadougou in Burkina Faso, in an area with a rainfall of 800-900 mm. This project is more recent and was started in 1986. The Nazinon forest now comprises around 100,000 ha, divided into a number of management units of 2,000-4,000 hectares. Each of these units is then divided into 20 parcels of which one is cut each year, giving a rotation of 20 years. Only 50% of the volume is taken out, leaving vigorous and well-formed trees of certain species which will provide a more valuable yield in the future. The wood is sold to private dealers who haul it on trucks to Ouagadougou for sale. The total sum received covers costs involved, including the management of the forest. The forest management includes training of the villagers/forest workers and some silvicultural costs like direct seeding of barren, earlier cultivated areas.

Research is in progress to study the effects of the presently applied cutting systems and the silvicultural operations and, as a result of this, it might be possible even to increase the annual yield. The most serious technical problem is, however, how to prevent the forest fires. It seems impossible to stop or even control them. Much research needs to be done to solve this problem.

Nazinga Game Ranch, Burkina Faso

Nazinga Game Ranch is situated within the big complex of natural forests in southern Burkina Faso, where the mean annual rainfall is around 900 mm. The 960 km^2 ranch is situated 200 km south of the capital, Ouagadougou.

In 1979, after several years of planning, a ranching project was started by C. Lungren and R. Lungren. The aim of the project was to improve the ecological situation for the wildlife in the area, by arranging for permanent water supply and control of forest fires and poaching. All the work was to be done by local inhabitants who would also reap the profits of controlled hunting/ranching.

As a result of these efforts, wildlife increased rapidly and so did tourism. The number of animals nearly doubled between 1983 and 1989, when there were close to 500 elephants, 300 buffaloes, 5,000 warthogs and nearly 7,000 antelopes. During the 1988/89 tourist season, there was 2,500 visitors to the area.

In 1988, the project started controlled hunting both as commercial hunting by the project personnel for the sale of meat, and as safari-hunting. Due to administrative changes there has been a break in development, but the results, so far, are very promising. They clearly show that when wildlife is given water and protection, it can be a basis for profitable ranching and sport-hunting in this region.

Parallell to the practical work more than 80 biologists have conducted studies at the ranch, producing more than 150 reports on soils, vegetation composition and production and on ungulate diets, habitat preferences, carcases decomposition, reproduction etc.

Concluding remarks

Already during colonial times, large forest tracts were set aside as reserved forests for government use. In these forests the neighbouring population was usually only allowed to graze their livestock, harvest minor forest products, dry wood and dead trees. Beside these regulations, the government seldom undertook any measures to manage the forest, usually only to demarcate the forests and employ forest guards and this was seldom effective. As a result, the remaining natural-forest areas are decreasing at a very rapid rate in many areas.

In all three studies summarized above, the forests are close enough to big cities to make the sale of wood and meat profitable, forming the basis of profitable management. But how can we make management profitable in forests further away from markets, where there is very little value on fuelwood or meat?

The problem is, that the need for new land for agriculture might have a higher priority, simply because of the decreasing productivity of the agricultural land already in use and increasing population. In a situation where there is a shortage of food, it is, naturally, hard for the farmer to make the choice that in the long run, would be in his best interests.

The importance of management of natural forests in the Sahel region as a means of supplying needs of fuelwood and other products, is stressed by Jackson *et al.* (2), who proposes that it should be given at least equal priority in the establishment, as that of large-scale plantations. Bonkoungou (3) is of the same opinion, based on the fact that management of natural forests compares quite favorably with afforestation with respect to wood production.

The possibilities of managing wildlife in sub-Saharan Africa are discussed by Asibey and Child (4). Lewis *et al.* (5) describe the positive effects of a new national policy of wildlife management introduced in Zambia. Beside these two examples "there has been little or no serious planning to develop the potential of wild animals to contribute to rural economies" Asibey concludes.

It has previously been mentioned that the management of natural forests in semiarid areas, has to be based on popular participation if it is to be successful. Planning has to be based on studies of the socio-economic conditions, and several methods have been designed for socalled rural appraisals (6).

The condition for a popular local participation is certainly that the population finds it useful to save and manage the forest. Two options for this interest have been mentioned. One is the possibility to harvest and sell fuelwood at a profitable price and the other possibility, also mentioned, is to manage a game reserve for profitable hunting either as meat for selling or renting out safari-hunting rights.

A third possibility is the use of forestry non-wood products like food, fodder and pharmaceutical products.

No quantitative studies of this possibility has, so far to my knowledge, been done, but Hagberg *et al.* (7) have studied the occurrence of forestry non-wood products on a market in Burkina Faso. They found around 40 products from 20 local species, of which 15 were sold at a price of at least half a US dollar a kilo. The study, although not giving any quantities, indicates that the forestry non-wood products may be of economic importance to a population living in access of a natural forest.

Traditionally, the natural forests are also of great importance as grazing areas. If a forest is managed for wood production, recently cut over areas or seeded areas must, however, be protected from grazing, but might instead be used for zero-grazing (harvesting of fodder for stall feeding).

The management of a forest area for wood production may even increase the fodder production and the application of the right silvicultural treatment may also increase the production of non-wood products of the forest area.

The following conditions must be fullfilled if the people living in and around a forest will be prepared to protect and manage it for sustained use (cf 8).

- It has to be in the interests of the inhabitants to use the forest for harvesting products and for employment opportunities, instead of turning it into agricultural land.

- The population must have legal rights to the forest products.

- There must be a legal protection of the forest enforced by the Government.

- To eliminate the pressures of shifting cultivation on forest land, farmers might have to be helped to increase the production on already farmed land.

It is obvious that much knowledge is needed to fullfill all these prerequisites and to protect and manage natural forests for sustainable use and, thus, a lot of research will be needed.

References

1. **FAO.** 1981. Tropical Forest Resources Assessment Project. Forest Resources of Tropical Africa. Part I: Regional synthesis, 108 p.

2. **Jackson, J.K., Taylor, G.F. and Conde-Wane, C.** 1983. Management of the Natural Forest in the Sahel Region. OECD/CILSS, 94 p.

3. **Bonkoungou, E.** 1987. Management of Natural Forest Versus Afforestation in the Sahel Region of Africa. Future Prospects. Report from UNESCO/CIER, Caracas, Venezuela, December 1987, p. 489-512.

4. **Asibey, E.O.A. and Child, G.S.** 1990. Wildlife management for rural development in Sub-Saharan Africa. Unasylva 161, Vol. 41, 3-10.

5. **Lewis, D.M., Mwenya, A. and Kaweche, G.B.** 1990. African solutions to wildlife problems in Africa: insights from a community-based project in Zambia. Unasylva 161, Vol. 41, 11-20.

6. **Freudenthal, S. and Narrowe, J. 1990.** Focus on People and Trees. A Guide to Designing and Conducting Community Baseline Studies for Community Forestry. Dept. of Social Anthropology, Stockholm University, 38 p.

7. **Hagberg, S. et Coulibaly nee Malo E.** 1989. Etude de marche des produits forestieres. FO: GCP/BKF/036/SWE. Doc. du travail no 8. 15 pp.

8. **Shepherd, G.** 1992. Managing Africa's tropical dry forests — a review of indigenous methods. — ODI Agricultural Occasional Paper 14. 117 pp.

Impact of World Market frozen meat imports on west African trade in livestock products

Henri P. Josserand

Club du Sahel

Paris, France

Abstract

Livestock raising and trade are historical and significant features of the west African economy, especially in the "central corridor" (Mali, Burkina-Faso, Côte d'Ivoire and periphery). The expansion of agriculture and successive droughts have induced an important redistribution of livestock, over space, in the region. Since about 1970, west Africa as a whole has been consuming more meat than it produces; the gap is expected to widen over time. Meat imports from latin America and Australia have been completely edged out by subsidized EEC products, which now satisfy a large share of the medium to low-income market in coastal countries. The latter have implemented a number of protective tariff or variable levy policies, which range widely in effectiveness, from the least (Benin, Togo) to the most effective (Cameroon).

Background

Livestock trade in west Africa is a long-established tradition. In 1923, for instance, a colonial administrator[1] described the "cattle traffic between the region of Tombouctou and the colonies of the Gold Coast and Nigeria". It was then clearly understood that the demand for Sahelian cattle was directly linked to the producer price paid for cocoa. Moreover, certain decrees designating traditional cattle trails (a number of which are still in use) between the south of Burkina Faso and the Plateaux region of Togo, date back to 1919[2].

---

1) Colonel Mangeot, quoted by Bellot, J-M. "Commerçants de bétail et Intégration Régionale: l'exemple de l'Ouest du Niger", CEAN/IEP Bordeaux, 1982.

2) Josserand, H. and Sullivan, G. "Livestock and Meat Marketing in West Africa", Vol. 2. University of Michigan, 1980.

Between 1950 and 1960, a number of factors — good rainfall, improved animal health, more watering points — combined to bring about a rapid growth in livestock numbers, which increased by 89% in Senegal, 125% in Mauritania and 62% in Mali[1].

As livestock numbers grew, so trade developed apace. Until the mid-1960's, for example, exporters in Niger sent animals to Ghana (the most dynamic market at that time), Côte d'Ivoire, Togo, Benin and Nigeria[2]. The list of countries then shrank gradually, reflecting new market conditions, national policies, changing income levels and effective demand. For instance, during the 1970's, Benin pursued a policy of self-sufficiency in livestock products, while Ghana adopted a similar policy with the Alien Compliance Act of 1968. The fall in Ghanaian real incomes contributed to the decrease in demand: although this country absorbed 55% of the cattle exported from Mali in the 1960's, the share fell to 22% in the 1970's.

Over the last twenty years, successive droughts have compounded the effects of a process already well under way: the disruption of pastoral societies and the weakening of their position in the rural economy.

In the case of Mali, a number of animals have been relocated in Côte d'Ivoire, while others shifted to other parts of the country. Significant changes occurred in certain regions following reduced access to the Niger Delta area, increase use of animal traction in farming, and the availability of agricultural by-products to feed cattle. Between 1965 and 1987, the number of cattle in the Sikasso region increased from 366,000 (7% of the national total) to 735,000 (16% of a herd of comparable size). The most recent estimates indicate a total of more than 1.2 million head of cattle in the region. By contrast, numbers in the regions of Tombouctou and Gao fell from 1,800,000 head of cattle in 1965 (37%) to 323,000 in 1987, i.e., 7% of the country's herd.

Conversely, in Côte d'Ivoire, the total number of cattle grew by 9.5% per year between 1975 and 1979. In the north of the country, the number of Zebu almost tripled during the same period[3]. Today, the region supports a transhumant cattle herd of 330,000 head and a sedentary herd of approximately 424,000.

---

1) Horowitz, M. "The Sociology of Pastoralism and African Livestock Projects". USAID/PPC, Washington, D.C. 1979.

2) see Bellot, J.-M. Op. cit. 1982.

3) Holtzman, J. and Kulibaba, N. "Preliminary Review of Livestock Exports from Burkina Faso and Mali to Côte d'Ivoire". Abt & Associates, Washington, D.C., 1990.)

Nigeria continued to import large numbers of Sahelian cattle until the mid-1980s; numbers peaking during the recent drought of 1984/1985. Since then, despite an increase in the price of meat, incoming flows have fallen considerably, for a number of reasons: some cattle coming from Niger and Chad have remained in northern Nigeria, the country has applied an aggressive national production policy geared towards diversifying sources of animal protein, and the devaluation of the naira has made imports extremely expensive. Nigeria also appears to have virtually stopped importing frozen meat from the world market.

As one may see from Table 1, 1990 cattle numbers in major producing countries (Mali, Burkina-Faso, Niger, Chad) had not quite caught up

REGIONAL FLOWS OF LIVE CATTLE FROM THE MAIN COUNTRIES IN WEST AND CENTRAL AFRICA AND MEAT IMPORTS FROM OUTSIDE AFRICA
(in thousand head)

	1970	1980	1985	1987
Exporting countries				
Chad	142	210	255	150
Niger	227	130	170	30
Mali	190	200	200	130
Burkina Faso	87	100	80	77
Central African Republic	0	30	70	70
Total exports	*646*	*670*	*775*	*457*
Importing countries				
Côte d'Ivoire	200	225	225	148
Nigeria	278	356	460	250
Benin	6	1	1	
Ghana	64	1	1	1
Sierra Leone	23	28	20	20
Togo	6	2	5	5
Liberia	18	16	10	10
West African total	*595*	*629*	*722*	*434*
Cameroon	43	30	20	40
Central African Republic	54	26	30	0
Gabon	2	4	4	4
Congo	6	0	4	0
Central African total	*105*	*60*	*58*	*44*
Total live cattle flows	700	689	780	478
Imports of non-African meat (equiv. heads of cattle)	124	370	670	740

with 1980 levels, whereas cattle numbers on the coast had risen by 25 percent over the same period. The coastal share of regional cattle numbers has gone from less than 60 percent to about 70 percent in ten years.

The rise of competition from the world market and EEC subsidies

Since the early 1970s, even though the region as a whole has had a meat deficit, Sahelian livestock exports to coastal markets have had to contend with two major economic constraints: low effective demand on the national and export markets (Nigeria being an occasional exception) and increasing competition from imported frozen meat.

Although regional trade picked up after 1980, due to the Nigerian oil boom, non-African meat imports also increased rapidly. Until 1974, imports came mainly from the EEC and South America, Argentina becoming one of the main suppliers up until 1980 before being replaced by the EC. After the 1984/1985 drought, regional trade stabilized at around 500,000 head per year, an overall reduction of approximately 200,000 head with respect to 1980. However, during the same period (post 1980), frozen meat imports in the region almost doubled, becoming roughly equivalent to 370,000 head of cattle.

The reason was that Sahelian countries (and other international suppliers) have been edged out by EC exporters, who operate with the benefit of large subsidies[1].

The EC has held a virtual monopoly on the sub-Saharan meat market since the beginning of the 1980s, meat being subsidized when sold to markets outside the Community. The AEGGF (European Agricultural Guidance and Guarantee Fund) grants these subsidies to make up the difference between the prices practiced in the receiving country and the considerably higher prices practiced within the Community. On the Atlantic market, which includes Europe and Africa, beef (particularly from Argentina) costs less than half the European price, i.e., between FF6 and FF8 per kilo. Without export subsidies, the EC would not be able to compete effectively with Argentina or India, on African markets.

---

1) *For this section of the paper I am heavily indebted to Jean-Paul Simier, of Solagral, Paris, who has been working on this issue for several years.)*

The European Commission sets the level of subsidies periodically on the basis of proposals made by market "management committees", comprising of civil servants and professionals in equal numbers, and in the light of the prevailing European or world market context and the trading ambitions of the Community. Subsidies tend to rise when European stocks are at their highest, but they can also fall, as when the price of pork rose sharply in 1989, for example.

Beef subsidies amount to FF10/kg, on average, as opposed to FF2/kg for pork and FF1/kg for poultry. They also vary according to the type of cut; an exporter receives more than FF17/kg on hind quarters of large male bovines, FF14/kg for boned flank (CAPA) and less than FF10/kg for front quarters. Similarly, pork traders receive a little more than FF2/kg for whole or half carcasses as opposed to more than FF5/kg for Parma ham. For poultry, subsidies total FF3/kg for chicken exported to the Near and Middle East as opposed to less than FF0.80/kg for whole wings sent to West Africa.

No less than two hundred products are entitled to subsidies. Pork holds the record for diversity, with more than ninety different categories. Not surprisingly, such a high degree of complexity invites fraud or simply allows exporters to select the most profitable form of packaging. For instance, exporters are nearly always paid for fresh meat, even if they export it frozen: all they have to do is to freeze it at customs — a perfectly legal procedure.

So are all these meat exports profitable? Certainly not from the viewpoint of the Community, whose objective is to manage the meat market rather than to generate export revenue. The situation must be considered in terms of the total volume managed by the Community market and not in terms of the cost of the subsidy per kilo of exported meat. The EC, thereby, uses an external market to manage its own internal market,

EEC EXPORT RESTITUTION EXPENSES, BY TYPE OF MEAT PRODUCT
(millions of ECUs)

	1980	1985	1987	1988	1989	1990	1991
Beef	715	1339	878	769	1343	977	1082
Pork	92	103	111	172	199	151	208
Poultry	85	63	152	194	234	213	262
Total export rest	*892*	*1505*	*1141*	*1135*	*1776*	*1341*	*1552*

which has been greatly destabilized by production surpluses. The table below summarizes the evolution of restitution expenses over time.

Estimated impact of frozen meat imports and countervailing measures

For Sahelian producers and exporters, the crux of the problem is not so much world market competition as the very weakness of effective demand in coastal countries, which is derived from the need for animal protein. When the price of meat rises in real terms (with respect to disposable income and/or the price of substitutes) many consumers shift to the least expensive cuts and to fish.

Recent work on the structure of demand in Côte d'Ivoire[1], suggests that the net effect of raising the price of imported frozen beef ten percent would have been to reduce frozen beef consumption by 19 percent in the 1970's and by 11 percent in the 1980's. However, the stimulative impact of this reduction in consumption of frozen beef, on consumption of Sahelian beef is thought to be small (3 percent in the 1980's). One of the reasons is that, in a period of shrinking incomes, the big substitute for west African beef (in volume and value) has been fish, rather than European beef.

On the other hand, the net effect of reducing the supply price in CFA of Sahelian fresh beef by 10 percent, would have been to increase its consumption by nearly 12 percent in the 1980s, (it would have been nearly twice as much in the 1970s).

The same study indicates that demand for sahelian beef remains strongly determined by factors over which west Africans have some control:

First, interventions that decrease relative prices for fresh, west African beef (reduction of transfer costs, for instance), would have at least as large an effect on the relative shares of European and west African beef, as a tariff on the former.

Secondly, a resumption of overall growth in coastal countries will probably lead to a greater improvement for west African beef than for other animal protein sectors, provided the relative price of this type of meat remains competitive.

---

1) *Delgado C. and Lent R., Coastal Demand Constraints for Sahelian Livestock Products: Côte d'Ivoire, paper presented at the IFPRI/ISRA seminar on Regional integration of agricultural markets in west Africa, Saly Portudal, Senegal, December 1992.*

However, comparative statics and the analysis of demand elasticities with respect to price and income don't tell the entire story. Much depends on the appropriateness and effectiveness of coastal countries' trade policies. The preliminary results of a study of trade policies in coastal west Africa[1] indicate the following:

Côte d'Ivoire

After at least two years of preparation, negociations with the World Bank on the one hand, and professional interest groups on the other, the countervailing duty system was implemented in Côte d'Ivoire in early 1991. Preliminary results are that:

a) The quantity of meat imported from the world market fell by 35 percent in 1991, compared to the previous year. This decrease was very likely due to three main factors:

i) the clearest and least arguable is shrinking disposable incomes,

ii) a continued reversal of the 1985-88 downward trend in CIF imported meat prices, which was somewhat mitigated by custom tax evasion by importers, and re-exports of little-taxed meat from Ghana; and,

iii) the price impact of the countervailing duties, although the rate, in response to shadow price increase and tension on Abidjan markets, was reduced, on "capa" for instance, from 200 to 80, and then to 20 FCFA/kg.

b) In a context of falling incomes and increasing CIF prices for frozen meat, the countervailing duty in Côte d'Ivoire first met with stiff resistance from consumers and importers. In the face of weak effective demand, the latter had to reduce profit margins on imported meat. Some went out of the meat import business, while others tried to recoup their losses by inflating the FOB prices of their parent European companies. Others yet have managed to circumvent the system (and continue to operate openly), while certain traders have either contacted or associated with importers in Ghana, to smuggle frozen meat into Côte d'Ivoire — Ghana's meat imports have approx. quadrupled in less than two years.

c) the combination of decreasing meat imports and downward adjustment of the countervailing duty, led to much lower Government receipts than

---

1) *IRAM/Solagral, Paris, study in progress financed by the French Ministry of Cooperation.*

anticipated. From early 1991, through the third quarter of 1992, counter-vailing duty receipts amounted to about 720 millions FCFA.

d) It appears that meat consumption has fallen in Côte d'Ivoire from just over 10 kg/cap/year, to about 9 kg in 1991; this is not startling. However, it seems that *fish imports and consumption have markedly decreased as well*.

e) A significant reinforcement of the effectiveness of the countervailing duty policy by the Government of Côte d'Ivoire, appears unlikely. Not only is there demonstrated resistance from importers and consumers, but the Government itself is in some debt to the meat industry. For instance, hundreds of millions of FCFA are owed to several suppliers of meat consumed in hospitals, the university, etc.

f) Under such conditions, and although Sahelian livestock exports appa-rently manage to hold their ground, prospects for a short-term impro-vement are about nil.

Togo
In Togo, the taxation of imported meat from the EEC first led to both a large increase in livestock imports from the Sahel, and in higher semi-industrial poultry and small ruminant production on the outskirts of Lomé. At the same time, the likely increase in price led to an overall decrease in meat consumption, and an increase in fish consumption (through higher imports). However, in 1991, the extent of protection of the local market has been reduced by several factors:

• mild enforcement in the face of rising prices and political instability;

• resulting smuggling into Togo by some importers, and;

• re-exports from Ghana or Benin by Togolese importers re-established there, or in association with local importers.

Finally, countervailing duties on meat imports were discontinued in April 1992, although the basic custom duty still applies.

Nigeria
Nigeria's experience, in the last few years, seems to contradict the usual assumption that the rate of urbanization is positively related to per capita meat consumption. Nigeria is about 50 percent urbanized, by now, but over the few years per capita meat consumption has fallen from

the already low estimated level of 6.5 kg/cap/year to just over 4 kg/cap/year.

Meat imports are prohibited, but this has had little impact on domestic production. In the first place, the scarcity of foreign exchange has severely disrupted most semi-intensive poultry and ruminant production, through lack of inputs. Drastically reduced incomes explain much of the resistance to meat consumption, especially since people have, so far, been able to find a partial substitute in fish. Although Nigeria has been exporting some fish in the past few years, this practice could quickly come to an end once more attractive sources of foreign exchange come on-line (oil and natural gas, for instance), and fish could switch from being a foreign exchange earner to a foreign exchange saver.

Cameroon
This is a country where potential for livestock development remains quite good. In fact, up to 1974, the country was a net exporter of livestock. After 1974, strong demand for meat fuelled an average 8.4% annual growth in cattle marketing.

From 1983 through 1987, frozen meat imports increased very sharply, while their price fell from 465 to 215 CFA/kg. Meat consumption in Douala and Yaoundé increased over the same period from 24 to 36 Kg/cap/year. The impact on the prices of locally available cattle and poultry was correspondingly clear and strong: 40 to 45% decrease in price over the period.

Since January 1988, there has been a complete stop to imports of frozen meat for the popular market (through a very high import tariff). The urban meat consumption level has fallen back to pre-1983 levels (24 kg/cap/year). For the moment, the refocusing on "local" meat has benefitted both local producers (south of the "quarantine border"), and neighbouring countries: since 1988, imports of cattle from Chad and the Central African Republic have increased by 50,000 head per year.

Year	metric tons
1985/86	80,000
1986/87	80.560
1987/88	79.000
1989/90	77.000

The experience of Cameroon has been rather unique among coastal countries. First, the fulani group has had enough political power to have this kind of policy enacted and enforced. Secondly, it is difficult to carry out clandestine imports of frozen meat, (although imports of live animals are only partially controlled). Finally, the import ban and resulting reduced availability of meat apparently did not lead to a strong substitution toward fish. Fish prices increased in the last few years, but total supply (domestic landings plus imports) apparently remained stable or fell slightly.

Conclusion

The IEMVT[1] estimates that the optimum stock carrying capacity in countries of the Sahel does not exceed 28 million standardized tropical livestock units, TLUs. This figure, which is not far from current levels, should provide the equivalent of approximately 560,000 tons of meat (carcass-weight). At current population levels, this quantity would correspond to approximately 10 kg of meat per capita per year. Note that in CEBV member countries[2], meat consumption is currently close to that level.

	Total Consumption (TEC)	Consumption (Kg/capita)	Nat. Prod. (%)	Imports: Live (%)	Imports: Meat (%)
EVOLUTION OF MEAT CONSUMPTION IN COTE D'IVOIRE FROM VARIOUS SOURCES					
1975	66.290	9.9	35.7	53.3	11
1980	102.200	12.5	38.2	49.7	12.1
1984	96.690	10.8	41.6	44.8	13.6
1985	109.810	11.8	38.4	42.7	18.9
1986	119.640	12.5	36.4	33	30.6
1987	120.420	12.1	37.1	28.9	34
1988	136.920	13.3	33.8	22.1	44.1

TEC: tons of equivalent carcass

1) IEMVT *"Perspectives et Orientations Prioritaires pour le Développement du Secteur Elevage en Afrique de l'Ouest"* 1986.
2) Benin, Burkina-Faso, Côte d'Ivoire, Niger, Togo.

Overall animal protein supply and demand projections for several countries in the region for the year 2000, suggest that the regional deficit is likely to worsen over the short and medium term:

Projected Deficit in Selected Coastal Countries (metric tons)

Côte d'Ivoire	80,000
Togo	9,000
Benin	7,000

Meat Equivalent from Livestock Surplus Countries:

Mali	11,000
Burkina Faso	5,000
Niger	3,000

Of course, Nigeria, with roughly 100 million people, is the "wild card in the deck". Meat consumption there, is currently very low, even by west African standards (6.5 kg/capita/year); an increase in 1 kg/cap/year would translate into 100,000 tons per annum...

There seems to be no compelling reason to believe that trade conditions will become more favorable to Sahelian countries, but even if this were the case, they would still need to improve the productivity of animal husbandry (small and large ruminants, poultry, pigs, etc.), to keep matching supplies with fluctuating demand, and to reduce transaction costs, including the unofficial taxes that hamper the livestock trade.

All the evidence we have indicates, that Sahelian producers and exporters have limited the loss in coastal market share by accepting a lower return on their labour and capital investments, and by working on the reduction of transfer costs from the Sahel to the coast. In addition, several Sahelian countries have already taken or are taking fiscal measures to reduce official transaction costs. Mali simplified export procedures for cattle in July 1989, although this measure is not yet totally applied[1]. Niger removed all export taxes on cattle in 1989.

---

1) Kulibaba, N. and Holtzman J. "Livestock Marketing and Trade in the Mali/Burkina Faso-Côte d'Ivoire Corridor". Abt and Associates, forthcoming.)

Official taxes, however, represent only a small percentage of transportation expenses. Most studies on the marketing of primary products describe unauthorized taxes in detail. Some new "transport clearing" companies have been emerging, which take care of all arrangements with public officials and secure a significant rebate in unofficial transit expenses, from the northern border posts to Bouaké or Abidjan. This is, however, rather a shift to a more efficient form of transfer than a real saving to the economies. Neither should one be too hopeful about the various Governments ability to reduce coercive practices through their multi-layered administrations. This can only happen when professional interest groups organize themselves to apply effective pressure for change.

Gender relations and economic transformations among the Hausa in Niger

Alain Lefebvre[1]
Copenhagen
Denmark

Introduction

This paper aims at contributing to the improvement of female participation in development programs, by illustrating through the gender analysis of a patriarchal West African society how women's economic betterment can be perceived negatively by men. The issue at stake concerns the men's strategy to preserve their dominating position in the decision-making process. I assume that development programs face the men's opposition if they bring a radical change to the traditional gender relations within a society, by transforming the distribution of power between men and women.

This hypothesis originates from two sources.

Firstly, my previous work about the relations between socio-cultural identity and economic development in Pakistani villages, i.e. communities built upon a social order, which has been characterized as classic patriarchy (D. Kandiyoti 1988). Honour and preservation of the kinship ties are some of the key concepts which explain the villagers' economic behaviour. In this cultural setting, a political economy of honour defines for both men and women a set of perceptions and practices which is logical in the villagers' meaning system. Economic improvement of villages,

1) Data for this paper was gathered from studies, monographs and reports about the Hausa society and from interviews with members of local NGOs and official institutions, during a two-month visit to Niger in 1991-1992. This was financed by the Scandinavian Institute of African Studies. Further from my personal observations of Hausa society during nine-months' work as socio-economist for the Danish Krüger company, in an integrated rural development project in several villages of the Zinder district in Niger in 1991.

thanks to the men's international labour migration, does not transform the women's roles and status as it has been the case in other societies. A migrant will never leave his household if his absence entails a change in the women's responsibilities. He makes sure that at least a male relative chaperons them. Any change which could affect the nature of the gender relations is feared by men, since they could lead to the decrease of their power (A. Lefebvre 1989, 1990 & 1992).

The second source originates from the contributions made by feminist studies in anthropology (see f.ex. H.L. Moore's compiling analysis, 1988). They have given a grass-root understanding of the economic strategies within the poor social classes and they have underlined the many facets of the women's role in the household. Without their ability to adjust to tremendous pressures, poverty will have even more dramatic consequences. Studies of poor, working women in Muslim societies have shown that the women's access to remunerated activities does not bring an overall improvement of their situation. Either the income is insignificant and part or all of it has to be given to the male head of the household (S. A. Khan and F. Bilquees 1976; N.H. Youssef 1977; K. Westergaard 1982; S. Feldman and F. E. McCarthy 1983). Or when men and women have a form of separate economies with the allocation of resources strictly controlled by each gender like in many West African societies poverty leads to the women's defavorable position (M. Monimart 1989).

However, irrespective of the strategy followed by the women, their role in the decision-making process concerning important matters remains subordinated to the men. Furthermore, many studies about female power (C. Nelson 1974, S. Deaver 1980, I. W. Boesen 1983, C. Braae 1984), illustrate that if the women have a joint consciousness of their common position in the society, their possibility of protesting against a patriarchal domination is limited to occur within the structural frame defined by the men.

On the basis of these findings, this paper aims at understanding the relations which exist between the men's perceptions of gender relations and the women's possibilities to improve their socio-economic status, through participation in development projects among the Hausa of the Zinder region in Niger.

Actual position of women in the rural Hausa society and their availability to economic development

Although one still finds, among the Hausa speaking people of Niger,

communities which are pagan like the Anna or the Maguzawa studied
by G. Nicolas (1975), J.H. Greenberg (1946 and 1947) and J.H. Barkow
(1972 and 1973) respectively, we are concerned here with the Muslim
Hausa of the Zinder area.

Zinder, the second largest city in Niger, lies within the Sahelian climatic
zone and is threatened by desertification. Zinder became important in
the late 19th. century, due to its position at the cross-road of the trans-
Saharan trade. The population is mainly sedentarized and engaged in
mixed agriculture of millet and sorghum as staple cereals, cow-peas,
cotton and groundnuts as main commercial crops. Beside these, a large
range of other crops are also cultivated spreading from various types of
pepper to several varieties of tubers. Sylvan products from the surrounding bush are also used as building material and for handicraft. Although the use of modern agricultural inputs is very limited, farming
techniques are elaborate with a combination of crop-rotation, inter-crop-
ping and double-cropping (M.G. Smith 1952:333), in order to obtain the
maximum from a regular seasonal cycle which has been, however, transformed in the last decades by the southward movement of the isohyet
boundaries. Handicraft and trade activities are also widespread, either
as subsidiary sources of income or as main occupations. The variability
in the economic activities depends on the punctual need for money of the
household, but more and more subsistence farmers and craftsmen have
become part-time, small-scale traders during the dry season so as to
supplement the unsufficient income from their primary economic activities (E.J. Arnould 1985 and 1986).

Village studies of rural Hausaland have shown that farmers do not
practice a subsistence economy but cultivate stapple foodstuffs and
garden crops partly for their own consumption, partly for selling them
on local and regional markets (E.J. Arnould 1985 and 1986; P. Hill 1972;
G. Nicolas 1970; C. Raynaut 1972; 1976 and 1977; E.P. Scott 1978; G.
Spittler 1977). A production for household consumption is combined
with a production for trade, because the villagers are always in search
of money since the colonization for the payment of taxes. The rapid
replacement of the traditional exchange of services by cash transactions, has increased this tendency. However, commercial crops like cotton
and groundnuts do not have the same priority for the earning of cash
income as previously, due to the low prices. C. Raynaut calculated that
the payment of taxes for one person required 17 kg of groundnuts in
1948, 27 kg in 1959 and 70 kg in 1971 (C. Raynaut 1977:161). It is very
difficult to obtain credits. Villagers have to find money through other
channels like petty-trade, handicraft and all kind of unskilled labour in

towns. Farmers sell part of their subsistence crops just after the harvest, i.e. at low prices and, therefore, have less for feeding their family, and have to buy them at high prices during the hunger season. Others sell or mortgage a piece of land, especially when it has a good commercial value due to its situation close to a town. The mercantile value of land is a consequence of the monetization of the society in all domains, as we shall see below. Before colonization, land did not have an intrinsic value. To own it did not give the right to the harvested products. Only farming gave the privilege to enjoy its fruits.

The social organization in Hausa villages
The Hausa society is stratified and hierarchical, with office holders on one side and commoners (peasants/craftsmen) on the other side. Further stratifications exist within each group with occupation, wealth and religious fervour being the criteria of difference (P. Hill 1972, G. Nicolas 1975, C. Raynaut 1972 and 1976, M.G. Smith 1959). The moral values, rights and obligations are shaped by a syncretism of Islam, with old traditional divinities where status inequality is stressed.

Traditionally, the Hausa social core is the patrilineage (*dangi*) which shares the same social space (*gari*) with other patrilineages under the authority of the village chief (*mai gari*), who, as a rule, belongs to the first patrilineage which settled there. A patrilineage is dispersed in several villages composed of different basic social and economic units, the compounds (*gida*, pl. *gidaje*). It is, in most cases, inhabited by several men, their wife/wives and their children and under the authority of and dependence on the senior male (the *mai gida*). Within the compound, one finds the women's individual houses located on a north-south line according to the order of their marriage to the common husband in the case of a polygynous household. These houses exclusively belong to each wife as well as all the furnitures and utensils, and the husband enters his wives' residence only as a visitor.

The term *gida* also refers to "those who farm as a single unit of production and close kinsmen who no longer reside together" (A.D. Goddard 1973; M.O. Saunders 1978). Ideally, the *gida* is an economic and residential unit based on patrilineal extended kinship ties, but, as we shall see below, trends towards the individualization of the economy transform the components of the family farming unit.

Social roles are very codified and an individual finds harmony when he/she exactly knows his/her position in the society, with the corresponding hierarchically organized rights and duties. According to M. G.

Smith a distinct system of social status exists for each gender (M. G. Smith 1959:245). A man's status is derived from his father's political position — either as ruler or as ruled — and from his occupational vocation with hereditary professions occupying a superior rank. A woman's status is mainly related to her marital career and her fertility. Within each gender, the individual relationships are determined by the necessity to maintain and increase one's honour and social prestige, and by following the ethics of reciprocity in gift-giving networks. Strong social ties are, in fact, formalized by an extremely codified system of customary gift exchanges (*bukis*) between people of the same sex, the same social status and the same age-group, during the daily interactions of bond-friendship and clientage relations. The female ties, known as *kawaye*, are started by the newly married woman, after she has moved to her husband residence. The closeness of the relationships between village women is, therefore, expressed by the frequency of these reciprocal exchanges of goods (gifts, food, kola nuts and other kinds of small tokens).

These exchanges turn into competitions — collective or individual — at the occasion of rites of passage and Muslim festivals. The redistributions of goods are, therefore, very costly but necessary for reaffirming individual bonds of social security and solidarity, as well as for reproducing the social relations as a whole. Nobody makes an economic profit in these gift-giving networks but it improves one's authority and respect by their ostentation. The economic behaviour within each gender group is, thus, based on the principle that economic wealth gives social weight, only when the individual redistributes a portion of it to cover his social obligations, which increase concomitantly with his economic resources instead of accumulating more and more.

Gender relations and economy in the Hausa villages

The gender relationships are regulated through social norms and values, where a syncretic form of Islam plays an important role. The perception of gender relationships, specific to Islam, was able to fall, without difficulties, into the sexual dichotomy of the Hausa pre-Islamic cosmology. The society, as well as the cosmos, is made of two opposite but complementary poles, the male and female poles, where the male element occupies the dominating place. Women have formally an inferior status in the Hausa society, in the domestic as well as the public sphere, even though they are complementary to men. They always live in a household for a transitory period, first as a daughter, then as a wife and later as dependent sister or mother.

Until her marriage, at a very young age (13-14 years), a girl is relatively free in her relationships with men. She is allowed to have, simultaneously, several fiancés who compete with each other for obtaining her favours through courting gifts, consisting of small amounts of money. Girls know how to make advantage of this game, and today the successful suitor has to reimburse the unlucky candidates, since the amount of money given has increased. Women's income is saved for establishing their daughters' dowry (E. Schildkrout 1983). The first marriage is arranged by the male head of the two involved households, while widows and divorcees may take the initiative to find a new partner, but the woman's inferior legal status entails that she is, however, always represented by a male chaperon in the matrimonial transaction regardless of her age.

Woman's virginity is a must, since to marry a virgin girl is the means which gives a man a full adult status. Today it is rare to find a virgin bride and consequently it is especially elder men who can afford to marry a young girl, because of the high bridewealth which has to be paid. Younger men without the adequate economic resources marry widows or divorcees. All in all, marriage is the first step which allows a man to start his independent adult life and women are very skilful to take benefit from the competition between men on the matrimonial scene.

Men may have up to four wives, whom he secludes if he has the economic means. The observance of woman's seclusion is considered, by both genders, as being the ideal way of life for women. It is perceived as being the form of conjugal life, which has been prescribed by Allah, and it also means a reduction of the woman's domestic work load, since her movements outside the compound must be as limited as possible. Being free of fetching water and of gathering fuel are advantages appreciated by women.

Marriages are virilocal and the husband has the absolute authority in the household, although, with the age the woman increases her power by the growing number of dependents, such as junior co-wives and daughters-in-law. Women obtain a higher recognition through their reproductive functions. They go then from the status of brides to the one of wives. Especially co-wives have to go through more hardships to achieve a respectable and individual status. They are under the control of both the husband and the senior wife who organizes the distribution of domestic work.

In polygynous households, the husband eats and spends the night following a two-day rotation with each wife in her own house, where her children also live. On one side competition between the co-wives is the rule, but on the other side they cooperate to take advantage of the husband's obligation to treat each of them similarly — for instance in the attribution of small gifts — so as to keep peace in the *gida*. Economically, a polygynous household has the advantage of providing more spare time for the woman.

Like the other members of the compound the woman is expected to be obedient, to show respect towards the head of the household, and to have a shame-respect relationship with her in-laws (J. H. Barkow 1972). She has to bear many children, to be skilled in all the domestic tasks and be always at the service of her husband.

Women must be faithful to their husband. Adultery is severely condemned and often ends with a divorce. The husband may repudiate his wife without further legal complications, while a woman has to provoke her husband if she wants to divorce him. She often uses adultery as one of the strategies to achieve this goal, when the husband refuses to agree with a separation. A man may remarry without a long delay if he can afford it, while a woman has to wait for a three-month period. He is allowed to keep the children if they have passed the age of weaning. However, all the possessions which she brought at the time of her marriage remain hers, and she takes them again in case of divorce.

The women's inferior status also determines their role in the agricultural production. This is ruled by a complex land tenure system, where the right to land property is limited. The Islamic rules of inheritance and land laws are not yet entirely followed, which represents a disadvantage for women. Although individual ownership of land has appeared among Muslim Hausa, it is still, in majority of cases, the right to land management which is patrilineraly inherited and not its ownership. Land was, in reality, the communal property of the village, with each male head of the *gida* in charge of its distribution and of the organization of the agricultural tasks. Within each *gida* one may distinguish between different types of land tenure.

The first type refers to the ancestral and communally-held land (the so-called *gandu* land), which is cultivated collectively during four days of the week by all the members of the compound, under the supervision of the *mai gida*. This land belongs to the patrilineage, and cannot be sold or alienated without the concensus of the male members of the lineage (A. D. Goddard 1973; C. Raynaut 1976). According to P. Hill (1972 and 1973) *gandu* is a volontary contract between individuals with mutual rights and obligations, in this case, between father and subordinated sons, and/or between brothers. It can be broken by any side at any time. In return of their labour, the *mai gida* is responsible for the distribution of seeds and tools, the adequate use of the harvest, the payment of the head-taxes and ceremonial expenses such as bridewealths, the provision of food, shelter and other services. He makes sure that each member of the production unit is fairly treated in this circulation of goods. Each wife receives a portion of the stapple crop from her husband, according to a quantity which is based on her number of children. When the husband's granary is empty, it is the woman's turn to provide the food for the family. It is either a gift or a loan according to the nature of the relationships between the spouses.

The second type of land tenure refers to the fields which are temporarily attributed from the communal land by the *mai gida* to adults members of the compound — women included, even though they are far from receiving the most fertile plots — and which are tilled individually, during the remaining three days of the week (the *gayamna* land). These plots are not owned privately even when they are lent out for several years but still belong to the *gida*. The products of the fields belong exclusively to the cultivator.

Finally, one has today, due to the transformations of the social relations wihin the household, a third type of land tenure. It points at fields and gardens which are owned individually because they have been purchased or inherited, or because they are plots cleared for the first time in the bush. Only land of this type may be sold by its owner. In other words, with the fission of households with extended families, collective fields are split into individual plots which enter into the market economy. One assists to the introduction of private land ownership, which opens new possibilities for women who are, in this case, no longer hindered by customs to acquire their own property.

The traditional economic relations between genders are characterized by the men's and women's separate budgets and by mutually reciprocal spheres of activities. The husband is responsible for providing food, clothes and housing for his wife and children, and for offering similar sexual favour when he has several wives. He is also expected to be generous in giving cash and small gifts. It is not rare that women return to their parents' *gida*, when they feel unfairly treated by their husband.

In return, the wife has a certain number of duties. Daily she fetches water, collects wooden fuel and prepares the meals, a very strenuous task, since it demands processing every food crop. In the last twenty years, she has had to feel directly on her body, the environmental degradations which have led to the dramatic increase of time required for assuring the domestic tasks, within the household. To earn some cash she transforms groundnuts into oil and cow-peas into flour for small cakes.

Traditionally, the woman works four days of the week on the communal fields, during five months yearly (from June-July to October-November) — this division of time is issued from the pre-Islamic time, since four is the feminine figure in the Hausa pagan cosmology and symbolizes the clitoris, the two *labia majora* and the vagina, while three is the masculine figure and refers to the penis and the testicles (G. Nicolas 1966). In exchange for this labour, the woman is provided subsistence from the *gandu* fields all year round and in supplement receives the poorest quality of millet heads and the remnants lying in the fields at the time of harvest (K. Amsatou 1989). The remaining three days of the week are devoted to the work on her *gayamna* plot. She keeps the products of her fields and the income they procure for herself. The husband has no right to alienate the yields of her private labour.

One has then, a traditional, sexual division of labour and a notion of private income, which make women partly economically independent from their husband. However, this situation does not give them the possibility to achieve a greater power in the public sphere, i.e. in the socio-political structure of the society as a whole. To know where and how women exercise power, is precisely relevant in the discussion about female-oriented projects, in order to discover the niches which could be relevant for their implementation.

Women's power in the Hausa society
J. Nicolas (1967) and M.O. Saunders (1978) have shown that women have different channels to exercise power, to increase their social values and, therefore, to raise their self-respect in the male dominated Hausa society.

The most respected social position for a woman is to be the first wife. She will be, in fact, the last one to be divorced in polygynous households. However, she feels frustrated when she becomes older and her husband takes a younger and more attractive co-wife. Next comes the father's sister, who plays an important role in the kinship structure because of her priviledged relationship with her nephews. Aunts and nephews "can count on each other in any situations" (J. Nicolas 1967:56). Another channel to achieve a social and economic autonomy is through the institution *kan kwarya*. It is a local form of potlatch which is performed through the distribution of cooked meals and exchange of small gifts among women, while the use of money and the prestige associated to it, is the rule in this type of exchanges between men today. This form of investment indicates each woman's status, strengthens the ties between women and ensures a kind of food-security for the future.

Finally, temporary prostitution, which, until the effects of urbanization, did not have a pejorative connotation, was a means chosen by some women to be autonomous. Prostitution refers, in this cultural context, to the status of courtisan or "free woman" taken by some divorced women and widows. It is a temporary stage between marriages for the women who have chosen not to return to their parents' household after such a life crisis and who are without resources. Several "free women" share the same compound and this gives them the possibility to be appreciated by men who find in their company an atmosphere, which is more opened than in their own household. However, with urbanization, the status of "free women" is devalued and transformed into prostitution on a western model. Many courtisans are, today, engaged in the *bori cult* so as to compensate this loss of social appraising.

In fact, even though the villagers are Muslim, they continue to practice the *bori* spirit-possession cult of the pre-Islamic *Anna* religion as a curative cult. The strong belief in supernatural power and the strong magical and religious aspects of illnesses, in the Hausa society, require the alliance of specialists who are able to protect individuals.

Illnesses are perceived as the punishments of angry spirits against evildoers. It is believed that very ill or barren women and the death of children are due to offended spirits. The only remedy is for the woman to become bearer of the particular spirit responsible for her difficulties and this way to become its ally.

The *bori cult* is mainly a female-dominated ritual, during which initiated women are possessed by spirits of the old divinities belonging to the *Anna* religion, who have been assimilated to the Islamic jinns. Women use these supernatural contacts for bodily and mental healing. It gives them the possibility to increase their power in the society, by providing charms for people. Spirits and initiated women communicate with each others through dreams during which the type of therapy is transmitted, such as the name of medicinal plants. It is not all the women who have the abilities to be initiated to the cult and it takes years of apprenticeship and learning as healers, after complex initiation rites, before a woman is considered as being totally a *bori*-woman.

When an illness or sterility do not have any psychological cause and, therefore, cannot be healed by a seance of spirit possession, the *bori*-woman has, nevertheless, improved her position in the society by being metamorphosed into a god while being watched by relative male spectators. Her sterility, which is disturbing for the social order since it hinders her to fulfill the woman's normal role in the society, is compensated by being socially useful at other levels.

The *bori cult* brings to the unbarren and/or old woman a psychological and social equilibrium, firstly for herself — by going from a negative to a positive role — but also for the society. She finds herself at an intermediary level in several aspects and her ambivalence fulfils important functions for the society. She has the ability to communicate with the supernatural world — the pre-Islamic as well as the Islamic one — and this reduction of the distance with spirits gives her respect and power in the society. She combines the Hausa past expressed in the *Anna* society — with its clan and pre-Islamic belief — with the present Islamic social order and this way helps to reduce the nostalgy for the traditional model of society.

The *bori*-woman also occupies an intermediary position between men and women. During the seance of possession, she combines male and female principles. Her status is different from the other women's and she is, therefore, allowed to interfer in the public sphere with the men's accept.

Transformations of the gender relations and their consequences for rural development

The economic changes, since the turn of the century, have led to a new management of land and to the disorganization of the socio-economic relations between individuals and genders in the villages.

We saw that the *mai gida* traditionally had the duty to assure the reproduction of the members of his household by providing the means to produce food, to obtain spouses and by paying the capitation tax. Since the integration of the rural economy in the world market, he has progressively met greater difficulties to cover all his obligations towards the members of the extended family with the income from the *gandu* fields. He has been constrained to depend on an income from cash crops more than women and, therefore, to be more exposed to the fluctuations of world prices. Confronted to the increasing taxation rates, the individual needs for more cash and the young men's preference to work for money in Nigerien and Nigerian cities than for food in villages, the collective units of production have slowly lost their importance (A. D. Goddart 1973; C. Raynaut 1976 and 1977; P. Roberts 1981).

The collective tasks are more and more considered as burdens imposed by the elders who therefore cannot mobilize the labour force of the compound members as previously. These tensions internal to the farming units have led to the fissioning of households with extended family into households with individualistic nuclear family and to a greater importance of non-agricultural source of income in the household economy. The transformations of these basic principles have brought an important change in the management of land. The leader of the household disposes of less male labour force for the cultivation of the gida communal land.

As a consequence of these economic difficulties, the household heads have adopted different strategies. Some have asked their male dependents to pay for their taxes themselves and this way provoke a faster disappearance of the collective solidarity (C. Raynaut 1976 and 1977). Others have allowed the women to work more on their *gayamna* fields and to be busy on the communal fields mainly, during the sowing and harvesting periods. These measures are not always advantageous for women. In fact, due to the shortage of land, the household head allocates plots which are so small and of so poor quality that they require a great effort from the women to improve their productivity. Men benefit of the female labour by taking back these fields when the level of fertility is acceptable (P. Roberts 1983). In exchange it is required that the product of the women's work is not enjoyed individually, but that it must also be at the disposal of the husband and their children. It has become a supplement to the husband's basic support. The 1975 IRAM study shows that many households in the Zinder district have managed the 1973-74 drought, thanks to the women's economic participation: more than one third of the production of stapple food originated from the women's plots (IRAM 1975:43).

However, the men's pride is hurt and tensions in the household can occur when a wife lends millet to her husband, since it makes clear that he was not able to fulfil his duty.

A third strategy, to compensate for the shortage of male labour force and the scarcity of land, is to limit the women's access to *gayamana* land in order to force them them to work on *gandu* fields (C. Raynaut 1976).

Regardless of the strategy chosen, the traditional rationale of the economic relations are progressively replaced by a new type of economic rationality based on monetary exchange which, added to the ecological changes, have social consequences (C. Raynaut 1990). The stereotyped roles specific to each gender are transformed and their relationships have taken a more autonomous and antagonistic nature. Men cannot, any longer, live up to their duties towards their household members and, therefore, see their authority weakened. It entails that they loose respect among their dependents and women do not feel to have the same obligations towards them as before. They become economically more independent and take over some of the responsibilities previously fulfilled by the husbands. One of the consequences of this new state of affairs is the greater instability of the marital life.

Conjugal conflicts and polygamy have in fact become more accute issues than previously. Men and women have opposite perception of polygamy. For the men to establish a polygynous household proves that he follows the Islamic ideal rule regarding conjugal life and thereby increases his status. At the same time he raises his power through the greater number of individuals under his control. It also is a guarantee to have access to at least one wife's labour throughout life. For the woman, it often means an insecurity for her social and economic status. There is always the risk of being repudiated, especially when the woman does not have the position of being the first wife. In case of divorce, she loses the parcel of land which she has been allocated. To hinder the men to make savings for a new marriage, the women's usual strategy is to abuse of the husbands' obligation to support their family by being very demanding with prestige expenditures. Another tactics, is the use of witchcraft against the eventual new wife.

Today, aware of their new economic power in the household, the women are less ready to accept the men's authority, control and whims to take co-wives. It results in a greater number of divorces. Women are now able to reimburse the bridewealth and to manage without a husband, thanks to their increasing economic independence. At the opposite, these new circumstances bring the man into an uneasy situation since he cannot function without a wife. Men are always dependent on a woman because, among other reasons, it is not respectable for them to cook in the Hausa society. For a man to be wifeless means that he was not able to keep his wife and that he failed to find another. In this situation he can easily loose his face in the community. As J.H. Barkow writes, appearance of woman's obedience is more important for the husband's respect than its reality (J. H. Barkow 1972:324). Insubordination is accepted as long as it is covered.

The increased number of divorces has become a channel used by women against their husband, since a dissatisfied wife can always remarry with another man. In other words, the actual women's power takes the form of economic independence and threat to provoke a divorce. These strategies do not, however, transform the overall gender relationships into a positive direction. The actual crisis between spouses hinders the economic improvement of the household and its receptivity to development projects. Neither spouse is sure of the other and thus no one takes the step to make financial investment which could be profitable for all. The lessening of cross-gender solidarity has entailed that no cooperation exist between them today.

Because of the high rate of divorce, women are not motivated to invest in agricultural production on their *gayamna* fields when they know that their husband may nowadays enjoy the product of their work. For instance, they do not spray manure on their fields when they know that another woman will benefit from their work in case of an eventual divorce, or they do not plant trees when the right to the harvested fruits is not given to the planter but to the husband. In fact, as soon as a new economic activity appears economically rentable, like for instance the off-season cultivation, men, who until then were not attracted by this kind of enterprise, want to take over the women's plots and to have the monopoly of this new source of income. As a rule a woman does not want to help her husband to become better off since he will likely use his savings for taking a co-wife.

The instable marital life also explains the women's economic dynamism which is profitable only for herself, her children, and which allows to compete for providing a greater generosity within the frame of female solidarity networks. Within each gender group the values of reciprocality and solidarity which rule the social relations have, in fact, not been disintegrated to the same extend as the relations between genders. C. Raynaut mentions, that food solidarity among men of the same ward and networks of food exchange among women still exists in Hausa villages (C. Raynaut 1976 and 1978). Nevertheless, with the penetration of money in all aspects of economic life, women are always interested in increasing independently their income through handicraft work, and through trading processed agricultural products, all in all through starting new endeavors independent from direct farm labour which remain out of their control.

Several studies (P. Hill 1969, E. Schildkrout 1979 and 1983, C. Raynaut 1978, P. Roberts 1983) illustrate how the monetization of the economy also affects the circulation of food between genders. Where one had previously the *mai gida* distributing the staple crops from the household granaries during the hunger season, the diminution of the quantity of farm products has substituted economic relationships between genders to the household members solidarity. Women sell ready-cooked meals prepared with the products of their *gayamna* fields, or with a part of the staple crop given by the husband, or also with the crops they have bought at harvest price from the poorest cultivators in need of cash for the payment of the head-taxes. Since the majority of their customers are male, women through this mercantilization of food distribution make the men pay for their cooking work and have indirectly access to their income.

Women's favorite forms of investment and saving are to purchase small animals (sheep, goats and poultry) and to sell them again in case of need. However, also in this domain they limit these investments.

According to the rationale of gender relations, men aim at maintaining their dominant position in the society and therefore are not interested by new possibilities for women to increase their income, because of the greater independence they achieve. The woman's improved economy is a threat to the husband's power in case of conflict since it gives her the initiative to demand the divorce. If men control women in many aspects of life, they have no claim on their income. Consequently women have to face the men's chicaneries in the agricultural tasks on the *gayamna* fields. For instance, a man can forbid a woman to use the organic manure of her animals because they are parked within the compound, which is his property.

According to the logic and the dynamic of power relations between genders, Hausa women cannot then expect the moral support of their husband, when they want to follow literacy courses, when they want to participate to meetings about topics relevant for the village well-being, when they want to have access to technical informations and modern agricultural inputs. They are kept out of credit facilities. They are not allowed to take part to the structure of agricultural cooperatives. The list of impediments could be long. In short, they do not have the permission to participate in all kind of activities which, in the long run, can also be beneficial for the household as a whole.

Conclusion

To sum up, the Hausa villages are confronted with a vicious circle. The bad economic conditions, which have historical and ecological causes, have lead to the deterioration of croplands and a disruption of the traditional social organization. Villagers' economic strategies have become more and more individualistic and money-oriented, while communal efforts are necessary to solve their problems.

Frustrations between genders are expressed through more frequent marital conflicts, whose consequence is the women's lack of motivation to invest their labour force in the family production unit and their aspiration to have access to new economic resources. Women thus do not require incentives for taking part to development programs, but have to cope with the limitations imposed by men. The control of the society has traditionally been in the men's hands. Therefore, they keep women excluded from land distribution according to the Islamic rules of inheritance, from agricultural informations, from the access to agricultural credit and machines, from decision-making in production cooperatives, from literacy programs and technical courses, from birth control policy.

Development programs which support a greater female participation to income-generating activities have, therefore, to take these changes touching the gender relations into account; they have to cope with the men's suspicion if not opposition to women-oriented projects, which might give them a greater economic dependence and concomitantly an increased possibility to escape from the male control. The immediate solution to this challenge seems to drop the idea of having development strategies where the men occupy a secondary position. One can no longer formulate projects where half of the population — either male or female — is left aside. Male villagers have, from the start, to be integrated into these projects, even though women will be the principal beneficiaries.

Another element for the success of extension programs, is to have key female persons who are respected and feared by men as allies, and it could be worth investigating whether *bori* women could fulfil such a role in the Hausa society.

REFERENCES

Amsatou Kansaye, 1989. Les Activités Sociaux Economiques de la Femme Hawasa dans l'Arrondissement de Magaria (Département de Zinder). Association Néerlandaise d'Assistance au Développement, S.N.V.-Niger.

Arnould, Eric J., 1985. Evaluating Regional Economic Development: Results of a Marketing Systems Analysis in Zinder Province, Niger Republic. The Journal of Developing Areas, vol. 19, pp. 209-244.

Arnould, Eric J., 1986. Merchant Capital, Simple Reproduction, and Under-development: Peasant Traders in Zinder, Niger Republic. Canadian Journal of African Studies — Revue Canadienne des Etudes Africaines, vol.20, No.3, pp.323-356.

Barkow, Jerome H., 1972. Hausa Women and Islam. Canadian Journal of African Studies — La Revue Canadienne des Etudes Africaines, vol.VI, No.2, pp.317-328.

Barkow, Jerome H., 1973. Muslims and Maguzawa in North Central State, Nigeria: An Ethnographic Comparison. The Canadian Journal of African Studies — La Revue Canadienne des Etudes Africaines, vol.VII, No.1, pp.59-76.

Boesen, I.W., 1983. Conflicts of Solidarity in Pakhtun Women's Life. Social Attitudes and Historical Perspectives. Copenhagen and London: S.I.A.S.

Braae, C., 1984. Degachia. En Undersøgelse af Tunesiske Oasekvinders Socio-Økonomiske og Ideologiske Status. Århus: Institute for Ethnography and Social Anthropology.

Deaver, S., 1980. The Contemporary Saudi Woman. in *E.Bourguignon* (ed.): A World of Women. Anthropological Studies of Women in the Societies of the World. New York: Praeger.

Feldman, S. and F.E. McCarthy, 1983. Purdah and Changing Patterns of Social Control among Rural Women in Bangladesh. in Journal of Marriage and the Family, vol.45, nr.4.

Goddard, A.D., 1973. Changing Family Structures among the Rural Hausa. Africa, Journal of the International African Institute, vol.43, No.3, pp.207-218.

Greenberg, Joseph H., 1946. The Influence of Islam on a Sudanese Religion. Monograph, American Ethnological Society. New York: J.J.Augustin.

Greenberg, Joseph H., 1947. Islam and Clan Organization among the Hausa. Southwestern Journal of Anthropology, vol.3, No.3, pp.193-211.

Hill, Polly, 1969. Hidden Trade in Hausaland. Man, nr.4, pp.392-409.

Hill, Polly, 1972. Rural Hausa. A Village and a Setting. London: Cambridge University Press.

Hill, Polly, 1973. Fra en Hausa Landsby i Nigeria. Den Ny Verden, vol.8, nr.2, pp. 70-87.

IRAM, 1975. La Participation des Femmes Rurales au Développement. A Propos d'une Action d'Animation rurale Féminine en République du Niger, 1966-1975. Paris: IRAM.

Kandiyoti, Deniz, 1988. Bargaining with Patriarchy. Gender and Society, vol.2, nr.3.

Khan, S.A. and F.Bilquees, 1976. The Environment, Attitudes and Activities of Rural Women: A Case Study of a Village in Pakistan. The Pakistan Development Review, vol. 15, nr.3.

Lefebvre, Alain, 1989. Tea Has Taken the Place of Love. Honour and Economy in Pakistani Villages. Copenhagen: Danish Development Agency, Research Council for Development Research.

Lefebvre, Alain, 1990. International Labour Migration from Two Pakistani Villages with Different Forms of Agriculture. The Pakistan Development Review, vol.29, nr.1.

Lefebvre, Alain, 1992. Women, Honour, and Money in Pakistani Villages. An Example of the Strengthening of Traditions through Economic Development. *O.Törnquist and K.R.Hællquist* (eds.): Asian Societies in Comparative Perspective. Nordic Proceedings in Asian Studies, nr.2, Copenhagen: Nordic Institute of Asian Studies.

Monimart, Marie, 1989. Femmes du Sahel. La Desertification au Quotidien. Karthala and OECD/Club du Sahel, Paris.

Moore, Henrietta L., 1988. Feminism and Anthropology. Polity Press, Cambridge (UK).

Nelson, C., 1974. Public and Private Politics: Women in the Middle Eastern World. American Ethnologist, vol.1, nr.3.

Nicolas, Guy, 1966. Essai sur les Structures Fondamentales de l'Espace dans la Cosmologie Hausa. Journal de la Société des Africanistes, vol.XXXVI (2), pp.65-107.

Nicolas, Guy, 1970. Circulation des Biens et Echanges Monétaires en Pays Hausa (Niger). Cahiers Vilfredo Pareto, No.21.

Nicolas, Guy, 1975. Dynamique Sociale et Appréhension du Monde au sein d'une Société Hausa. Paris: Institut d'Ethnologie, Musée de l'Homme.

Nicolas, Jacqueline, 1967. "Les Juments de Dieux". Rites de Possession et Condition Féminine en Pays Hausa. Etudes Nigériennes No 21, Paris: IFAN-CNRS.

Raynaut, Claude, 1972. Structures Normatives et Relations Electives. Etude d'une Communauté Villageoise Haoussa. Paris: Mouton.

Raynaut, Claude, 1976. Transformation du Système de Production et Inégalité Economique: le Cas d'un Village Haoussa (Niger). Canadian Journal of African Studies, vol.X, nr.2, pp.279-306.

Raynaut, Claude, 1977. Circulation Monétaire et Evolution des Structures Socio-Economiques chez les Haoussas du Niger. Africa, 47 (2), pp.160-171.

Raynaut, Claude, 1978. Aspects Socio-Economiques de la Préparation et de la Circulation de la Nourriture dans un Village Hausa (Niger). Cahiers d'Etudes Africaines, 68, XVII (4), pp.569-597.

Raynaut, Claude, 1990. Inégalités Economiques et Solidarités Sociales. Exemples Haoussa au Niger. *Didier Fassin and Yannick Jaffré* (eds): Sociétés, Développement et Santé. Paris: Ellipses.

Roberts, Pepe, 1983. Rural Women in Western Nigeria and Hausa Niger: a Comparative Study. Subordination of Women Editorial Collective: Serving two Masters. Lonfon: Routledge and Kegan Paul.

Saunders, Margaret Overholt, 1978. Marriage and Divorce in a Muslim Hausa Town (Mirria, Niger Republic). Ann Arbor: University Microfilms International.

Schildkrout, Enid, 1979. Women's work and children's work: Variations among Moslems in Kano. *Sandra Wallman* (ed.): Social Anthropology of Work. London: Academic Press.

Schildkrout, Enid, 1983. Dependence and Autonomy: The Economic Activities of Secluded Hausa Women in Kano. *Christine Oppong* (ed.): Female and Male in West Africa. London: George Allen & Unwin.

Scott, Earl P., 1978. Subsistence, Markets and Rural Development in Hausaland. The Journal of Developing Areas, vol.12, pp.449-469.

Smith, M.G., 1952. A Study of Hausa Domestic economy in Northern Zaria. Africa, vol.XXII, No.4, pp.333-347.

Smith, M.G., 1959. The Hausa System of Social Status. Africa, vol.XXIX, No.3, pp.239-252.

Spittler, Gerd, 1977. Traders in Rural Hausaland. Bulletin de l'Institut Fondamental d'Afrique Noire, vol.39, sér. B, nr.2, pp.362-385.

Westergaard, Kirsten, 1982. Pauperization and Rural Women in Bangladesh. A Case Study. Copenhagen: Center for Development Research, Project Paper A.82.5.

Youssef, N.H., 1977. Women and Agricultural Production in Muslim Societies. Studies in Comparative International Development, vol.12, nr.1.

The impact of demographic changes on the inter-relations between health, water and the environment — the schistosomiasis experience

Jerry Ndamba
Blair Research Laboratory, Harare
Zimbabwe

Abstract

Vector borne parasitic diseases are endemic in many parts of Africa. The arid conditions in these countries requires that irrigation schemes be set up in order to facilitate agricultural development. However, most of these water conservation programmes have the undesirable effects of creating optimum conditions, conducive breeding and survival of vectors that are responsible for the transmission of diseases. High levels of morbidity and in some cases mortality, inevitably impede agricultural development programmes by reducing the productivity of the human hosts. Schistosomiasis, a disease that is not characterised by acute readily recognisable episodes of disability which can be counted and measured, is given as one such example. Data on some of the adverse effects of high schistosomiasis infection intensities on infected agricultural workers is presented. The local knowledge of the people, regarding schistosomiasis, is outlined together with examples of the economic significance of high infection levels. Various possible control measures are outlined with special reference to the Primary Health Care to disease control. The possibility of modulating the Ethiopian traditional uses of a plant, *Phytolacca dodecandra*, for the control of the snail, intermediate host of schistosomiasis, is briefly discussed. Sociological studies carried out in order to assess the community attitudes towards the proposed use of the plant in self-help schistosomiasis control programmes is presented. Although most of the data presented is obtained from studies carried out in Zimbabwe, it is argued that similar conditions are most likely to occur throughout most African countries, where these diseases are endemic. It is concluded that the lessons learned from schistosomiasis can also be used as a basis for initiating similar control programmes for other vector borne diseases.

Introduction

In most parts of Sub-Saharan Africa, a number of infections uncommon and/or eradicated in other parts of the world are prevalent amidst poverty, poor housing and non-existent or inadequate sanitary conditions. The arid conditions, in most of these countries, have resulted in a number of water conservation schemes necessary for agriculture development, being initiated. However, such well-intentioned schemes have had the undesirable effect of increasing the potential for the transmission of water borne parasitic diseases such as malaria, schistosomiasis, onchocerciasis (river blindness), filariasis, trypanosomiasis, leishmaniasis and guinea worm. Despite the availability of a number of control strategies, very little priority has been given to the initiation of control programmes for most of these diseases. The reasons range from the insidious nature of the infections and lack of drama usually associated with other spectacular diseases, to lack of financial resources by most developing countries to effectively deal with the problem. This, coupled with the underestimated overt morbidity and mortality, and scarcity of convincing evidence regarding the benefits of low morbidity levels results in most governments diverting their scarce human and financial resources to tackle other, more pressing, health issues where the 'dollar benefit' is clearly visible.

It is, therefore, apparent that an estimate of the socio-economic implications of high prevalence and incidence coupled with initiation of cheap and effective control strategies, could be powerful arguments in favour of granting priority to the control of such diseases. However, the evaluation of the public importance of most diseases is difficult, especially in cases where the condition is not solely characterised by acute, readily-recognisable episodes of disability, which can be counted and measured. The problem can be worse when the disease occurs in areas where hospital and pathological services are scarce. Such problems are clearly evident in the case of schistosomiasis, sometimes called bilharzia, a vector borne parasitic disease widely spread in most parts of Africa (Kloetzel 1962; Ongom and Bradley 1972; Jordan 1972).

The schistosomiasis life cycle

The human schistosomes or blood flukes are digenetic trematodes with a complex life cycle that involves alternating parasitic and free living stages (Figure 1). The dioecious adult worms are parasitic stages which reproduce sexually and live in the human body. They are about 2 cm long and occur in pairs, with the female lying in the gynecorphoric canal of the male. There are two types of human schistosomiasis in Africa namely *Schistosoma haematobium* and *S. mansoni*.

The worms are found in the vescical venules around the urinary bladder in the case of *S. haematobium*, while adult *S. mansoni* live in the portal system, primarily in the superior mesenteric veins. The worms themselves are not very important in inducing the pathological changes

Figure 1. The schistosomiasis life cycle.

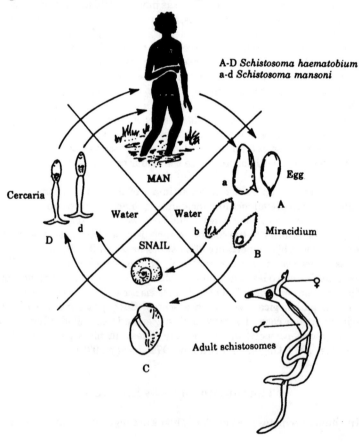

A-D *Schistosoma haematobium*
a-d *Schistosoma mansoni*

often associated with schistosomiasis, but it is the accumulation of the eggs produced that gives rise to most of the symptoms of the disease. The female worms produce about 300 eggs per day, per worm, which through a combination of enzymatic secretions and peristalsis, pass out of the blood vessels through the tissues and into the urinary bladder, in the case of *S.haematobium* or lumen of the gut, in the case of *S. mansoni*. The eggs leave the body through either the urine or faeces. When the urine or faeces reach fresh water and when the temperature is right, the eggs hatch into free swimming miracidia which must locate an appropriate snail, specific for that type of schistosome within 24 hours after being hatched or die. The intermediate host snail for *S. haematobium* in most parts of Africa, is *Bulinus globosus* while *Biomphalaria pfeifferi* is the host for *S. mansoni*. Inside the snail, asexual reproduction takes place that results in thousands of cercariae from one miracidium. The cercariae can penetrate the skin of humans who come into contact with the infested water in the course of daily water related activities.

Infection through drinking infected water is possible but this is thought to be a rare mode of transmission. Once inside the skin they gradually change into mature pairs of female and male trematodes or schistosomes which can be lodged in the blood vessels of the intestine or urinary tract. The pair will eventually mate and the female lays eggs to continue the cycle.

The significance of schistosomiasis in Africa with special reference to Zimbabwe

Schistosomiasis represents a real threat to agricultural development in almost all countries of Africa and is often second only to malaria in terms of morbidity. Over 40 million persons living in rural and agricultural areas are estimated to be infected and 15-16 million are exposed to the infection. Prevalence studies carried out over the years in the Sub-Saharian African region have shown high levels of infection among women and children.

Schistosomiasis cases are increasing due to the spread of the snail intermediate hosts as new irrigation schemes and water conservation projects, needed for economic and agricultural development, are established. The disease can have severe effects on man resulting in paralysis or death. Studies in various parts of Africa have shown the debilitating effects of schistosomiasis which reduces the capacity for work, increases susceptibility to other infections and exacerbates malnutrition. In a study conducted in Zimbabwe to assess the major causes of absenteeism among agricultural workers, although the occupationally related backache was found to be the most common cause, abdominal pains and diarrhoea, all manifestations of *S. mansoni* infection significantly contributed to the rate of absenteeism (Table 1).

Recent work has shown, by ultrasound examination, that a lot of previously unknown pathological changes take place in cases of high infection intensities resulting in fibrosis of the liver and bladder (Figure 2). High schistosomiasis infection intensities, it has been argued, could have severe economic implications for agro-based developing country economies. In Egypt where the prevalence of both *S. mansoni* and that of *S. haematobium* is high, the loss of labour output among the 14 million infected people is estimated to be as high as 35% (Farooq 1967) and in mainland China where the more pathogenic *S. japonicum* is endemic, an average loss of 40% of an adult's capacity for work has been reported (Cheng 1971). Furthermore in the Philippines, it is estimated that 13 million pesos are lost annually due to *S. japonicum*, a much heavier economic burden than that due to malaria (Farooq 1963).

In a more recent study, *S. mansoni* infection was determined among agriculture workers in Zimbabwe. Prevalence of *S. mansoni* infection

	Intensity of *S. mansoni* infection (eggs/gm of stool)							
Complaint	23-100 n=82	101-200 n=75	201-300 n=49	301-400 n=32	401-500 n=29	500+ n=48	T n=315	C n=120
Abd pains	25.60	14.70	26.50	25.00	24.10	29.20	24.50	14.20
Diarrhoea	15.90	22.70	16.30	31.30	17.20	16.70	19.40	10.80
Backache	28.00	25.30	22.40	28.10	27.60	31.20	27.00	24.20
STDs	14.60	16.00	12.20	3.10	10.30	4.20	11.40	16.70
Malaria	6.10	9.30	8.20	6.30	6.90	8.30	7.60	13.30
Other	9.80	12.00	14.30	6.30	3.40	10.40	11.10	20.80

n= total number of people in the indicated category of infection while **T** indicates the total number of infected subjects and **C** indicates uninfected control subjects.

Table 1. The major causes of absenteeism during the last two weeks among agricultural workers infected with S.mansoni in Zimbabwe. The figure shown is the percentage in the respective infection category claiming absenteeism due to the given complaint.

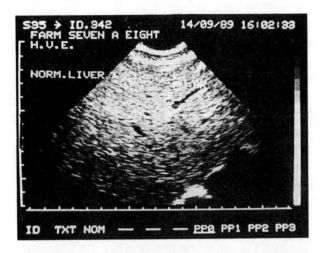

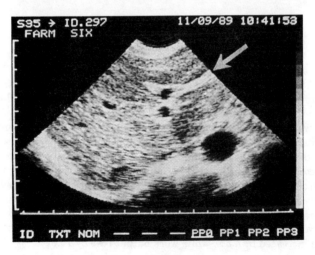

Figure 2. *Ultrasonographic pattern of (A) a normal liver and (B) of a 42 year old agricultural worker with severe Symmer's peri-portal fibrosis (ppf). The deleted portal vein is indicated by the arrow in picture (B).*

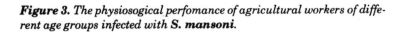

Figure 3. *The physiosogical perfomance of agricultural workers of different age groups infected with* S. **mansoni**.

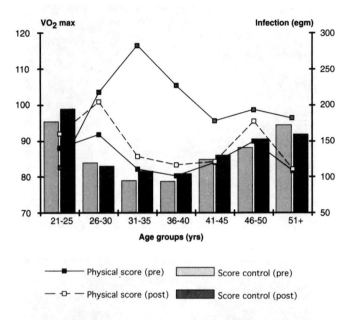

was 15.8%. Morbidity due to *S. mansoni* was determined by ultrasonography, stool consistency, blood and mucus in stool. The prevalence of periportal fibrosis (ppf) and other *S. mansoni* related morbidity indicators was higher among the infected subjects. Blood loss had no anaemia producing effect as determined by haemoglobin and red blood cell counts. Physiological (VO_2max) and work performance was assessed on infected and uninfected workers. Although all the subjects were found to be of good nutritional status and generally physically fit, paired t-test showed a significant improvement ($p < 0.01$) in the post treatment physiological performance among the infected cutters as measured by the Harvard Step Test (Figure 3). The age related physiological performance increased by 4.3%, while work output rose by 16.62%.

However, although there was a general increase among uninfected controls who also received the same anti-schistosomal drugs as the infected subjects, this trend was not significant ($p > 0.05$). Work output also followed the same trend (Ndamba *et al.* 1992). *S. haematobium* infection among school children also decreased their running performance while treatment with praziquantel had a dramatic improvement on their physiological performance (Ndamba 1986). Similar studies that showed the adverse effects of schistosomiasis have been reported from a number of African countries (Siangok *et al.* 1976; Karim *et al.* 1980).

As a basis for formulating a schistosomiasis control programme and realising that the success of such a programme would depend on the affected population's knowledge about the disease and their appreciation of the extend of the problem, sociological studies, as they relate to the transmission of schistosomiasis, were carried out in various social groups of rural parts of Zimbabwe. It was apparent from these studies that most rural people associated blood in urine with urinary schistosomiasis but knowledge about the other form of the disease was not wide spread. Other manifestations commonly associated with schistosomiasis in rural areas of Zimbabwe have been established to include frequency of micturation, dysuria, headache and weight loss. The methods of transmission given ranged from jumping across the fire, taking too much salt, using toilets without shoes to drinking dirty water. Only a few people indicated some involvement of snails in the transmission of schistosomiasis (Table 2). The high *S. mansoni* infection prevalence and intensity figures among the adult population could be attributed to this phenomenon (Figure 3). The lack of obvious manifestations of *S. mansoni* poses problems, even for rural health service centres, as microscopes are usually not available for diagnosis. On the other hand,

Table 2: Knowledge (percentage) of the rural people in various parts of Zimbabwe about the signs and symptoms often associated with *S. haematobium* by province.

Signs and symptoms	Province where traditional healer practices					Total cases
	Masvingo	Manica land	Matebele land	Midlands	Mashona land	
Haematuria	55.20	18.30	8.90	10.20	8.10	99.20
Dysuria	50.00	26.70	7.10	10.00	6.70	21.90
Frequency	28.60	28.60	28.60	14.30	0.00	2.60
Weakness	54.20	17.80	9.90	12.70	5.00	35.00
Blood in stool	12.80	40.00	13.40	33.30	0.00	5.50
Abdominal pains	53.30	20.80	5.40	13.30	8.00	43.10
Other	70.00	16.90	7.00	0.00	7.00	11.10

the association between increase in age and *S. haematobium* infection prevalence among children of school-going age has been ascribed to both changing social habits, as well as acquired immunity.

Schistosomiasis control strategies

Over the years, there has been a shift from the previous emphasis of eradicating the disease to that of control of morbidity. It would appear that the most effective method of morbidity control is a combination of snail control, safe water supplies, adequate sanitation, health education and chemotherapy through the primary health care (PHC) system. The PHC system is a broad based approach to health care which recognises that many factors affecting health are inter-related. This inter-relationship is most clearly appreciated in the areas of water supply and sanitation, which are related not only to schistosomiasis but to other major health problems particularly diarrhoeal diseases, malaria and guinea worm. It is believed that such an approach will be cheaper, as financial and manpower resources for strengthening water and sanitation activities can be shared by different disease control programme areas and the cost savings channelled to the other components of the schistosomiasis control programme. However, chemotherapy and snail control, the key components in the implementation of schistosomiasis control, should be co-ordinated primarily to achieve maximum and sustained reduction in prevalence, incidence and intensity of schistosomiasis infection.

Molluscicides as the most effective snail control method and the potential of plant molluscicides

Jobin (1973), proposed snail control as the most effective method of schistosomiasis control as this forms the 'weak link' in the *Schistosoma* life cycle. Jordan and Webbe (1969), divided snail control measures into three categories, namely environmental, chemical and biological control. It has been demonstrated, in a number of studies, that the use of snail killing compounds (molluscicides) is the most dramatic of all the snail control strategies. The undesirable broad-spectrum faunal toxicity inherent in the use of molluscicides is believed to have been lessened by the now commonly practiced focal and periodic, rather than area wide blanket, application (McCullough *et al.* 1980).

The continued availability of the currently used synthetic molluscicides is in doubt, due to lack of interest in industry to sustain their production as a result of high production costs and lack of an assured market. Most countries that might otherwise need to import these synthetic compounds are developing countries that have depleted resources. The insidious nature and lack of drama associated with schistosomal infections, coupled with the underestimated, overt morbidity and mortality are not clear indicators of the 'dollar benefit' to most governments for initiating control programmes. This coupled with increasing concern over the possible build-up of snail resistance to the synthetic compounds, their persistence in the environment and toxicity to non-target organisms has given new impetus to the study of plant molluscicides. The most promising of such plant molluscicide are the berries of *Phytolacca dodecandra* L'Herit, a plant indigenous to many parts of Africa.

Adaptations of social practices for disease control — lessons from Ethiopia

In 1964, while studying the distribution of snails, an Ethiopian scientist observed that in areas where women were using the berries of *Phytolacca dodecandra* for washing clothes, only dead snail shells could be seen. However, large snail colonies were recovered up and down stream from the washing points (Lemma 1965). Since this observation, a number of research activities have been undertaken to assess the feasibility of using *P. dodecandra* in community self-help schistosomiasis control programmes. The plant, called *endod* in Ethiopia, *gopo* in Zimbabwe and *ipoko* in Zambia, is a member of the *Phytolaccaceae* family. Its distribution is said to cover most of Sub-Saharan Africa (Dalziel 1936). It has since been established that if the sun-dried berries are crushed and minute quantities (10 to 25 parts per million) mixed with water, the solution is molluscicidal. International conferences have since been held in Zambia, Swaziland and Ethiopia to review research progress that has been made in this area. The World Health Organisation's Special Programme in Tropical Diseases Research has endorsed *P. dodecandra* as the leading candidate both in terms of molluscicidal promise and number of previous studies.

Toxicological data has shown that beside being an eye irritant, the berries exhibit no mutagenicity, very low mammalian toxicity, and moderate but acceptable aquatic eco-toxicity (Lambert *et al.* 1991). Unlike most promising molluscicides, the berries of *P. dodecandra* are highly molluscicidal against all types of snails, water soluble and easily biodegradable. Recent studies by Monkiedje *et al.* (1990), showed stability of *P. dodecandra* molluscicide potency at various W radiation levels and low pH values. Furthermore, although piscicidal at molluscicidal concentrations, saponins could be detected in the water for only five days after application, while a synthetic molluscicide persisted for up to 14 days.

From the wild to domestic fields — the Ethiopian experience

The major strength and potential of plant molluscicides is their application in village self-help schistosomiasis control programmes. Such programmes require that agronomic characteristics under various environmental conditions be known in order to provide cultivation guidelines to overcome the stress that might be imposed on the plant by the new circumstances. It is a well established phenomenon that domestication may result in lose of specific plant characteristics. Agronomic studies have resulted in the desirable strains being selelcted for further studies in Ethiopia (Lugt 1981).

Search for indigenous and adaptation of the Ethiopian varieties

The news from Ethiopia generated a lot interest in Zimbabwe, where the national schistosomiasis control programme was short lived due to the expenses of the synthetic mollusicides. Studies were initiated to assess the feasibility of using *P. dodecandra* in the revitalised control programme. Numerous natural varieties were identified but their distribution and molluscicidal potency was were closely associated with certain climatic and edaphic features of the country (Chandiwana *et al.* 1986; Ndamba *et al.* 1988). Preferential areas of natural growth were found to be anthills and hilltops at altitudes of over 900 metres, with berries of the highest concentration of saponins collected from poor rainfall areas. The natural preference of *P. dodecandra* in Zimbabwe for orthoferrallitic soils, which are highly leached and acidic with no reserves of weatherable minerals, is consistent with those made in Ethiopia. Local varieties have been identified in Zambia and recently Uganda, although the berries were less potent than those harvested from Ethiopian plants.

Adaptation trials using clonal material of an Ethiopian variety carried out in Zimbabwe, revealed good growth performance and high berry productivity under these foreign conditions. The plants grew well and produced berries when introduced to different altitudes and soil types of Zimbabwe. Limited trials of the Ethiopian varieties carried out in Zambia revealed higher survival rate of the local strain, while the same plants adapted well to conditions in Swaziland, but in both cases propagation was from seeds.

Sociological evaluations of *P. dodecandra*

A central research question is whether a traditional practice can be modulated in such a way as to have a positive health impact. One of the fundamental issues to be addressed before embarking on programmes to encourage community use of any plant, are the socio-cultural and economic implication of such practices on the community. This is essential to design health education material that will achieve maximum results. Against this background, a study was initiated in order to assess the knowledge and uses of *P. dodecandra* and the community attitudes towards the proposed use of the plant. The study was conducted in two communities, where the plant is known to grow naturally and in a further two communities, where no records of the natural occurrence of the plant exist.

It was apparent that the knowledge and uses of the plant was widespread among people that were normally resident in the areas where natural growth of the plant has been reported. Of all the people interviewed, 44.20% had prior knowledge of *P. dodecandra* while 55.80% had never seen or head of the plant before. Only a few immigrants, who were at the time of the study resident in areas where no records of the plant

Table 3. Number of people interviewed and percentage of who had prior knowledge of *P.dodecandra*.

Area of respondents residence	Females		Males		Total	
	Number per area	% of total	Number per area	% of total	Total responses	% of total
(A)	79	98.70	66	80.30	145	90.30
(B)	86	3.50	24	0.0	110	2.7
(C)	61	14.70	41	4.90	102	10.80
(D)	45	80.00	37	35.10	82	59.80

The plant is known to grow naturally in areas (A) and (D) but not in (B) and (C)

have been made, had knowledge of the plant from their previous areas of residence. However, 90.30% of the people resident in one of the areas where *P. cdodecandra* grows naturally and 59.80% from the other area knew about the plant (Table 3). The extend of the knowledge of the plant seemed to be dependent upon the frequency of natural occurrence in each of the two areas.

The most frequent use reported was that of the leaves as a floor polish. Other uses ranged from that of the roots and leaves as a medicine to growth of the plant near the homestead to act as a lightning deterrent and in some cases as a snake repellent (Table 4). It was, however, of interest that unlike in Ethiopia, none of the people interviewed were aware of the use of the berries as a soap. Further, none of the people knew of the piscicidal nor molluscicidal properties of the berries. Asked about their opinion regarding its cultivation, 77% of the interviewees were willing to cultivate it for snail control purposes. However, of the 23% that had reservations, scarcity of land (47.70%), lack of adequate knowledge about the plant (21%), indifference due to age (20%) and lack of confidence in a wild plant to control a life threatening disease (11.20%), were cited as some of the major obstacles to its cultivation.

Strategies for the future

It is realised that the future control activities for most vector borne diseases is through the (PHC) system. However, as is evident in the case of schistosomiasis, such an approach would not succeed unless the concerned governments appreciate the extend of the problem and therefore prepared to provide financial resources necessary for financing various components specific for that disease control programme. In the absence of such resources, alternative and cheap methods, therefore, need to be established. Furthermore, the importance of chemotherapy as an integral part of a schistosomiasis control strategy is realised and funding for this aspect inevitable. However, snail control, although equally important but as previously highlighted, could be achieved through other means.

It is evident that a lot of work has been done to prepare for the eventual use of the plant molluscicide in schistosomiasis control programme. However, the major question is whether a traditional practice can be modulated to have a positive health impact. Besides a five year field trial by Lemma (1977) in Adwa, where the berries were purchased from the local market women and demonstration of the efficacy of *P. dode-*

Table 4. The most common uses of *P.dodecandra* in 2 rural areas where the plant grows naturally.

Use of *P.dodecandra*	Area (A)				Area (D)				Total % (A+D)	
	Females (n=78)	% Total	Males (n=66)	% Total	Females (n=45)	% Total	Males (n=37)	% Total	Females (n=123)	Males (n=103)
Floor polish (leaves)	61	78.20	24	36.40	33	73.30	6	16.20	76.40	29.10
Medicine (roots + leaves)	2	2.60	2	3.00	2	4.40	2	5.40	3.30	3.90
Domestic animal disinfectant (leaves)	4	5.10	14	21.20	0	0.00	0	0.00	3.30	13.60
Emetic (roots \berries\leaves)	0	0.00	0	0.00	0	0.00	2	5.40	0.00	1.90
Lightning protector (whole plant)	0	0.00	7	10.60	0	0.00	0	0.00	0.00	6.80
Snake repellent (whole plant)	0	0.00	5	7.60	0	0.00	0	0.00	0.00	4.90
Abortifacient (leaves\berries)	6	7.70	0	0.00	0	0.00	0	0.00	4.90	0.00
Flea repellent (leaves)	0	0.00	3	4.50	0	0.00	0	0.00	0.00	2.90
Don't know	9	11.50	19	28.80	11	24.40	17	46.00	16.30	35.00

n = number of people that were interviewed. A further 2.70% and 10.80% females only from area (B) and (C) respectively gave floor polish as the only use of *P.dodecandra*. The natural density of the plant was higher in area (A) than in area (D).

candra berries under laboratory and field conditions in reducing the snail population (Ndamba *et al.* 1989), most of the information so far available on the subject has been speculative. It is important that studies are initiated to demonstrate the efficacy of domestically produced berries in reducing the disease in the human population. To this effect studies have been completed in Zimbabwe to assess and determine the best cultivation method for use under village conditions, as a basis for formulating guidelines for the widescale production. It is envisaged that a further study, where the villagers will be encouraged to cultivate the plant and the berries thus obtained used to control schistosomiasis, will be implemented in collaboration with scientists from the Royal Danish School of Pharmacy and the Danish Bilharziasis Laboratory. The major objective would be to evaluate the efficacy of the plant material produced, processed and applied by the community in significantly reducing the prevalence and incidence of schistosomiasis in the human population. It is hoped that the information gathered will be used throughout Africa, as a basis for initiating community oriented schistosomiasis control programmes.

Acknowledgements

The author is grateful to the organising committee of the SAHEL workshop for the honour of being invited to the workshop. The studies, whose results are discussed here, were made possible with financial assistance from the Government of Zimbabwe (Ministry of Health), the Old Mutual (Zimbabwe) Ltd and DANIDA through the Danish Bilharziasis Laboratory (DBL). My sincere thanks are due to DANIDA, the DBL and the Royal Danish School of Pharmacy (DFH) who have all made it possible for me not only to carry out most of the work presented here, making it possible for me to come to Denmark to complete this work, but also to attend this workshop. I would like to extend my thanks to the Director of the Blair Research Institute for his assistance and support during the implementation of these studies. I am indebted to Ian Robertson of the University of Zimbabwe for his unwavering support during my pursuit of the Endod studies. I extend many personal thanks to Niels Christensen, Director of the DBL, Per Molgaard and Else Lemmich all of the DFH and Peter Furu (DBL) for providing me with a good working environment while in Denmark. The inspiration and motivation provided by Leon Brimer, former Director of the Blair Research Laboratory, Paul Taylor and Henry Madsen, in developing the Endod project will always be remembered.

References

Chandiwana, S.K., Mavi, S. and Ndamba, J. (1986): A preliminary report on the distribution of *Phytocacca dodecandra* (L Herit) in Zimbabwe. Zimbabwe Agricultural Journal 83:1-2.

Cheng, T.H. (1971): Schistosomiasis in mainland China. A review of research and control programs since 1949. American Journal of Tropical Medicine and Hygiene 32

Chimbelu, E.G. and Shehata, M.A. (1987): A review of research in Zambia on *Phytolacca dodecandra* (Endod). Endod II (*Phytolacca dodecandra*); Report of the Second International Workshop on Endod, *Phytolacca dodecandra*, Mbabane, Swaziland, April, 1986. Council on International and Public Affairs, New York, 1987: 109-126.

Clarke, V.deV., Taylor P, Sviridov, N. and Richardson, M.A. (1981): The importance of an integrated approach to the control of bilharzia. Central African Journal of Medicine 27: 198-202.

Dalziel, J.M. (1936): The useful plants of West Tropical Africa, Crown Agents, London.

Farooq, M. (1963): A possible approach to the evaluation of the economic burden imposed on a community by schistosomiasis. Annals of Tropical Medicine and Hygiene 57: 323-331

Farooq, M. (1967): Progress in bilharziasis control. The situation in Egypt. World Health Chronicle 21:175-184.

Jobin, W.R. (1973): Cost/benefit analysis for application of molluscicides in the prevention of schistosomiasis. WHO Document WHO/SCHISTO 73: 24.

Jordan, P. (1972): Schistosomiasis and disease. Pages 17-23 in MJ Miller (Editor). Proceedings of a Symposium on the Future of Schistosomiasis Control. Tulane University, New Orleans.

Kloetzel, K. (1962): Splenomegaly in *Schistosomiasis mansoni*. American Journal of Tropical Medicine and Hygiene 11: 285-294.

Lambert, J.D.H., Temmink, J.H.M., Marquis, J., Parkhurst ,R.M., Lugt, C.B., Lemmich, E., Yohannes, W.L. and De Savigny, D. (1991): Endod: Safety Evaluation of a plant molluscicide. Regulatory Toxicology and Pharmacology 14: 189-201.

Lemma, A. (1965): A preliminary report on the molluscicidal property of endod (*Phytolacca dodecandra*). Ethiopian Medical Journal 3: 187-190.

Lemma, A., Goll, P., Duncan, J. and Mazengia (1978): Control of schistosomiasis by the use of endod in Adwa, Ethiopia: Results of a 5-year study. Proceedings on the International Conference on Schistosomiasis 1: 415-436. Cairo, Ministry of Health (1978).

Lugt, C.B. (1987): Feasibility of growth and production of molluscicidal plants. Plant Molluscicdes. UNDP/World Bank~WHO Special Programme for Research and Training in Tropical Diseases pp 231-244. Mott KE (Editor): John Wiley & Sons Ltd. 1987.

Lugt, C.B. (1981): *Phytolacca dodecandra* berries as a means of controlling bilharzia transmitting snails. Litho Printers, Addis Ababa, 1981.

McCullough, F.S., Gayral, P., Duncan, J. and Christie, J.D. (1980): Molluscicides in schistosomiasis control. Bulletin of the World Health Organisation 58: 681689.

Monkiedje, A., Wall, J.H., Englande, A.J. and Anderson, A.C. (1990): A new method for determining concentrations of Endod-S (*Phytolacca dodecandra*) in water during mollusciciding. Journal of Environmental Science and Health B25: 777-786.

Ndamba, J. and Chandiwana, S.K. (1988): The geographical variationin the molluscicidal potency of Phytolacca dodecandra in Zimbabwe. Tropical and Geographical Medicine 40: 34-38.

Ndamba, J., Chandiwana, S.K. and Kanyande, C. (1992): Factors influencing the natural distribution of Phytolacca dodecandra (L' Herit) plants in Zimbabwe. Zimbabwe Science News 25: 59-61.

Ndamba, J., Chandiwana, S.K. and Makaza, N. (1989): The use of *Phytolacca dodecandra* berries in the control of trematode-transmitting snails in Zimbabwe. Acta Tropica 46: 303-309.

Ndamba, J., Makaza, N., Kaondera, K.C. and Munjoma, M. (1991): Morbidity due to *Schistosoma mansoni* among sugar cane cutters in Zimbabwe. International Journal of Epidemiology 20: 787-795.

Ndamba, J., Makaza, N., Munjoma, M., Kaondera, K.C. and Chadukura, V. (1992): The physiological and work performance of agricultural workers infected with *Schistosoma mansoni* in Zimbabwe Acta Tropica (in press).

Ongom, V.L. and Bradley, D.J. (1972): The epidemiology and consequences of *Schistosoma mansoni* infection in West Nile, Uganda,I. Field studies of a community at Panyagoro. Transactions of the Royal Society of Tropical Medicine and Hygiene 66: 835-851.

Trees as Tools for the Reconstruction of Sustainable Rural Production Systems

Gunnar Poulsen
Hillerød,
Denmark

Basic Predicament

Not so very long ago only a relatively small proportion of available farm-land in the semi-arid tropics was cultivated in any single year. More than three quarters of the total area was left to fallow, being the best known means to maintain fertility at a satisfactory level. This traditional production system, applied in many parts of the world since time immemorial, was indeed characterised by a high degree of ecological stability. In fact, since the large fallow areas of those days were typically covered by a protective mantle of grasses and shrubs, there was little risk of water or wind erosion ever getting seriously out of hand. In addition to ensuring upkeep of fertility and erosion control, the fallows also served as an adequate source of fuel, small construction timber and, of course, pasture requirements for a not too numerous rural population.

During the long fallow to which all cropland was being periodically subjected, the top soil did not only get replenished with organic matter, but its content of plant nutrients were refurbished by recycling of deep-rooted grasses and shrubs and, not least as a result of nitrogen-fixation by rhizobia on legume plants, and various bacteriae and algae. Even the tilled fields were probably less exposed to erosion in the past. After harvest, livestock was usually let in to feed on the stovers and fertilize the soil with their waste products. Neither straw nor dung was carried away in large amounts to be marketed as fodder or serve as kitchen fuel, as has become the custom. As a result of these gentle management practices, the amount of plant nutrients annually removed from a field never reached excessive levels, being confined almost exclusively to those elements encompassed within grain, pulses and animal produce. Another significant feature of the traditional pattern was the fact that the farmers of yore hardly ever let the soil become seriously exhausted before they shifted to another plot, abandoning the field to a good, lengthy, fertility-restoring fallow. When endeavouring to circumscribe the characteristics which ensured, most decisively, the stability of the old production system, two features in particular stand out, viz. —

1) An adequate biomass equilibrium, and
2) A rotational pattern where relatively short cropping periods were succeeded by long fallows.

N.B. By adequate biomass equilibrium we understand an ecological state where a sufficient surplus of biomass, above what is taken away as crop and animal produce, is being produced annually to ensure the regular and sufficient replenishment of the topsoil with organic matter.

Where the traditional system was operated correctly, the combined effect of a "healthy" balance between biomass production and removals, and the limitation to only a few years for the continuous cultivation of any plot of land, ensured that the infiltration capacity and the resilience of the topsoil to erosion and leaching remained sufficiently high to prevent any kind of excessive degradation.

With respect to large tracts of land in the semi-arid tropics, the ancient cultivation practice began to deteriorate already many years ago under the impact of changing socio-economic circumstances, an unfortunate development which has tended to accelerate in the course of time. As a consequence of increasing demands for cropland from steadily growing populations, cropping periods have been extended and conversely, fallow periods, shortened far below the critical threshold for the regular upkeep of fertility. Trees and shrubs have been lopped and chopped destructively for the provision of both fodder and fuel. Fields have been swept almost clear of dung, straw and other organic substances that might serve a useful function under pots and pans in the kitchen. Intense grazing of an already impoverished pastoral resource has furthermore resulted in the soil often becoming almost totally denuded of vegetal protection, before the onslaught of the first heavy showers of the rainy season.

What probably strikes elderly farmers most, when observing such an unfortunate development, is the steady decline of yields per hectare which is taking place as well as the no less disturbing fact that much more land will be needed for feeding a family than when they were young. In addition to the often intractable problem of acquiring access to more cropland and to till and weed larger expanses for satisfying the needs of a family, the present-day situation confronts farmers with several other adversities. More work is required to collect fuel for the kitchen. Construction material is harder to come by. Seeds and eventual fertilizer are frequently blown or washed away. Springs and watercourses, where the women used to fetch water, dry out more often than before, etc. etc.

Curing underlying causes far more important than treating symptoms

The most conspicuous symptom of environmental deterioration, at least to most outsiders, is the destruction of the original forest cover which typically precedes and accompanies the breakdown of rural ecosystems. From observations of this kind, the conclusion is very often drawn that remedial action must be centered around ways and means to reinstate the tree, an argument which probably, to most people, seems sound and irrefutable.

In the opinion of the writer of these lines, the "reforestation solution" must, in most cases, be written off as unrealistic. It overlooks the basic fact that the interaction of adverse factors that caused the disappearance of the forest in the first place, will still be operating and can even be expected to exercise more destructive pressures than just a few years previously. Many more people require more land now, and not just in total but also per family unit, to satisfy basic needs. That such a predicament cannot be overcome by "taking land out of farming" on a considerable scale and returning it to forest utilisation, should be evident to all and sundry — notwithstanding all the numerous benefits, also agriculturally, that could be derived from having some forest land within easy reach again.

As in the case of medical science, remedial action should also in the environmental sphere, be directed foremost at treating the underlying causes of the malfunction. Expressed briefly it should be aimed at helping farmers to develop and practice sustainable production systems that may enable them to produce essential necessities at optimum levels without putting the most essential functions of the supporting ecosystem into jeopardy.

Farmers production-related motivation

In the agricultural domain, and if we except the special case of commercial farming, the production of as much food as possible is probably the main consideration of most rural people. It may not be too far fetched, in fact, to say that the heart of motivation of most smallholders is located in their stomach. — it is of the greatest importance to have this in mind when designing a strategy for environmental rehabilitation.

Farmers usually listen politely to sensible proposals for measures directed at controlling erosion, improving fuelwood supply, and similar praiseworthy innovations, and may even accept to participate quite enthusiastically in such activities, particularly if encouraged to do so by certain favours, financial or otherwise. Nevertheless their interest in such ventures will dwindle into insignificance when compared to their response to an eventual proposal of a new practice, within their technical and economic means, that would enable them to double or triple crop yields and correspondingly raise output from livestock.

In order now to achieve an impact which is commensurate with the huge dimensions, area-wise, of the environmental catastrophy that is hitting whole regions and even countries, it is recommended to concentrate development planning and extension, even more than hitherto in most places, around the promotion of sustainable production systems aimed absolutely foremost at supplying food at optimum levels. Only by doing so will we have a chance of obtaining that multiplier effect which will ensure that the innovation gets disseminated among tens of thousands of farmers within a minimum of time. — Directing the main focus towards food production does not mean, though, that attention should not be paid, eventually, to tree planting. On the contrary, in the context of the establishment and operation of sustainable production systems, trees and shrubs may often serve as extremely useful tools, a subject which we shall later return to.

Principal constraints to remedial action

When it comes to an eventual change of production method, the freedom of choice of most farmers is limited by the usually modest size of the holding, the numbers and characteristics of the available manpower, and not least, by shortcomings with respect to capital. Moreover, soil and climate and eventual access to irrigation water, put other clear restrictions to their freedom of action. When elaborating an improved rural production system, an additional problem should be taken into account, the great importance of the time factor to smallholders should be not overlooked. For a man, or woman, who often must struggle, almost continuously, for the survival of their families from one rainy season to the next, any activity which does not promise a fairly short interval between initial investment of land and effort and the first return of tangible benefits, may not seem feasible at all. For an operation to be attractive to such people, the investment period must be very short — not exceeding one to two years at the very most. If the activity does not involve any great proportion of available resources and, in particular, if the expected recompense is spectacular, people may be prepared to twist this general rule quite considerably. Even a very poor man may be willing to plant and nurse a few mango trees with little hope of being paid for his efforts, except in the world of dreams, within at least five years. However, such cases only constitute the exceptions which confirm an important rule of wide application.

Appropriate rural production systems

In order to be attractive to the typical smallholder, an agricultural production system must combine optimal yield of desired goods, as well as an economically satisfactory balance between input and return, with practical answers to the following basic problems:

1. Upkeep of a crumby top soil presenting favourable conditions both to water infiltration and nutrient retension.
2. Control of erosive surface run-off.
3. Prevention of the occurrence of erosive or desiccating winds at ground level.
4. Promotion of favourable conditions for nutrient recycling, including the fixation of atmospheric nitrogen.
5. Securing efficient utilization of rainwater.
6. Ensuring the upkeep of soil fertility by maintenance of a sound equilibrium between nutrient replacement and nutrient removals.

This may seem quite a long list of problems — many of which furthermore are quite complex. Nevertheless, if we exclude point 6. temporarily, 1-5 may be summarized, with some indulgence from the reader, into one single requirement. The farmer must combine satisfaction of his production needs with careful maintenance of the most essential features of a forest ecosystem. — More easily said than done, many would argue. It is the contention, however, of this writer, that all that is needed to achieve this goal, oversimplifying a little perhaps, is the scrupulous upkeep of an adequate biomass equilibrium by the farmer on his crop and pasture land. If this is done, natural biological mechanisms will take care of the rest — with the only exception of not providing a solution for problems arising from an imbalance in the supply and removal of plant nutrients. If nutrients are taken away at a pace which exceeds their replacement by weathering of mineral particles and other natural processes, such gradual exhaustion of the fertility of the soil cannot be remedied (with exception made for N) by biological means alone. Consequently if P, K, Mg and other necessary elements are being removed regularly as elements of crops and animal produce, it will not normally be possible to ensure the upkeep of fertility by other means than some kind of fertilisation. In this context, it should be added, however, that both the efficiency and economics of fertilizer application may be greatly influenced by the status of the biomass equilibrium on the area in question — a subject to which we shall later return to.

The function of trees on crop and pasture land — what they may accomplish and what they cannot do

Trees on farmland may serve a wide range of useful purposes, such as: helping to control wind and water erosion, protecting crops against desiccating winds, sheltering livestock against wind and sun, and yield all sorts of products, including fruits, fodder, fuel, timber, honey and even medicine. They may also, by means of rhizobia, act as efficient binders of atmospheric nitrogen and equally, through their deep root systems, to recycle nutrients that have been leached out of reach of most ordinary crop plants. In the same context, ligneous vegetation may help decisively to maintain an adequate biomass equilibrium.

Trees do not render all these services completely free of charge. They occupy land at the "expense" of crops, and compete with neighbouring herbaceous vegetation for light, water and nutrients. They may also harbour pests like Quelea birds and rodents. A competent farmer will endeavour to ensure, through his choice of species, spatial arrangement and management practices, that the advantages he expects from growing trees on his land always outweigh the negative aspects by a reassuring margin.

When planning a production system involving the intercropping of ligneous and herbaceous crops, the farmer must furthermore avoid subscription to the widespread but erroneous belief, that certain tree species possess some sort of magical quality which enables them to restore and maintain the fertility of cropland, regardless of an eventual imbalance between nutrient supply and removals. No tree is (naturally) able to synthesize P, K, Mg or any micro-element out of thin air. Trees may, it is true, bring elements up from deep soil layers for the benefit of more shallow-rooted crops. They may even carry out such a beneficial effect for several years before an eventual "hidden store" of nutrients is "pumped" dry. However, in the long term all agricultural production systems, whether including a ligneous component or not, will be subjected to the same basic law. The fertility of the land and the growth of ligneous as well as herbaceous plants will deteriorate, if removals of basic nutrients are permitted to exceed the rate of replacement for any extended period of time. But what, then, about the well-known capacity of trees, particularly of the legume order, to fix atmospheric nitrogen? Does the extremely valuable mechanism in question not escape the "law'. Unfortunately it is not so. The rhizobia, and other microorganisms that may be involved, are just as dependent as other vegetation on a well balanced supply of phosphorus, potassium, magnesium etc. — with the obvious exception of nitrogenous substances. Unless the indispensable elements are present in appropriate concentrations, the organisms will develop poorly and worst of all, in the present context, be unable to carry out their most beneficial function optimally. A set back in this sphere will again, which should surprise nobody, be directly reflected by a reduced growth-rate for the rhizobia-supporting tree. However, a no less severe adversity, in a farming context, is also bound to occur. With a disrupted supply of fixed nitrogen, a basic element of amino acids, the trees in question will produce foliage and fruits with a lower protein content than otherwise. In the case of fodder trees, this will reduce the nutritive value of the produced livestock feed very seriously. Similarly, the value of the foliage and twigs for mulching purposes will be affected adversely. Before leaving this specific subject, it should be mentioned that, according to Australian observations, tree fodder grown on exhausted land will also be less palatable to livestock than foliage originating from a more fertile locality.

Spatial arrangement of shrubs and trees on farmland

For centuries, most farmers in the semi-arid tropics grew their crops and pastured their livestock under and among trees or within the open spaces of an irregular mosaic of forest and woodland, disrupted only here and there by small, cultivated fields. In such a well wooded landscape, wind or water erosion rarely reached serious proportions. Furthermore, fields hardly ever became severely depleted as farmers usually abandoned them to a long fertility-restoring fallow in good time before total exhaustion of the soil.

In greater outlines it may, therefore, be no exaggeration to state that the farmers of those times applied an agricultural production system which was characterized by a respectable level of ecological stability. — these days are gone as we all know. Most rural landscapes have become almost totally denuded of shrubs and trees. Not ecological stability, but ecological disruption reigns supreme in far too many regions. One of the most intriguing problems which confronts many modern farmers, as well as development planners and advisors, is whether it may not be possible to bring some of the trees back, together with the useful functions they carried out, without causing unacceptable conflict with present-day realities in a far more crowded countryside.

In order to succeed in such a venture, the choice of an appropriate spatial arrangement of the ligneous vegetation will be of the greatest importance. Any turning back of the clock will obviously be impossible. People are crowded too densely into the modern farmscape for that. It is out of the question to return to a pattern of vast areas of bush-fallow or of trees and shrubs scattered unevenly across people's fields, where they would constitute too much of an obstacle to the operation of modern farm equipment, whether pulled by animals or machines.

If we want many trees back in the rural areas, some alternative pattern must be worked out which takes these new realities into account. Basically three types of spatial arrangement deserve consideration.

1) A savanna pattern
2) A zebra pattern of hedges
3) A grid of shelterbelts.

A savanna pattern would differ from the real, natural savanna by the trees being spaced much more regularly, like a checkerboard, in order to cause minimum obstacle to cultural practices. The spacing would, furthermore, be varied in accordance with the characteristics of the utilized tree species and intended management practice. A typical spacing may be of the order of 10×10 metres.

The term "zebra pattern of hedges" has been chosen to describe a spatial pattern, where closely spaced hedges (6-10 metres apart), are established regularly across crop and pasture land, making it look, from the air, like a quietly resting zebra. Various models may be applied within this category. Instead of using a single pattern of evenly spaced rows, it may be preferable, according to the circumstances, to establish double or triple rows relatively far apart (8-12 meters). The application of this last model is of particular interest where it is intended to intercrop ligneous vegetation and grain crops or pulses, while the single row alignment will be ideal for the creation of a purely pastoral production system.

"Shelterbelts", also called windbreaks should usually be aligned at right angles to the most feared wind direction and spaced at distances of, at the most, ten times the height of the trees composing the belt. It is of great importance, in the tropics in particular, that the belts are given a fairly open structure. Otherwise there will be a risk of the stagnant air, causing harmful overheating of the crops close to the belts. Another disadvantage of a very dense belt is that it will not provide nearly as effective a protection against desiccation and erosion at extreme wind velocities.

Although most people, when considering planting trees for the control of wind erosion, only think of shelterbelts, it is a fact that the savanna and zebra models will provide as good, if not better, protection in this domain. — so why chose one spatial arrangement rather than another? In reality all three present advantages and disadvantages that need to be weighed carefully against each other.

The savanna and the zebra models are undoubtedly best suited for ensuring the upkeep of biomass equilibrium, recycling of nutrients and nitrogen fixation. Against such very distinct advantages they may be blamed for causing a far greater obstacle to the execution of many agricultural practices than a widely spaced grid of shelterbelts.

Strongly in favour of opting for the zebra pattern, is the fact that it can be established and made fully operational very rapidly — within 2-3 years — under reasonably favourable circumstances. The farmer will usually have to wait twice as long to harvest any distinct benefits from newly established savanna plantings or windbreaks.

All three spatial models mentioned here can, in addition to serving their principal environmental function, be expected to yield fuel on an appreciable scale, and also small timber and possibly several other types of produce. For the purpose of ensuring a regular supply of fuel and timber, the shelterbelt system may, nevertheless, be considered the most appropriate. When, on the other hand, the interest is directed principally at creating a stable source of livestock feed, the zebra pattern presents distinct advantages.

While the farmer, in a planning situation, must pay great attention to the advantages and disadvantages presented by various systems, his decision making will inevitably rest upon the extent to which the application of one or another of the suggested spatial patterns fits most appropriately within the framework of the main production goals, which normally will be oriented towards the production of certain crops or varieties of livestock, or eventually some kind of mixed farming.

Management practices for ligneous vegetation on crop and pastureland

Trees and shrubs have a tendency, if left unattended to shade the ground to the detriment of herbaceous crops growing under their canopy and also, in the case of shallow-rooted species, to compete strongly, with neighbouring vegetation for water and nutrients. For this reason, the successful intercropping of ligneous and herbaceous plants will usually require the subjection of the tree or shrub component to specific management practices. The intervention, in this context, will usually be directed, at the same time, at creating nearby optimal conditions for growing crops under and among the trees, and deriving as much benefit from these in the form of fodder and other useful produce.

Farmers, accustomed to producing crop on open land, will often initially object to growing any trees at all. They will argue, sensibly enough, that they need every tiny bit of their land for producing the amounts of sorghum, cassava or beans, needed to feed their family. They may be prepared to change their mind, however, if it can be demonstrated to them convincingly, that the "sacrifice" of say 15% of their land to tree planting may result in raising crop yields by a higher percentage, and in addition provide the farmer with substantial amounts of useful tree products, such as fodder, fuel and timber.

In order to maximize the benefit to the farmer of such mixed production systems, a variety of exploitation practices may be applied to the ligneous component, viz.

1) Direct and rotational browse by livestock of hedges of legume shrubs, supplemented by periodic pruning back at close to ground level keeping the fodder resource within reach of the animal.
   N.B. unpalatable branches may be carried away for fuel purposes.

2) Periodic pollarding (every two or three years), or pruning up to top shoot of trees grown in a savanna pattern.

3) Lopping of savanna trees according to need, aimed at the same time, at obtaining produce and reducing shade-effect. — in this same context it may be added that trees producing valuable fruits, and in this manner giving good compensation for land occupancy, normally will be left untouched.

4) Rotational exploitation of timber and fuel resources of shelterbelts, carried out as felling at ground level and in rows with attention to minimizing an eventual reduction of the shelter-effect.

Fertilization of mixed ligneous/herbaceous production systems

Any exploitation of agricultural land with little or no fallowing, as often necessitated by high population densities, will almost unavoidably result in the removal of more plant nutrients, together with harvested produce, than being replaced through weathering and other natural processes. Unless compensated for by appropriate means the consequence of such a development will be the steady decline of the fertility and productive capacity of the land.

As pointed to earlier, an imbalance of this nature cannot be redressed, as is sometimes advocated, by the introduction of trees, and more particularly of nitrogen-fixing varieties, into the farming system. Some immediate betterment may, in reality, be achieved, in some cases, as a result of the trees recycling nutrients from deep soil layers. However, such improvement will always be of a temporary nature unless some additional measures are brought to bear on the problem. For any long term upkeep of fertility, the regular replacement of removed nutrients, through manuring or the application of artificial fertilizer, is indispensable. In this context, it is however of the greatest importance to note that a production system involving the intercropping of ligneous and non-ligneous plants and characterized by an adequate biomass equilibrium, will present far better conditions for economically satisfactory fertilization, than those occurring on open, windswept farmland. There are at least four good reasons for this state of affairs, viz. Firstly, the application of N-fertilizer can be totally dispensed with, if the system involves the growing of legume plants (trees and herbs) on a significant scale, and sufficient P, K and other basic minerals are provided to sustain efficient nitrogen-fixation by rhizobia.

Secondly, far less unproductive losses of added nutrients can be expected from a soil whose cation-exchange-capacity and resistance to erosion and leaching is kept high by almost continuous replenishment with organic matter and which also, in other respects, is being protected by the presence of many trees.

Thirdly, the trees can be expected to recycle those nutrients which, despite all, should have been leached to deeper soil layers.

Fourthly, but no less important, where production systems involving a substantial tree component are involved, it will make good sense to apply relatively cheap, slow-release types of fertilizer, rather than the most commonly used, rapidly dissolving types.

The benefits of all these quite complex interactions, can be quite startling. From Western Australia it is reported (personal communication by Dr. L. C. Snook) that the establishment of legume shrub hedgerows across sandy, windswept pasture land, receiving only 500 mm annual precipitation, has led to a tripling of the carrying capacity for wool sheep on the basis of total omission of nitrogen fertilizer and reduced application of P, K and other basic elements, when compared to conditions on neighbouring, conventionally managed farmland. Comparable results are also reported from the region of Adelaide in Southern Australia, where a slightly different production system involves the cultivation of grain crops among the hedgerows during the humid season.

"Trees as tools" versus "Trees are good for you"

As it has been attempted to explain on the preceding pages, trees and shrubs may serve extremely useful functions in the context of operating sustainable rural production systems with the main emphasis oriented at optimal yield of food products — in accordance with the motivation, in the agricultural domain, of most farmers.

When carrying out, eventually, collaborative extension to bring this message out to farmers, it is suggested directing their attention, foremost, on the prospects for using trees as tools principally for reaching an agricultural goal, rather than approaching the rural people with the more conventional "Trees are good for you" gospel.

Carefully selected, in respect of species, and appropriately managed, trees and shrubs may indeed be used for raising the productivity, in a substantial manner of both crop-cultivation and animal husbandry quite considerably without requiring unrealistic inputs of either capital or manpower. Show me the farmer who would not like to get hold of such tools and learn to apply them efficiently?

Pastoralism as an Underestimated Aspect of the Sahelian Production System

M.A. Mohamed Salih
Nordic Africa Studies
Uppsala, Sweden

Resume

This brief presentation attempts to assess pastoralists contribution to the economies of some of the Sahelian countries and to answer questions pertaining to the factors which ushered their political and economic marginalization. It, therefore, examines three inter-related areas of concern: First, why, despite their substantial contribution to the national economies of their states, pastoralists have not been accorded sufficient attention by policy-makers and planners. Second, the linkages between the externalities and internalities which produced a pastoral economy incapable of coping with an increasing economic and ecological pressures. Third, responses to the crisis which has largely been heralded by the neglect and underestimation of pastoral production systems, and the possibility of a linkage between environmental degradation and underdevelopment, and the underestimation of pastoralists in the Sahel.

Pastoralists contribution to Sahelian economy

In most Sahelian countries, pastoralists represent a minority, except in Djibouti, Chad, Mauritania, Mali and Somalia (Table 1). However, even when they are a majority, pastoralists are largely marginalized and their welfare neglected as far as the allocation of development projects is concerned. This occurs despite the common knowledge that over 90 percent of the national herd, in most Sahelian states, is owned by pastoral nomads (Table 2). In that sense the pastoral sector provides between 10-25 percent of livestock protein intake in Burkina Faso, Chad, Ethiopia, Mali, Niger and Senegal and between 40-65 percent of livestock protein intake in Kenya, Mauritania and Somalia, in the form of milk, meat (Table 3). Moreover, trading in livestock and hide as an export commodity, play an important role in the national and local markets. Livestock are exchanged for cash, grain and other range of commodities which cannot be produced by the pastoralists themselves.

The national accounts of the Sahelian countries give contradictory reports as to the share of livestock production in their Gross Domestic Product (GDP). In most cases, livestock production is subsumed under agriculture, added to that fisheries and hunting. However, my own calculations of the share of milk and meat production in the GDP, shows that the role of livestock in the national accounts is greatly underestimated. Table (3) suggests that the GDP of most Sahelian countries, either does not consider important food items such as meat and milk as products or that the planners are not concerned about their contribution to the national economies. The underestimation of the contribution of any sector of the economy in the national accounts, often has some serious implications on how that sector is perceived by policy-makers and planners. It would also have some negative implication for the allocation of development priorities and the direction of investment. Apart from

Table 1. Pastoralists as percentage of the total population and TRLU per pastoralist

Country	Population (in million)	Pastoralists (in million)	As % of total population
Burkina Faso	9.001	1.10	12.2
Djibouti	0.54	0.16	25.0
Chad	5.428	1.40	25.7
Ethiopia	49.2	3.90	7.9
Kenya	24.0	3.50	14.5
Mali	9.2	1.00	10.8
Mauritania	2.0	1.25	62.5
Niger	7.7	1.00	12.9
Senegal	7.0	0.60	8.5
Somalia	7.5	4.50	60.0
Sudan	25.2	3.50	13.8

Source: *(1) FAO, Yearbook, 1990.*
          (2) ILCA, Handbook of Livestock Statistics, 1991
          (3) Europa, Africa South of the Sahara, 1993.

Table 2. Estimates of Livestock population and TRLU in some Sahelian countries (in million)

Country	Cattle	Goats	Sheep	Camels	TRLU	TRLU per pastoralist
Burkina Faso	2.90	5.70	3.15	0.05	2.92	2.08
Djibouti	0.70	0.50	0.414	0.068	0.20	12.93
Chad	4.173	1.90	2.80	0.54	3.93	2.80
Ethiopia	29.0	18.00	24.00	17.00	26.20	6.71
Kenya	13.45	7.50	6.32	0.80	11.59	3.31
Mali	5.00	5.80	5.80	0.241	4.90	4.91
Mauritania	1.263	3.32	4.20	0.82	9.71	7.77
Niger	3.609	7.617	3.539	0.42	4.06	4.06
Senegal	2.741	1.20	3.920	0.15	2.58	4.30
Somalia	4.90	20.00	14.30	4.90	11.76	2.61
Sudan	18.00	13.10	15.40	2.71	18.16	5 18

Source: FAO Yearbook, 1990

Kenya, Sudan and Nigeria which spent over 10 percent of development allocations in livestock development projects. All other Sahelian countries have spent or proposed to spend less than 5 percent in the livestock sector (ref. EIR 1992, Europa 1993). Ironically, about 75-90 percent of livestock development projects are externally, and at times one gets the feeling that they have been imposed by foreign donors, which the national planners would have preferred that investment to go to agriculture or agro-industry. Except for a few cases, the bulk of the investment was allocated to livestock production with little interest in pastoral development. For instance, recurrent expenditure on livestock services, during the 1980's as percentage of agricultural services expenditure was as follows: Burkina Faso 16.2%, Chad 4%, Ethiopia 10%, Niger 7.9%, Senegal 4.9% and 8% in the Sudan. Kenya is the only country which spent 34% in recurrent services, table (4) below. All percentages are grossly disproportionate with livestock contribution to the national economy.

If this substantial contribution to the national economies has not satisfied the national planners and policy-makers, the contribution of livestock to the local communities is far from being assessed. The Sahelian pastoralists have been successful to eke out their living from such a harsh and unpredictable environment, for centuries. Livestock provided

Table 3. The Value of meat and milk production and their value as percentage of the contribution of agriculture to GDP

Country	Meat 000' MT	Price/MT in USD	Value in million USD	Milk 000' MT	Price/MT in USD	Value in million USD	Total Meat and or Milk Value in million USD	Agriculture (GDP) in million USD	Meat and or Milk % of Agri GDP	FAO, World Bank and World Resources Liv. GDP as % of Agri. GDP
Burkina Faso	60.0	1 690.0	101.40	99.0	850.0	84.15	185.55	213.97	86.7	24.0
Chad	69.0	-	-	236.0	840.0	198.24	198.24	12.24	1619.6.	34 0
Djibouti	6.0	-	-	9.5						
Ethiopia	600.0	510.0	306.00	794.0	410.0	325.54	631.54	4,665.70	13.5	35.0
Kenya	466.0	490.0	228.34	2,467.0	330.0	814.11	1,042.45	2,271.30	45.8	33.0
Mali	120.0	850.0	102.00	164.0	450.0	738.00	840.00	204.60	410.5	33.0
Mauritania	44.0	-	-	253.0	-	-	-	-	-	84 0
Niger	104.0	-	-	252.0	540.0	136.08.	136.08	219.07	62.1	78 0
Senegal	211.0	-	-	138.0	-	-	-	-	-	-
Somalia	146.0	-	-	1,545.0	-	-	-	-	-	80.0
Sudan	395.0	1,150.0	454.25	2,875.0	400.0	1,150.00	1,604.25	5,456.05	29.4	37.0

Sources: (1) Annual Meat and Milk Production, FAO Yearbook, 1990.
(2) Meat and Milk Prices, compiled and mean prices computed from ILCA, Handbook of African Livestock Statististics, 1991.
(3) World Bank, World Development Report, 1990
(4) World Resources Institute, World Resources, 1990-1991.

Table 4. Livestock Services Recurrent Expenditure (LSRE) as Percentage of Agricultural Services Recurrent (ASRE)

Country	LSRE as % of ASRE
Burkina Faso	16.2
Chad	4.0
Niger	7.9
Senegal	4.9
Ethiopia	10.8
Kenya	34.0
Sudan	8.0

Source: Anteneh, A. The Financing and Staffing of Livestock Services in Sub-Saharan Africa, ILCA, 1991.

not only a valuable source of food, but also acted as a wealth reserve, a redeemer from damage, a sacrificial gift and a means for marriage and other ceremonial payments. The exchange value of livestock and its conversion into grain has provided, in some instances, the only means to gain access to grain. Not to mention the high transport value of the burden beasts and their silent contribution to local and regional transport systems in the Sahel.

To stop at enumerating the virtues of an underestimated production system, says nothing than stating the obvious. My task from here on is to establish a link between the underestimation of pastoralists and its effect on their ability to cope with the harsh conditions of the Sahel. Therefore, it is argued that the neglect of pastoralists has compounded the problems confronting them and made them vulnerable to the rationality (or irrationality) of the market economy, the ill-planned large-scale mechanized schemes and the deteriorating socio-economic conditions as a consequence of the deteriorating prices of their stocks, relative to the manufactured goods. These and other issues will be highlighted in the following section of this essay.

The eco-economy of neglect

The eco-economy of neglect, refers to the underestimation of pastoralism, its contribution and subsequently the effect of that on their ecology and economy. The main contention here, is that most interpretations of the relationship between ecology and economy in the Sahel are based on explicit or implicit recognition of the modern market economy as a factor external to the local communities (Franke 1980; Sen 1981; Redclift 1984; ICHI 1985; Watts 1987; Hjort and Mohamed Salih 1989; George 1990; Winpenny 1991; Thomas 1992). In the process of incorporating the Sahelian communities into the market economy, they have lost much of the characteristics of the so-called self-sustaining societies. The exchange of products such as gum arabic, sesame, groundnuts and livestock for cash, also points out that the use of general purpose money has been transformed into an entry into general purpose economic arrangements, which invite structural change in the traditional economy and its relationship to society and ecology.

Many a society have been compelled, by economic reasons, to put more land into pastoral or agricultural production to maintain the status quo, cut more wood for sale or for charcoal making to satisfy an increasing need by urban dwellers and an accelerating need for commodities manifold expensive than their own products. In Hutchison's (1991:145) words, "with few options of survival, they have little choice but to exploit key environmental resources to provide food and income for survival". Tree felling for sale in the form of firewood, charcoal or construction material, land "mining", overstocking in preparation of long spells of drought or over-cultivation etc...

Excessive utilization of resources, both in the modern and the traditional sector, has been heralded by unfavourable climatic conditions which, in the long-run, ruined the very basis of survival. The Sahelian people's willingness to expand agricultural production and multiply their herds has increased in order to be able to avoid the bad years which may be laying ahead.

Although many studies have shown that the traditional systems of range management and pastoral production are well suited to the Sahelian ecology (Ahmed 1979; Baxter 1991; Hjort 1985, Mohamed Salih 1991; Behnke, *et al.* 1992), such views have always been neglected. The argument that pastoralists have developed through the years an efficient system of resource management and that social development services can be provided to pastoralists while they are on the move, have in most cases fell on deaf ears. There is also the predicament of appropriating land from the traditional producers, both peasants and pastoralists, and its allocation to the already wealthy and powerful large-scale farmers for the production of cash crops to satisfy the demands created by the international market economy.

An answer to the dilemma of appropriating land from pastoralists and its allocation to pastoralists is to establish grazing reserves and allocate them for pastoralists. Imposed or ill-conceived settlement projects for pastoralists, with their negative ecological impacts, has dominated livestock development projects. The objectives of such settlement projects include livestock-agricultural integration and an intensive interaction with the market economy to increase off-take, while securing a reliable system for the provision of health, water and education facilities. These policies were adopted under the guise that the traditional systems of herd management represent a waste of labour and valuable land resources. Hence, the settlement is expected to make available vast stretches of land for cultivation and the production of food crops. An association between social development and settlement has, therefore, been perceived as the most pertinent way of developing pastoralists.

The Decline of pastoralism

As has been shown earlier, there is a clear linkage between the deteriorating socio-economic conditions of the Sahelian communities and the decline of the productive options available to them. Markakis (1993) argues that the neglect of pastoralists by the state has contributed to their decline. However, it is equally plausible to argue the reverse i.e. the state intervention has also contributed to the demise of pastoralists. In this sense, the ecological dimension of the disastrous impacts of the incorporation of the pastoralists into the modern market economy, has resulted in political crises which challenged the societal structures, their survival as well as their ethical and moral foundations.

Poverty, hunger and destitution of such a preponderant magnitude have also been accompanied by aggressive pursuance of political goals. In the process, the state became an arena of competing interests and political objectives, inconsistent either with its role as the main monopolizer of the use of coercion or the sole arbiter of divergent ethnic and regional interests. The intersection of ecology, economy and polity has produced an unprecedented wrangling over the control of any of three factors to gain access to the others. Access to political power facilitates the use of its decision-making capacity to gain access to the control of natural resources. A similar principle may apply to the utilization of natural resources, not for mere subsistence, but for commercial and large-scale production with less interest in ecological sustainability.

One of the striking features of pastoral development policies, which continued from the colonial legacy to post-colonial or independent Africa, is the state's ownership of land and its bias towards large-scale agricultural enterprises *vis-á-vis* the small-scale producers. This in itself shows a conspicuous disregard of pastoralists and lack of appreciation of their production system.

In this respect, most African states have created a small group of privileged farmers, parastatals or private enterprises which monopolized agricultural production, marketing and distribution. Most African states have a free hand to evict traditional peasants and pastoralists from their farming and grazing lands to establish projects "of national interest", such as mining and large-scale plantations for the production of cash crops, without compensation. Eviction of peasants and pastoralists from their cultivable lands and pasture is a common practice, which has been very well documented in the literature (Bernstein and Campbel 1985; Lawrence 1986; Henderink and Sterkenburg 1987, Glantz 1987; Mohamed Salih 1987 and 1991). The end result is the emergence of a tendency towards the concentration of land in the hands of a few, financially-able wealthy farmers. Consequently, social differentiation increased and the income gap between those who solicited the support of the state to gain access to better landed resources and those who are evicted from their lands, became apparent.

The expansion of large-scale mechanized schemes in the Sahel has meant that a large number of the small peasants and pastoralists (Mohamed Salih 1991b), have been denied access to local resource rights which are based on traditional activities, such as seasonal grazing or the seasonal extraction of materials for food, medicine, fuel-wood and construction purposes (Hutchison 1991:145). Pastoralists and peasants are instead forced to settle in more poorly populated areas, some of which might have already been targeted for conservation (*ibid*). An illustrative example is the case of some parts of South Kordofan, where 6 million acres of large scale mechanized schemes owned by the private sector have been allocated since 1968 (Mohamed Salih 1987, 1990 & 1991). These have created the all too familiar environmental mismanagement which usually accompanies such schemes (Redclift 1984; ICHI 1984).

More alarming is the pastoralists and peasants response to the decrease in the fertile lands available to them due to the expansion of large scale mechanized schemes. These include continuous cropping which consequently contributed to the reduction of fellow periods. Second, shifting cultivation, which was adopted in the past to regulate land fertility, is no longer practiced. Fixed farming or large-scale clearance of tress and shrubs have now been adopted to solve the problems engendered by the low fertility induced by the short fellow periods or lack of sufficient land to practice shifting cultivation. The ecology-economy linkage here is self-explaining.

It is by now obvious that state policies are of vital importance to any integrated approach towards understanding the association between poverty and the manner in which people utilize their natural resources. Economic rewards, in this case, seem detrimental to long-term sustainable environment. The political relationship between states and civil societies can be translated into attitudes towards economic opportunities and their ecological consequences. The context of this relationship in the Sahel is a clear case of contradictory perceptions of resource management objectives. For instance, the state ownership of land has reinforced traditional patterns of ownership, therefore denying the rural populations the potential of transforming production systems into investment assets that invite initiative. The persistence of labour exchange arrangements, which involves little cash (Ziche and Mohamed Salih 1984), is a clear indication that peasants and pastoralists prefer not to be dependent on cash transactions which might radically transform the social basis of production. Certainly the reduced peasant and pastoralists capacity to cope with economic pressures is a direct response to the state agrarian policies, as far as land and the rural labour markets are concerned.

Scarcity of fertile lands due to appropriation by the state has, in some areas, contributed to malnutrition as land, which supports subsistence became scarce. Small producers were pushed to lesser fertile lands and in some instances were compelled to expand horizontally in order to be able to survive (Hjort and Mohamed Salih 1989; UNICEF/UNSO 1991; Hutchison 1991). Land appropriation policies have encouraged rural/-urban migration, as land without title can also be considered a land with little or no commercial value. In some areas, traditional producers have lost their lands to the large-scale commercial sector, while they were deprived the commercial value of that land which eventually became an economic asset owned by "outsiders". State-controlled or restricted land markets have slowed down agrarian transformation at the local level and restricted it either to state capitalism or to the business class which enjoyed the fruits of more fertile lands, credit facilities, subsidies and access to imported inputs. There is no reason to separate the impact of such policies from the overall development/environment *problemtique* since each has an intimate relationship to the other.

A limited exchange of land for cash was adopted by the peasants as a response to external factors rather than to factors pertaining to internal transformations. Such transactions represent a piece-meal solution which aggravates the problems of the rural poor. Although such change may be capable of solving immediate problems within the peasant family budget, it may not be in a position to provide long-term solutions to the agrarian crisis. In short, the present land policies are not conducive to factor changes in production. Land markets have an intimate association with rural labour markets which are, in most cases, fragmented. Rural wages were kept low to reduce costs and hence secure cheap food for the politically-vocal urban consumers. Low wages usually reduce the already limited purchasing power of the rural labourer, which is not conducive to the expansion of trade and enterprise. This has contributed to the alienation of the rural households from their production and hence relegated many to poverty and destitution. In retrospect this implies that, in a situation of near stagnating technology, more land has had to be put under production, not to improve the standards of living, but to maintain the status quo. A depleted countryside cannot readily afford the labour, nor the land required for such an undertaking.

The national context within which the Sahelian system operates has imposed three major externalities which have re-shaped society and its relationship with ecology. These are: the expansion of the market economy and the encapsulation of the rural areas into the international division of labour. Second, agricultural policies and their bias towards large-scale mechanized agriculture *vis-à-vis* pastoralists and arable cultivators. Third, recurrent drought which aggravated the impacts of the economic and ecological pressures exerted by the state agricultural policies and its interferences with the environment. Such externalities have invited an array of regional consequences and responses, which are in themselves a product of a larger international context.

An important aspect of resource management pertains to the fact that conflicting interests over natural resources, whether between individuals, groups or states, have increasingly been taking a regional dimension as a result of peoples movement from the degraded ecology to regions more suitable for sustenance. This has also another dimension of conflict not only over the exploitation of natural resources (for subsistence or commerce), but also over their sustainability, conservation or long-term objectives versus short term needs. The Sahelian region is a case in point, where its fragile environment has to cope with responses to market economy, large-scale production and the demands of the more disadvantaged rural poor.

Agro-pastoral production in the Sahel offers an ample evidence of regional inter-dependence between farming and pastoral or nomadic communities. While riverine regions and valleys are important for the production of food crops, pastoral communities depend on these very resources as dry season pastures. Pastoral communities which inhabit the more drier regions in the northern frontiers of the Sahel, depend on imported grain for a greater part of their subsistence, and in many instances on the local markets and water sources outside their nationally perceived political boundaries. Ecological variations within and between states militate, especially for people for whom the existing political boundaries represent a hindrance rather than a facility, have to be met with careful utilization of resources (land, labour, inputs and herds), wherever they may exist. Such arrangements include cross-border farming, grazing or trading with the communities on the other side of the border, and who in most cases might not be of a different ethnic stock.

State policies have far-reaching impacts on the regional context of resource management, administration, use and control. Ecological crises which result from human interferences, are not country-specific and their consequences can be felt by distant communities within the region (mass flight of refugees to neighbouring countries) or even by communities in different continent (Third World refugees in the North). I argue elsewhere that (1991b:118), "environmental conflicts are inter-related to the extent that it is impossible to divide the world into fragmented regions, hoping that one nation or continent would survive the consequences of a major disaster". Hence, the most obvious regional response to ecological crises (drought, floods, epidemics etc...) is mass population movement in search of new survival opportunities, strategies and mechanisms to make ends meet amidst staggering deteriorating socio-economic conditions.

If similar market mechanisms operated, among pastoral communities, in more than one country, then ecological inter-dependence is ultimately linked to economic inter-dependence between those inhabiting various ecological zones. The regional context of livestock/grain terms of trade is one such mechanism which links pastoralists inhabiting the arid zone and agro-pastoralists and farming communities inhabiting the more wetter savannah. The regional context of production-cum-ecology has been enhanced by the linkages between the local economies and large national and regional economies. And due to the fact that different ecological zones (are likely to) produce different goods, ecological inter-changability is a very important factor in creating dependency between various sets of consumers. It is also linked with the regional context of trade between livestock and grain; an argument which has been on the agenda for quite some time (Swift 1979; Hjort 1981; Sutter 1982; Little 1983; Mohamed Salih 1988; Kerven 1992). The argument presented here is that livestock prices tend to deteriorate relative to grain prices during drought periods and when grain is most needed by pastoralists. Such a price mechanism is not determined by local communities, but influenced by the regional context of trade on grain and other goods of services.

References

Ahmed, A.G.M. (1979), Some Aspects of Pastoral Nomadism in the Sudan, Khartoum University Press, Khartoum.

Ahmed, A.G.M. 1987, "National Ambivalence and International Hegemony: The Negligence of Pastoralists in the Sudan", in M.A. Mohamed Salih (ed) **Agrarian Change in the Central Rainlands, Sudan**, SIAS, Uppsala.

Ahmed, J.Y. 1991, "International Policies to Respond to Global Environmental Threats: An Economic Perspective", in Winpenny (edt), Development Research: The Environmental Challenge, ODA, London.

Baxter, P.T.W (edt), 1991, When the Grass is Gone: SIAS, Uppsala

Behnke, R.H. et al.. 1992, Rethinking Range Ecology: Implications for Range Management in Africa, Dryland Network Programme, IIED, Issue Paper No. 33.

Bernstein, H. and Campbel, B.K. (eds), Contradictions in Accumulation in Africa, University of California, Berkeley.

Bohannan, P. and Dalton, G. (eds) 1962, Markets in Africa, Northwestern University Press.

Brandt Commission, 1983, North- South Dialogue. A Programme for Survival, Pan Books, London.

Brandt Commission, 1983, Common Crisis, Pan Books, London.

Bruntland Report, 1988, Our Common Future. Oxford University Press, Oxford and New York.

Cooper, D.E. and Palmer, J.O. (eds), The Environment in Question: Ethics and Global Issues, Routledge, London and New York.

Franke, R.W. and Chasin, B. 1980, Seeds of Famine: Ecological Destruction and the Development Dilemma in the West African Sahel, Allaheld, Osmun, Montclair (New Jersey)

Firth, R. 1961, "The Social Framework of Economic Organization", in R. Firth (edt), Elements of Social Organization, 3. edition, C:A: Watts and Co. Ltd. London.

Glantz, M.H. (1987) Drought and Hunger in Africa, Cambridge University Press.

George, S, 1990, Ills Fair the Land, Penguin Books, London (second edition).

Global 2000, 1980, United National Environment Programme, Geneva.

Hinderink, J. and Sterkenburg, J.J. 1987, Agricultural Commercialization and Government Policy in Africa, KPI, London and New York.

Hjort, Anders af Ornäs, 1981, Herds, "Trade and Grain: Pastoralism in Regional Context", in J.G.Galatly et al. (eds), The Future of Pastoral Peoples, IDRC, Ottowa.

Hjort, Anders af Ornäs, 1986, Pastoral Life in Drylands, Input Report, SAREC workshop on a Research Programme on Deforestation and desertification.

Hjort af Ornäs, A. and Mohamed Salih, M.A. (1989) Ecology and Politics: Environmental Stress and Security in Africa. Scandinavian Institute of African Studies, Uppsala

Hutchison, R.A (edt), 1991, Fighting For Survival, Insecurity, People and the Environment in the Horn of Africa, The World Conservation Union, Geneva.

Jong Boon, 1990, Environmental Problems of the Sudan, Institute of Social Science, The Hague. 2 Volumes.

Kerven, K. 1992, Customary Commerce, A Historical Re-assessment of Pastoral Livestock Marketing in Africa, ODA, London.

ICHI (1985) Famine, a Man-Made Disaster. International Commission for Humanitarian Issues, London.

Lawrence, P. 1986, World Recession and and Food crisis in Africa, Review of African Political Economy, (special issue)

Little, P. 1983, "Livestock/Grain Connection in Northern Kenya: An Analysis of Pastoral Economics and Arid Lands Development in Africa", in Rural Africana, Vol. 15/16.

Markakis, J. 1993, The Decline of Pastoralism in the Horn of Africa, Macmillan Press, London and Basing Stocske.

Mohamed Salih, M.A. 1991a, "Governmental Development Policy and Options in Pastoral Development in the Sudan", in P.T.W.Baxter (edt), When the Grass is Gone, SIAS, Uppsala.

Mohamed Salih, M.A. 1991b, "Environmental Conflicts in African Drylands, cases from Sudan and Nigeria in J.Kakonen (edt), Perspectives on Environmental Conflict and International Politics, Pinter Publishers, London and New York.

Mohamed Salih, M.A., 1990, "Pastoralism and the State in Africa", in Nomadic Peoples, No. 25-27.

Mohamed Salih, M.A. 1989 "Political Coercion and the Limits of State Intervention: Sudan", in Hjort af Ornas and Mohamed Salih, M.A. (eds), Ecology and Politics: Environmental Stress and Security in Africa. Scandinavian Institute of African Studies, Uppsala, pp. 101-116.

Mohamed Salih, M.A. ??, "Camel Production in the Drylands of the Sudan": National and Local Level Perceptions of the Potential, in A. Hjort (edt), Camels in Development. Sustainable Production in African Arid Lands, SIAS, Uppsala.

Mohamed Salih, M.A. 1987, "Introduction", in M.A. Mohamed Salih (edt), Agrarian Change in the Central Rainlands of the Sudan, Scandinavian Institute of African Studies, Uppsala.

Mohamed Salih, M.A. 1985, "Pastoralists in Town", Pastoral Development Network No. 21b, Overseas Development Institute, London.

Nash, M. 1966, Primitive and Peasant Economic Systems, Chandler Publ. Co. Chicago, 1966

Palmer, J.A. 1992, "Towards a Sustainable Future", in D.E. Cooper, and J.O. Palmer (eds), The Environment in Question:Ethics and Global Issues, Routledge, London and New York.

Redclift, M. 1984, Development and the Environmental Crisis, Methuen, London and New York.

Sen, A. 1981, Poverty and Famine, Clarendon Press, Oxford.

Spooner, P. and Mann, H.S. (eds), 1982 Desertification and Development in Dry Ecology in Social Perspective. Academic Press.

Sutter, J. 1982, "Commercial Strategies, Drought and Monetary Pressure, in Nomadic Peoples No. 2.

Swift, J. 1979, "Development of Livestock Trading in Nomad Pastoral Economy: the Somali case, in Pastoral Production and Society, Cambridge University Press, Cambridge.

Timberlake, L. 1984 Natural Disasters: Acts of God or Acts of Man? Earthscan, London.

Thomas, C. 1992, The Environment in International Relations, The Royal Institute of International Affairs, London.

Trusted, J. 1992, "The Problem of Absolute Poverty: What are Our Moral Obligations to the Destitute?", in D.E. Cooper, and J.O. Palmer (eds), The Environment in Question: Ethics and Global Issues, Routledge, London and New York.

UNEP, 1981, Environment and Development, Pergamon, Oxford.

UNEP, 1987, Environment, Growth and Development, Geneva.

UNICEF/UNSO, 1992, Pastoralists at Crossroads: Survival and Development Issues in African Pastoralism, Project for Nomadic Pastoralists in Africa, Nairobi.

Watts, M. 1987, 'Drought, Environment and Food Security: some reflections on peasants, pastoralists and commercialization in dryland West Africa', in H.G. Michael, *et al.* (eds), Drought and Hunger in Africa, Cambridge University Press, Cambridge.

Winpenny, J.T. (ed), 1991, Development Research: The Environmental Challenge, ODA, London.

World Bank, 1989, Sub-Saharan Africa: From Crisis to Sustainable Development, Washington DC.

Ziche, J.and M.A.Mohamed Salih, 1984, "Traditional Communal Labour and Rural Development in Africa South of the Sahara", in Quarterly Journal of International Agriculture, Vol. 23 No. 4.

Natural Resource Management and Livestock Development in agro-sylvo-pastoral zones

Poul A. Sihm.
PIA Consult, Kibæk
Denmark

Natural Resource Management and Livestock Development are inseparable in agro-sylvo-pastoral zones, and the rational procedure is to promote management of livestock and agro-sylvo-pastoral resources by the people who exploit those resources and whose existence depends on the advancing degradation of the environment being brought to a halt. This can only be done by the introduction of a rational management of the natural renewable resources, which form the basis of their livelihood — soil, water and vegetation.

The purpose of this note is to draw your attention to an encouraging experience regarding pastoral development which I had during a mission to Mauritania this year.

Arid- and semi-arid zones constitute about 70% of the total surface of Africa and are home to about 40 million pastoralists who have the ability to utilize, productively, the environment in which they live. In the absence of alternative employment the options open to the State are; to rehabilitate the agro-sylvo-pastoral environment and to make its exploitation a viable proposition or to deal with the increasing influx of destitute and unemployable pastoralists.

The model for the rehabilitation of the environment and the improved management of natural resources, including livestock, is based on thirty years of trial and error and consists of the following elements:

*   the creation of an enabling political and legal environment;
*   the organization of the population *on the basis of*
*   the allocation of usufruct right and responsibility for the dry lands

in the agro-sylvo-pastoral zones to those who traditionally exploit them, *and the*

- encouragement of and support for identification, planning and action by the user groups in accordance with their own priorities, *which requires*
- improved, decentralized agricultural support services remodeled to offer technical support in the form of consultancies for producers on demand.

This is rural development integrated from the base up. It needs to be integrated, since it must be prepared to respond to the development priorities of the rural population. The key difference is that the producer changes his role from a recipient of aid, on Governments terms, to being the master of his own destiny and a consumer of services and inputs which he himself considers relevant and for which he is prepared to make an investment.

The enabling environment must be established by Government policies and by legislation institutionalizing the voluntary organization of the rural population and the allocation to them of responsibility for and priority rights of utilization regarding their traditional grazing and wells, including the support of the authorities for the maintenance and defense of these rights.

Groups of pastoralists must also be helped to plan and execute actions in accordance with their own priorities. This would normally be the responsibility of a capable and motivated extension service, executing projects together with the groups. This has not worked because the extension services are mostly badly trained, under funded, underpaid and de-motivated.

It is the weakness of this important factor, in the development process reinforced by the fact that aid organizations predominantly act at the level of the central Government services, that has inhibited progress. The introduction of decentralized agricultural services must be accompanied by a rigorous screening of extension agents and deployment in accordance with their competence.

The case for the village extension worker, the agent who is the link between the service and the community must also be reviewed. With a desirable quality and quantity of subject matter specialists, at the regional and sub-regional level, it is likely that better results could be obtained by training a member of the village association to perform this role.

It is at the level of the village associations that progress can be achieved by investing the time and effort and limited resources to:

* encourage and assist the population to organize themselves;
* educate and help the groups to plan and act for their own improvement in accordance with their perceived objectives;
* participate in the design of projects and the establishment of a revolving fund for their execution on the basis of a negotiated contract;

So far nothing much new you would say. We have done all this and it does not seem to work as we expected.

Yet, encouraging progress is being made in Mauritania, where I have just had the opportunity to work with a GTZ financed project Gestion Integre des Ressources Naturelles de l'Est de Mauritanie (GIRNEM).

What was noteworthy was that the work which is underway in that particular region, by the Livestock Department in the framework of the Second Livestock Development, financed jointly by the World Bank, the African Development Fund and OPEC, which organizes the livestock owners in pastoral associations in order to give them a political presence and the ability to manage their own resources, is now being combined with the work which GIRNEM has started at the micro-level in the villages and camps, of which there are on average 20 per pastoral association. The combination of the political organization of the producer and support for development action at the village level, provides a viable model in integrated rural development from the base up.

The key to this achievement is that the relationship between the groups and the extension services has been reversed, so that the groups, with the help of the project, have become the planners and implementers of activities and have been put in the position of being able to select and procure the technical assistance they require. The extension services are becoming consultants who provide technical assistance to the groups — but only when the group wants them to do so.

The GIRNEM project consists of two experienced local staff, a natural resources specialist and a sociologist, assisted by an expatriate project adviser. The role of the project adviser is to educate and support his two counterparts. He alone releases funds thereby protecting the national counterparts against the ever present pressure from the local authorities.

His main role, therefore, remains that of the motivator, the coordinator and the supporter of ideas and the provider of funding for critical inputs more than being the implementor. He always keeps himself in the background and his counterparts centre stage.

The project staff educates the groups through a continued dialogue, and coordinates the assistance of the extension services by keeping all parties informed and by acting as a catalyst in bringing the group and the extension services together in a joint planning exercise on the basis of a map of the village area, designed as an inventory of its natural resources.

In this manner a formal development plan is drawn up. The village group provides the identification of its needs and is assisted in the elaboration of the plan by the regional extension service and the project staff. The plan, subsequently, becomes the basis for a negotiated contract between the group and the services on the development activity which has the highest priority for the group.

In accordance with this contract the village group undertakes to execute a project, e.g. sand dune fixation or grazing management. GIRNEM provides some very modest but essential subsidies in the form of hard to get inputs as well as the reimbursement of the petrol and per diem cost of the consultancies of the subject matter specialists from the regional extension service.

This support for the extension services is on a case by case basis and only concerns the actual cost of per diem and travel. The procedure is that an advance of 40% is followed by the reimbursement, in full, only when the groups have certified that the job has been carried out in a satisfactory manner.

Experience shows that a positive response at the level of the rural groups to a genuine show of interest and extension of a good technical assistance may confidently be expected.

This case is no different. In the first year, the activity chosen by nearly all groups was dune fixation executed by men women and children of the village, with only a 20% subsidy in the form of hand tools and the installation of a tree nursery.

During my three weeks in the area, I had the opportunity to visit, together with the project staff, the organizing committees of ten villages. We inspected the impressive communal efforts in dune fixation, which we found had yielded other benefits in the form of a greater cohesiveness of the group and a more durable organization of the village. We held meetings and frequently spent the night in the village, which gave us time for a real exchange of experience.

I believe that the close collaboration between the two projects, described above, provides the model for natural resource management activities not only in Mauritania but for the agro-sylvo-pastoral regions of the entire Sahel, provided the Governments concerned are willing to create the enabling environment for this development.

Ignoring turbulence in planning: some lessons, experiences and principles of chaos, hazard and conflict from the Horn of Africa

Bryan Spooner
Independent Consultant
Near Brook Ashford, U.K.

*"A new scientific truth does not triumph by convincing its opponents and making them see the light, but rather because its opponents eventually die, and a new generation grows up that is familiar with it." — **Max Planck***

Introduction

When dealing with the implementation of development projects, whether in the Sahel or elsewhere, the changes that have cascaded from social and economic turmoil, recurrent famine and droughts, and civil war and banditry have been seriously under-estimated. Over the last 30 years various degrees of stress related to these conditions have prevailed in many parts of the Horn of Africa. The ultimate demise of societies subjected to mismanagement of politics, economy, society, resource management, technological interventions, aid relations and development policy is anarchy and deprivation at the scale experienced in Somalia and the Southern Sudan.

In planning and implementing development tactics and strategies, the international agencies, the donors, the NGOs and local governments have ignored the basic fact that, when put under stress, both human and ecological systems exhibit much that is apparently irrational. Almost without exception the roots of insecurity, conflict and chaos have been treated as short-term phenomena, or as external forces not essential to the good planning and feasible implementation of projects and programmes. In essence, the role of turbulence has been shied away from or ignored because it is difficult to measure, predict or manage. As a result military and development interventions have apparently unwittingly converged to actually increase social disintegration, economic collapse in favour of alternative parallel economies, and ecological disruption at the expense of biodiversity.

The growing scale of turbulence and the rate of change of social, ecological and technological conditions is forcing a re-evaluation of the basic thinking behind development. Unless the inter-relationships between political, social, economic and ecological processes of change are better understood and their realities acted upon, little can be done to re-establish or maintain stability, or to have faith in the removal of human rights abuses or the promotion of such obtuse ideas as "sustainable" development. In many areas of the Horn the official economy and even access of outsiders has little legitimacy. The powerful have gained more power from exploiting the complex of disasters that provide the basis for their control over resources.

The issues only become apparent fully through a historic and holistic perspective. The insights gained show that conventional academic theories, education, training and decision-making practices are inadequate when instability is so widespread. Media coverage and much professional analysis feeds only on the plight of the oppressed through humanitarian eyes. Little attention is given to the winners and indigenous systems of management of chaos in these areas of economic, social and ecological turbulence. As a result field workers, academic researchers, aid practitioners and policy makers (inside and outside of government circles) are poorly equipped and orientated to deal with the real problems of ensuring basic human needs, let alone promoting notions of sustainable development.

This paper is based on some selected aspects of research undertaken by the author in drawing together for the World Conservation Union (IUCN) a study of the inter-relationships between insecurity, survival strategies, people, environment change and the historical management of aid and development policy in the Horn of Africa (Fighting for Survival: Insecurity, People and the Environment in the Horn of Africa. Bryan Spooner and Nigel Walsh, ed. R. Hutchison, IUCN 1991).

This paper examines where new thinking is needed in areas where turbulence and insecurity abound. The issues are numerous and complex in their interplay and poorly researched. The paper explores three areas. First, the principles of chaos theory are examined and the need for these to be taken in concert with, and as complementary to, conventional forms of analysis, policy making and project design. Second, a brief overview is given of the outcomes for the region when planning and science have so consistently ignored insecurity and non-linearity. Third, the need to focus on mechanisms for inter-disciplinary and inter-agency information flows is stressed, as is the need to assess conflict and conflict resolution in both ecological, social, political and economic processes.

Insecurity, Turbulence and Non-Linearity as Real but Ignored Issues

Turbulence and non-linear systems pervade and, in many ways, characterise life itself. They are as evident as periods of apparent stability and order. Both phenomena occur in different phases and time scales of dynamic patterns of cyclical evolution. They are manifest in the events and unfolding change in just about any theme of life-sustaining or human processes we could choose. The proviso to recognise turbulence is that reality must be perceived in its fullness of both time, space and dynamics of change. The following selected examples have been subjected to varying degrees of research or no research at all. Their relevance to the design of development tactics and strategy ought to be clear to policy makers and technicians alike:

- weather patterns and the dynamics of macro and micro-climate
- soil and land formation
- river, floodplain and delta hydrology
- price and production cycles
- land use and biological structure
- population dynamics and structure
- disease pathology and incidence
- martial and economic growth and decay
- refugee and migration movements

The role of turbulence in these systems has, until recently, been consigned to the back-burner of research, theory and education; mainly because non-linear systems proved too difficult to measure and model and thus encapsulate into simple concepts for popular educational dissemination.

The theoretical world, which supplies the tactics and strategies for development investment and activities, has consistently focused research on periods and phases of apparent stability in social, economic and biological processes. A range of tools are also employed to reduce the diversity of change to conveniently packaged "perverse response" — "statistical insignificances" — "external influences" — "acceptable errors".

Decades of bias for the easier, measurable and potentially predictable systems in all the development sciences and state education systems have produced at least two generations with few tools, and even less vision, to recognise, assess and respond to turbulence, insecurity and non-linearity.

The result has been a perverse view of life based on often blind abstractions from reality that has reached deep into the basic paradigms across science and development. This has been ably assisted by the divisions between the sciences in ministries, companies, agencies and planning teams. Effective cross-fertilisation of ideas has been long stifled and mainly remains so, despite shifts in attitude towards multi/inter-disciplinary activities.

A widely-held paradigm expects development to be a simple, ordered, uni-directional, cumulative, and evolutionary expansion of "civilised" behaviour and technological progress. This belief has been applied in the fields of resource use and management, as much as it has to the moulding of the lifestyle and culture of rural and urban people alike. As such, the discussion can refer as much to economics as it might to agronomy or hydrology, as to about relief as it might to development, as much to trade as it might to aid.

This tradition has had severe repercussions for the people's of the Horn and elsewhere. These paradigms in the history of development tactics and strategy are important contributory factors destabilising the social, economic and ecological conditions throughout the Horn. The development environment, since it has developed no provisions for turbulence in policy, programme and project provisions, has actually fuelled insecurity to fill the void created by the lack of attention to it.

The Features of Turbulence

Virtually all processes periodically pass through phases of turbulence. To see turbulence in its entirety requires the world to be viewed as a continual process of dynamic change over time. If the perception of reality is to remain initially neutral, no time-preference can be imposed. Some processes enter turbulence in short cycles that can be measured in time scales of less than a day, others exhibit successions measured in months or years, and others in time scales of decades through to millennia. When conditions favour a change of state into turbulence it is common for the rate of change to increase disproportionately as a threshold is crossed.

It is the apparent rate of change and the crossing of thresholds that determines just how apparent turbulence is to the time scale of human life. The nodes of change determine how insecure conditions are for men, women and children and the likelihood that normally resolvable disputes can turn into conflict.

The general principles of chaos theory would identify the following features of turbulence:

The systems will exhibit COMPLEXITY and MULTILINEARITY; that is they are being influenced by a multitude of factors that interact to change the conditions and nature of the system and thus the tenets of which model of the systems can be applied to understand what is happening. Example: pastoralist stocking, grazing and drought coping systems.

The systems exhibit unexpected SENSITIVITY to even small changes in conditions in any one of the influencing factors. This is known as the "Butterfly Effect" and means that these systems are inherently unpredictable as small events can produce disproportionate effects — i.e. the sum of the parts being greater than the whole. Example: 1983 Rindapest scare in Somalia — the 1988 United States arms delivery to Somalia — the development of instant global media and financial communications.

Whilst prediction is impossible, patterns and shapes can be discerned that do exhibit a regularity establishing points of stability, structure and order if one knows where and how to look for them. These have become known as strange attractors and fractal patterns. This aspect of research has not been tried or tested outside of the pure physical sciences, but may have some value as a conceptual tool. Potential examples: Watering points and vegetation and livestock systems — border routes/differentials and parallel marketing systems — mountain ranges and rainfall systems.

The evolution and adaptability of these systems is regulated by the quality of information FEEDBACK mechanisms between influencing factors. The capacity for feedback determines the adaptability and survival status of the system in times of rapid, unpredictable change. Example of successful system: Pastoralist communication networks — Commerce and asset transfer in crisis situations. Example of unsuccessful systems: Donor and NGO programmes in insecure crisis situations.

The systems exhibit DISCONTINUITY and PERSISTENCE meaning that when conditions change they do so almost arbitrarily fast cascading across a THRESHOLD but, having reached a new state, that state will tend to recur or remain until the next phase change. This means that the idea of statistical randomness must be carefully reassessed in each case where it is applied. Examples: Economic depression and growth — rainfall and drought cycles — occurrence of seismic events.

A Brief Look Back

Four decades of postwar international development have heralded a series of fashionable objectives and rhetoric for the academic and development intellectuals and their readership. Yet, with each passing decade, the scale of warfare, abuse of human rights and inability to deal with the world's basic needs has increased. Development, as it is commonly understood, has been the least visible process of change in the poorer countries, particularly in Africa.

All too frequently development policy and resource investments have been structured around illusions of manageable, fixed, stable resources owned by asset builders who could provide consumptions products rationally in response to local, regional and world markets. Absolutely no integration of social, economic, political and ecological planning or arrangements have been made for dealing with periods of stress. Similarly, no explicit reference has been made to the relationships between excised rangelands and the riverine and urban areas. This process has been politically supported by government to the advantage of powerful political and commercial elites, and by the burgeoning development, welfare and food aid industries. The result has been dramatic change. The following features are associated with recent turbulence in the Horn.

- the maximum economic and social dispossession of people from natural resources through asset grabbing and transfers.
- the breakdown of many "norms" of social organisation — juxtaposed with the international social, technological and information revolution.
- the disempowerment of local natural resource managers and dispossession of them from their survival resources — juxtaposed with new commercial and political values of the new legal custodians and managers of these resources.
- the major re-structuring of indigenous survival and disaster response strategies, inter-relationships and reciprocation to deal with times of stress — juxtaposed with relations based on the official, parallel, relief and disaster economies at local, regional and international levels; these frequently being hijacked by the least desirable forms of political and commercial interests.
- the destabilisation of long evolved forms of conflict resolution through poor governance and arms trading.
- the disempowerment of familiar means of leadership and dispute mediation exhibiting well-tried and trusted sanctions — juxtaposed with imposed "state and international" forms of governance, legislation and repression.

With cynical hindsight the scientific and development contribution might be highlighted as:

Social and Political

The social and political sciences have played out decades of capitalist-communist charades to enact superpower foreign policy and thus the underlying tenets of the financing of development activities. The Horn was always a regional centre for fickle manipulation of allegiances and as a result fickle measures to promote development through aid, trade and fiscal policies. Meanwhile, indigenous political contradictions have been exacerbated by the ignorance of them as the key features determining the capacity for indigenous development at an international interface.

It has been in the interests of many for the arms trade to remain external to the mainstream of economic and development analysis and planning. The rapid growth and economic success of this industry in the Horn has occurred at the expense of economic development capacity, by the finances it diverts and the insecurity it feeds. These operations should be brought into the open for analysis and debate and declared in policy strategies for the allocation of scarce resources. No real development progress will be made until there is both a national and an international commitment to policies to target the sources and stem the supplies of modern weapons systems.

The New World Order is, in fact, one of heightened insecurity and chaos as regional, ethnic and religious forces vie for position to fill the vacuum created by the demise of the Eastern Block, the ravages of international and corrupted national financial strategies, and the effective withdrawal of any committed and coordinated donor support.

The international wastelands of the Horn are now reformulating around the coherence of self-determination established in Eritrea and Tigray where order is returning after 30 years of organised conflict. Apparently less coherent restructuring is taking place around the religious and ethnic exploitation of warfare and welfare chaos in Sudan and Somalia. The flames of this strife have already spread and linked with the seeds of turbulence beyond the boundaries of the Horn.

The Natural Sciences

The natural sciences have continued to unwrap the technological tunes of international commerce and industry. They have been mostly unaware of, or uninterested in, the political and humanitarian consequences of the often socially and ecologically divisive technological systems promoted in the rural hinterlands. The often exclusive promotion of intensive agricultural systems, the settling of societies and the enclosure and legitimising of land ownership has, through a range of policy measures, effectively expropriated the most crucial survival resources from pastoralists, agro-pastoralists and smallholders in many areas across the Horn. There is a strong bias towards commercial and research claims for high productivity from mechanisation and chemical inputs, which have significant costs in terms of displaced labour, foreign exchange and environmental pollution.

With the era of "environmentalism" this irresponsible and uncaring position is being challenged. Research and planning should be made more accountable through the wider application of holistic impact assessments prior to the introduction of any development interventions; through improved holistic monitoring and evaluation; and, above all, through programmes determined and managed by local people themselves and supported through committed donors and government intentions. As long as poor leadership, state repression and regional insecurity maintain their historic and present levels, environmentally sustainable development in the Horn is unlikely to make any headway.

Outside interventions to reduce the pressure on soil and grazing resources usually involve a model approach based on research in highly controlled situations, incorporating crops, fallow and grazing. However, local variations in land and ecology, household needs and capacities, and the varying impacts of social and economic pressures, imply complex indigenous systems that are difficult for these model solutions to accommodate. They are, thus, irrelevant to the local reality.

Economics

Economists have forged a world from abstract and selective theories legitimising industrial and commercial flows of trade, aid and technology packed with self-interest, many unquestioned values and the hidden dominance of the industries of death and mass destruction. Historically, a diverse basket of value systems (based on local environmental and resource conditions) prevailed and moulded a range of social contact, resource management and conflict resolution systems. Increasingly these have been replaced by a monetarised and materialist set of values that give priority only to control over access to resources. They embrace little social or cultural mediums for assisting the transformation, or for encouraging new forms of conflict resolution. Meanwhile, the technicians and policies of development have devalued a wide diversity of critical coping strategies to a level of non-developmental subsistence. Similarly, unrepresentative leadership and policies have undermined diverse forms of functioning local governance and sanctions.

It would be of great interest to analyze resource values attributed by local communities and international organisations to determine how and why they differ; how resource values affect resource use and marketing systems; and the impact these patterns have on conservation, economic development and social integration.

Waves of blinkered economic policies for aid and trade have legitimised state bureaucracies, unrepresentative political leadership and created systems of pervasive structural indebtedness, not only between states and donors, but also amongst the socio-economic relations within states. The most adaptable and success response has been witnessed in the growth of powerful, thriving, parallel financial and trade networks at the local, regional and international levels. These often are unaccounted in the theory. The fiscal and policy responses attempt to excise them, in spite of their obvious ingenuity and success. These political economies have become naturally adapted to crisis situations. Those who operate and manage these successful parallel economies have become perversely geared to the propagation of absolute poverty and human degradation feeding on the growth of the international donor and NGO programmes whether these be relief, welfare or development programmes.

Natural disasters, violence and displacement will remain closely interconnected as instruments for exploitation and manipulation by many parties. This will continue as long as the Horn remains a loose association of poorly integrated states without an official, dignified and productive role to play in international affairs.

Relief and Development Operations
The dominant model of development still assumes that all nations can profit equally and harmoniously from development investments and trade based on comparative advantage. It assumes that strategies to maximise economic growth can benefit all through redistribution mechanisms. It assumes that transfers of modernising technology can support the process at little or no social or environmental cost. It does not deal with the manipulations and distortions imposed by vested interest groups who also control the allocation and flow of resources, both internationally and nationally. It does not deal with the perverse decision-making imposed by personal and corporate greed. It does not deal with the utility value which power brings to oppress and coerce. Yet these, amongst many more ignored factors, are the real, dominant forces which shape people's lives and possibilities.

The separation in planning and policy between relief, rehabilitation and development is not valid. Each represents a continuum of integrally linked processes responding to the legacies of the past, the needs and momentum of the day, and the visions and inevitabilities of the future.

The institutionalisation of public welfare is potentially divisive in undermining local organisational capacities. It has been all too easy for the agencies involved to dictate the organisation, administration and content of relief because their institutional management systems are controlled from funding and administration centres in the northern hemisphere. Too infrequently is the question asked as to what local people would do if they managed and controlled the response by their own criteria. This bypassing of local participation and initiatives is exacerbated by cases of agency arrogance, or ignorance of the manipulation by the state of these agencies and their resources.

The diversion of aid funds away from governments and through NGOs, introduces a structural relationship between donors, governments and NGOs. NGOs' targeting of resources towards the poorer and less able groups has structural and political implications, as does their involvement in supplying humanitarian aid into opposition areas. The lack of research and policy response concerning the winners in crisis situations is evidence enough that the "industry" is missing the point, loosing the game and foregoing the opportunities to evolve successfully for its own interests.

Maintaining Missing Links and Illusions

Each scientific and policy specialisation has sought immutable theories, figureheads and heroes by which to market their ideas. In the face of the glaring irrelevance and inappropriateness of past theories and policies, the search is on to find the MISSING LINK to assign as the new fashionable rhetoric to keep the flame of intellectual activity and hope alight.

Missing links there certainly are; but the insights are generally all as old as history itself and, thus, present nothing new. There is no shortage of facts, but an obvious dearth of appropriate mechanisms by which the process of development and fact collection can feed into more meaningful inter-actions between development givers, planners and receivers, and between them and the natural world around them. Human empathy with the resources and forces of nature has long been politically and economically defunct in profound structural ways.

The lack of cross-fertilisation of tactics and strategies between sciences, ministries and communities is equally defunct. This demise is based on a long-standing bias towards divisible theories, education and employment in the now global education and development industries.

These structural and intellectual deficiencies are seldom represented in either social, political or economic analysis, or training for development. They are very really acted upon in the tenets of inputs into development planning or strategies, whatever the rhetoric and propaganda may be. If so, the conclusions might well be that the real missing link is the ILLUSION being maintained within the "development industry" as the only constant in an atmosphere of increasing change, turbulence and insecurity. But this is the stifling of information flows and thus our ability to evolve successful with effective feedback. It is not difficult to trace how these limitations have fed into the state of insecurity that exist in the Horn through the structure and output of the development workers, both foreigners and nationals.

The age of media and communication technology has linked the world into a global entity. Whatever the formulation of this new world may become, dealing with its realities as realities is vital if order is to develop out of the chaos that now exists. In a world of monopolised mass media and education *we would all be wise to question very careful how these illusions are introduced, operated and maintained, and for whose interests.*

New Awareness and Approaches

Managing Turbulence to Minimise Chaos

Recognising where and when turbulence is, or might become, important requires a new approach to thinking about the nature of development. There are no panaceas for a solution, but there is a need for a better understanding of process, in addition to the continuing collection and monitoring of facts.

Individually or institutionally it requires sufficient holistic input to balance the details of specialist thinking and analysis. This must have scanned and previewed history and spacial linkages, initially without preference for either the future or the past; the short or the long term; the local or the international; the micro or the macro. It is an approach that, first, must allow reality to talk for itself and, then, let relevant priorities fall out accordingly. Having established what is, the process of establishing *what might realistically be* after human intervention can then start to have a reasonable chance of a sustainable interface.

A reorientation can take place by raising an awareness of how history, and the current realignment of power and economic brokering through manipulation of aid, relief and local resources and assets, shows us WHY previous conditions have led to a deterioration, and not an improvement, in the quality of life; this is the lesson of experience and hindsight. Secondly, this new awareness needs translating into future approaches of HOW and WHEN individuals or organisations can respond whether independently or collectively. These elements cannot and should not be separated.

The implications of accepting change and turbulence as an equal rationale to stability and order are many. It means that the framing of an understanding of "sustainability" must become an approach that deals with processes and conditions that are constantly changing and that have the ability to evolve through living with turbulence, but with effective feedback. Greater stress is required in a global education forum for ensuring that all forms of production and consumption deal with the realities of living empathetically with forces of change so that they become integrated into the future paradigms of "sustainable" development.

A new approach demands that policies determined as suitable for a situation at one time are not necessarily suitable for a similar situation at another time or in a different place. Also, clearer distinction needs to be made of the rationale and relationships between tactics and strategic outcomes when non-linear analysis becomes more relevant than linear analysis.

To cope with the periods of recurrent instability, international and national policies, like traditional local coping strategies, should be planned around using the good times to overcome the ravages of later adverse conditions. Important regulatory controls should remain in the hands of the communities and they should be known to be in agreement with them. The state must also withdraw from interfering with the evolution of sound, locally-appropriate survival strategies and concentrate on its national responsibility to support these strategies. Local communities should not have to have strategies to enable them to also survive the adversities of the state and global economies. The role of the state and international agencies should be to ensure a diversity of policy measures which can enhance local environmental management capacities and shift rapidly to supporting traditional coping strategies when periods of adverse conditions arise.

Improved food security in the villages could affect many other fundamental problems adding to national and economic insecurity. This requires a re-introduction of community grain storage, using national and international stocks only as a supply of last resort or to stabilise prices.

Research needs to identify how best the state and international community should intervene in the exchange market for food, seed, livestock, tools, other assets and wages and labour, to support local ability to minimise risks and avoid destitution. The policies need to take on the challenge of both competing with, and complementing, the operators in this marketplace of asset transfer who thrive on developing crisis. The policy of investments in health, education, infrastructure and marketing services needs to be made in the same light.

The policies promoting settlement must be reassessed in cultivation and pastoral areas requiring mobility and flexibility for survival. Infrastructure investment must fit the realities of environmental change and not a predetermined human image of a world that assumes environmental change might somehow stop through an illusion of human domination over nature. Programme designs should incorporate mobility and flexibility, and focus deliberately on contingency arrangements and insurance strategies. Any baseline surveys for planning and policy need to guarantee at the minumum that ALL users of local resources have been identified; no matter how infrequent or how geographically distant this relationship may be.

Information Flows and Feedback
Systems need to be established that allow for more effective feedback and information interchange in projects and programme development. Monitoring and evaluation need to feed more directly into assessments that deal with tactical and strategic issues and the views of local people, in addition to their measurable technical components. Holistic and impact analysis should accompany all planning, evaluation and review studies.

The shifts in attitudes to conserve or develop resources for future generations should not be the preserve of international action and lobbying. Regional, national and local action is required through cooperation, research, lobbying, and education. The current education programmes are usually formal and devised from a top-down approach. They are usually compiled by outsiders and often deal with the measurable symptoms, rather than underlying causes and processes, of social, ecological and economic change.

Promoting local action and participation is essential in planning and implementation in relief and development, both in terms of establishing a wider body of cooperation and as a more informed source of information on local environmental conditions and possibilities. Satellite interpretation and occasional social and economic surveys are no substitute for a life long familiarity with a local area. Which development workers today spend more than a glimpse of time within the areas that they plan for or operate in? This argues for programmes to devolve more, and not less, responsibility to those who are the daily managers and users of these local resources. This will require much greater emphasis on establishing networking systems capable of reaching these peripheral areas.

Establishing communication systems, local institutions and information networks would provide local people with the necessary knowledge and power to lobby more effectively for change in local development and conservation programmes.

Conflict Avoidance

Where there is a clear separation of ethnic or economic activity between pastoralism and cultivation, tensions and conflicts are a fact of life which must be dealt with. Local, collective responsibility should be built up and supported by national measures desirous of mobilising resources for the common good. This requires dialogue and participation from all involved. The political and commercial interests which have exploited natural resources, dispossessed people from their land and divided communities, are unacceptable. Especially when supported by force of arms, they guarantee that true development and food security will remain an unattainable objective as long as they proceed unchecked. Any shift in development attitudes will only have meaning if there is widespread commitment to reforming contemporary paradigms; to curbing exploitative interests; to prohibiting the sale of sophisticated military weaponry; and to transferring the innovative skills of the arms industry to more productive development purposes. Above all, the major commitment should be to ensuring that the people of the Horn have the possibility of creating their own development processes in a dignified way. This demands that their access to assets, resources and coping strategies is protected and developed.

The approach must examine the checks and balances and be more aware of those elements that act as fuel for conflict. If these dissipate the ability for conflict mediation and resolution then increased turbulence will inevitably result.

Traditional conflict situations positively integrate societies when carried out within well-recognised traditional means to arbitrate and resolve. Once these systems are undermined or dismantled by transformation in production systems, commercialisation and/or state interference, or the scale of conflict is changed through arms technology and trade, the time frame for conflict can become indeterminate and the potential for escalation is greatly increased.

The primary fuels are the weapons of mass destruction and automatic weapons. The proliferation of the former has traditionally been confined to an elite of states where maintaining "order" has been possible through weapon parity and sanctions of the Cold War. With the proliferation of automatic weapons amongst individuals and the weapons of mass destruction to a multitude of states, the scenario is now one of a complex system showing multiple lines of cleavage and engagement; this being one necessary feature of turbulence. When juxtaposed with collapsing economies and networks of information flow the systems will become more sensitive to unpredictable changes and more thresholds into instability.

When the threshold of conflict resolution and leadership ability is crossed, a point is reached when all choice is denied for any form of rational social or economic behaviour. All that remains is the stark dilemma between fight or flight. When offered an organised military stratagem of opposing, but organised, political forces funded through sufficiently stable official economies, the chaos is organised through an apparent ordered organisation of armies whether regular, guerilla, terrorist or militia in nature. When ethnic or social divisions run wide and coincide with the demise of official economies, true anarchy and parallel disaster economies rapidly thrive.

The revitalising of indigenous strategies for dispute resolution and survival should not hark back to the past, but should be seen as a process of redressing imbalance in a forward-looking, evolutionary, way. The old systems may have been appropriate in their historical social and economic settings, but to integrate these methods into modern global networks will require considerably more analysis if this is to be effectively achieved.

Legitimacy
As long as the international community upholds the credibility of narrow-based, unrepresentative governments, and continues to see national resources simply supplying the global marketplace, little progress can be made towards reconciliation and peace in the Horn. As long as state repression and regional insecurity maintain their present levels the integration of international conservation and development interests is unlikely to make much headway.

There is a need to develop policies which revitalise and strengthen government responsibilities and legitimacy in the realms of local communities for their sense and not solely their apparent economic gains. Longterm policy needs to transfer power to local communities that have, until now, had little influence in deciding their own future. A broader base of networking and linkages with representative local organisation is required at both grass roots and national levels.

Pastoralists and Cultivators
Survival capacities of the pastoralist are dependent on the riverine grazing systems and diverse systems of rangeland management, which are supplemented by hunting, gathering and rainfed cultivation. The increased pressure of population, expanding settlement and economic marginalisation have led many to withdraw from pastoralism, drifting or being forced into settlement, labouring, destitution or conflict. Re-establishing and integrating opportunities are essential to good resource management in the marginal and insecure rangeland systems.

The future must seek new and innovative arrangements to resolve these problems, through better market and social integration and with the direct participation and approval of the pastoralists themselves. The modern credit and banking systems offer little to advance traditional strategies of savings and insurance, and the dynamics of the monetary terms of trade do not have adequate checks and balances to prevent the continued demise of this environmental management system. The evolution of land and water tenure systems has promoted conflict and unsustainable use patterns, along with the penetration of absentee owners uninterested in resource conservation. Water point programmes are often based on irrational criteria of value and usefulness. The insecurity problems and distorted investment strategies deny access to important veterinary and technological support services which could deal effectively with the pastoral and rangeland problems, at a regional or local level.

Until resource tenure reforms and legislation are introduced to protect pastoralist rights, and more is done to include them in the debate on development policy, there can be little or no further alleviation of the problems in this sector.

The majority of cultivators in the Horn have developed sustainable forms of dryland farming based on fallowing techniques. Increased population, land shortages and economic needs have reduced these fallow periods, cleared many areas of natural vegetation and opened up widespread and sometimes irreversible erosion hazards.

The basis for food security is either, to provide traditional cultivators with a protected and productive environment to carry out sound environmental management, or to replace them with large, modern farming operations. If local people are to be dispossessed, they must be offered viable forms of alternative employment elsewhere, if their meaningful participation in the global economy is to be maintained. However, the experiences of leaving food production to the state or the commercial private sector in the Horn, have been the source of wholly destructive agricultural mining, food insecurity and the economic marginalisation and unplanned displacement of indigenous peoples. The large farming schemes have also proved generally unsound in economic and environmental terms. The commercial farming methods employed have been developed in more temperate climates or in higher rainfall tropical areas. In their present form these are not sustainable in the Horn, were fragile soils and unreliable rainfall patterns are common.

Both options require strict lands reforms to protect the rights of indigenous peoples and to ensure their participation during any land registration processes. Much greater education and/or control is required to ensure that the excesses of absentee and commercial farmers, using unsustainable forms of agriculture, are stopped.

Interlinkages

The importance of the links between livestock and crop farming systems as a rational and wholly suitable multipurpose strategy for income generation, diverse savings and economic investment is under-rated in research, planning and policy. It is a system of communications, interchange and reciprocation which helps riverine and hinterland societies bind together and provides for diverse forms of conflict resolution in areas where the inter-action is competitive. Its wider acceptance would help shift attention to more appropriate forms of cultivation, cropping patterns, and the development of integrated food crop, fodder and browse systems.

The value of livestock as animal draught power and cheap sources of biologically appropriate manure for the soil processes and the recycling of energy and nutrients is often overlooked. The loss of trees as fuel is having a severe impact on the return of animal manure to the soil. In many areas of the Horn increasing amounts are being used as a fuel substitute.

There are important interactions between cultivation and pastoralism for maintaining a healthy and productive ecology and biological diversity. Their potential for producing wealth and establishing a varied ecology, is also underrated by the agricultural specialists and engineers responsible for the diversion of agricultural policy and investment into a limited strategy for agricultural crop development. This wealth derives from a variety of crops and famine foods, crop residues, livestock products, firewood, timber, fruits, medicine, resins, and bee products with significant economic and survival value.

There is need to promote research and policy support for multipurpose mixed production systems integrating crops, livestock, tree crops and other economically important vegetation producing wild products. Improvements are needed to improve the efficiency of land and crop use for fodder production in, and outside of, cultivated fields. A better understanding must be gained of locally appropriate farming systems based on their ability and links to coping strategies in good, average, poor and disaster years. A better understanding is also required of the mechanisms and effects of energy and nutrient transfers, the role of fire and the implications of vegetation composition and structure for crop and livestock production.

Conclusion

Using the insites gained from the outcomes of development experience in the Horn and chaos theory the following can be concluded:

- Development and welfare planning, policy and practice need to be more dualistic and holistic. They need to accept and reflect that unpredictable and dynamic change are the only reliable features of reality. Non-linear analysis needs to complement linear analysis and, at appropriate times, replace it as the main means of ensuring adaptible and successful forms of problem solving and opportunity creating tactics and strategy. Such insites affect researchers, technicians, administrators, policy makers and politicians alike since it calls for a change in thinking at the level of paradigms.

- Chaos theory and logic identify the need for expanding the basis of positive contact, dialogue and feedback between the international, national and local communities. The evidence shows that the interfaces have been far from positive. They have been poorly developed as no value has been placed in them. The current response of the international community is one of actually retracting contacts and as a result the interface with will less evolutionary capacity.

- Both official and unofficial networks of commerce, aid, trade and welfare develop in response to crisis. The offical networks deal with the loosers, while the winners and successful networks are in the unofficial sphere. This reflects their ability for flexibile and rapid response to change and new opportunity.

- The unofficial networks maintain a hidden order of trade and commerce in a world of apparent human disaster and chaos; but they also feed and thrive on this misery. Their methods of organisation, operation and management of assets and information flows potentially hold the keys to more successful forms of official development and relief operations. This is receiving no attention in research or policy circles.

- Critical points of potential stability (the strange attractors) that could bind societies together in an ordered evolution of change are ignored in strategic policy and financing. This is because of considerable bias in time-preference and the desire to legitimise ill-founded nation states and their attendant bureaucracies and infrastructure. Interim measures to maintain community controls over food security, access to resources, reciprocation and conflict resolution mechanisms have been ignored with the inevitable result that rampant insecurity and conflict has evolved.

Further Reading

Coveney, Peter. & Highfield, Roger. 1991: "The Arrow of Time" Flamingo, London.

Duffield, Mark. 1992: "NGOs, Disaster Relief and Asset Transfer in the Horn: Political Survival in a Permanent Emergency." Paper to the 1992 Annual Conference of the Development Studies Association. University of Nottingham, U.K.

Gleik, James 1987: "Chaos: Making a New Science." Cardinal, Sphere Books

Howell, P. & Allan, J. 1990: "The Nile: Resource Evaluation, Resource Management, Hydropolitics and Legal Issues." Royal Geographical Society/School of Oriental and African Studies Conference, London.

May, Robert, M. 1977: "Thresholds and Breakpoints in Ecosystems with a Multiplicity of Stable States." Nature 269. pp. 471-477.

Mearns, Robin. 1990: "Structural Adjustment and the Environment: A Study in the Nature of Scientific Explanation." Institute of Development Studies, University of Sussex.

Milne, A. 1989: "Earth's Changing Climate — The Cosmic Connection." Prism Press, U.K.

Roche, Chris. 1992: "Operationality in Turbulence" Draft Paper ACORD-RAPP, London

Spooner, Bryan & Walsh, Nigel 1991: "Fighting for Survival: Insecurity, People and the Environment in the Horn of Africa." Original consultancy research report to IUCN. Paperback Edition, Ed. R. Hutchison, IUCN, Gland. (This contains an extensive bibliography for each country in the Horn and general references).

Population & social conflicts — household strategies for dealing with risk and ensuring survival in the Sahel

Camilla Toulmin
Drylands Programme,
IIED, London, U.K.

This presentation will deal with household strategies for dealing with risk in the Sahel, the main forms of risk faced, and means by which these can be accommodated. The three kinds of risk examined here are:

- climatic/environmental
- institutional, particularly in relation to resource tenure
- demographic, concerning health and reproduction.

Two main kinds of adaptation to changing risks and circumstances will be noted: through changing patterns of household organisation, and the central importance of large household size; and the critical role played by income diversification, including incomes earned by labour migration.

The presentation will emphasize the importance of retaining flexibility within production and social systems, and the need to maintain a diverse range of activities in order to hedge against risk. It should also be remembered that Sahelian society is very diverse, with great differences between social groups, and within each village or camp. People's ability to protect themselves from risk is usually strongly associated with wealth.

The discussion will assess the implications for certain areas of policy of understanding risk and how people try to adapt. This is particularly important given the recent and currently great emphasis placed on the "Gestion de Terroir" approach throughout the Sahel. I shall argue that we need great flexibility in how such approaches are put into practice, so that they can build on people's own strategies, rather than hindering them.

Unlike the previous two speakers, my talk will concentrate on areas of the western Sahel which are relatively unaffected by civil or military conflict. Clearly, where major conflicts exist, this provides an additional and dominant dimension to the problems people face and how they must adapt. People's risk coping strategies will, therefore, be described under what might be called "normal" conditions, remembering that normality is a very relative term. Normality encompasses great variability and risk related to environment, economic, demographic, and other conditions.

Inevitably, the presentation will deal with issues at a very broad level of generalisation, but I hope that in the discussion which follows, people can provide evidence which supports or contradicts this general discussion. This presentation will also avoid many issues that are very important, such as those related to the economic context both at national and international levels, and the constrains this context places on herders' and farmers' ability to make a decent living.

Risk and coping strategies

Climate and other environmental risk.
These include rainfall variability, pests, and disease attacks. The main strategies adopted to combat this risk include the diversification of activities to ensure that even if one activity fails, others may have greater success. Diversification takes place within the farming system — as when different crop types are grown, crops and livestock are kept, and mixed animal herds are maintained. Diversification also takes place outside the farming system, through the development of trade, crafts, and other forms of income earning. In such activities, the role of migrants' earnings is particularly important.

Other forms of adapting to environmental risk include:
- maintaining mobility, particularly where livestock assets are important, and
- maintaining and expanding a network of social contacts through which help may be sought in times of crisis.

Risks associated with institutions and systems of resource tenure
The main risks considered here involve the use and misuse of natural resources by members of the local community and by a range of outside interests. A number of strategies have been developed to try and deal with these risks which include:

- maintenance of customary rules and sanctions aimed at controlling who has access to certain resources, for what purposes and on what

terms. However, for this strategy to be successful requires that the administration supports these rules in cases of conflict.
- use of threats and violence to protect access, of decreasingly significant use
- development of links with the local administrative structure, and use of bribes to ensure that decisions in cases of conflict are made in a direction favourable to that particular community.

Currently, there is considerable debate regarding various reforms to resource tenure, new codes and legislation. These are intended to bring clarity to a confused situation and, in the long term, should provide much clearer and more enforceable systems of resource tenure. However, in the short term, there may well be greater confusion and conflict, as people try to assert their rights and test the new framework.

Demographic risk.
These include ill-health, risks with child-bearing, and problems with maintaining a viable household unit, able to feed itself now and ensure its longer term survival.

Various means are used to protect against such risks:

- in times of illness, resort is had to traditional and modern medicine
- to ensure production of descendants, men can practice polygamy. For women who have not produced living children, their options are more limited, though divorce and remarriage may be possible.
- to expand and maintain a large household, which provides greater protection to the group from the illness or death of any individual, ensures a greater spread of labour available for different tasks, and reduced vulnerability to changing dependency ratios. Large household size also provides major advantages in the economic sphere, by providing a large work force which can be spread amongst a range of different activities, hence reducing overall vulnerability of household income to risk.

The research on which this presentation is based was particularly concerned to examine the link between large household size and successful economic performance. In the field studies, it was intriguing to find households of 40, and sometimes 50 or more people who worked and ate together, farming a common field and investing in a common estate of assets — typically ploughs, Yells, and a trading business. A very strong correlation was found between household size and wealth, with animal holdings per person highest in the largest households and lowest in the smallest ones. Household size and food production also were linked, the smallest households being much the poorest and most liable to food deficit. Since larger households tend to have greater food security, their members are given considerable freedom to develop their own income generating activities. As a result, people are happy to stay living, working and contributing to these large successful domestic groups.

Work elsewhere suggests that such large domestic groups are liable to break down into their component parts. For example, on the death of the elderly father, a household containing his three sons, their wives and children, would split into three separate units. Such patterns of breakdown are usually seen as the inevitable result of 'modernisation' and increased emphasis on individual, as opposed to social goals, and increasing economic pressures which have meant that many household heads can no longer ensure payment of taxes, food, and marriage costs for household members.

However, evidence from my work in Mali (Toulmin 1992) and that of a colleague's recent work in the Diourbel region of Senegal, shows that the opposite process of household consolidation may also occur (David 1992). In the Bambara villages of central Mali, households which in the 1950s and 60's had been working as separate units were now working as a single group. People explained this as being a means by which they could respond more effectively to some of the risks they faced, given the decline in rainfall and the need to accumulate a sufficient surplus to take advantage of the economic opportunities available, such as through investment in a plough team. Similar evidence comes from the work of Rosalind David in Senegal, where she has been looking at the impact of high levels of male migration on household resource management. She had assumed at the start of the research that she would find many households effectively headed by women. In fact, she found these units were absorbed into the larger family group to which they were related. Male outmigration in this case led to a consolidation of those left behind into more viable production units (David 1992).

The broader policy context

I shall turn now to the broader policy context of natural resource management and the current vogue for 'gestion de terroir' approaches throughout the Sahel. I want to discuss some of the underlying assumptions and risks of this approach, given the very diverse, risk prone and highly variable Sahelian context. In comparison with previous attempts to improve rural livelihoods, the GT approach offers a very promising new framework for attaining more effective natural resource management in the Sahel. The approach is based on certain assumptions summarised here.

1. that you need to establish firmer rights over land and other resources if people are to have the incentive to manage and invest in improvement of these resources. Linked to this assumption is the expectation that governments are ready in practice to achieve such a transfer of power to the local level.

2. that there are investments which people can make which will bring returns that are sufficiently high to encourage further investment and improved resource management, leading to rising rural incomes and welfare.

3. that the GT approach can respond in a sufficiently flexible manner to the highly diverse physical, economic, social and political situations found in the Sahel. Such flexibility is particularly important to maintain a high degree of flexibility and mobility of people and their livestock between different areas, to allow them to respond to variable physical conditions.

However, there are *certain drawbacks to the GT approach* which need to be addressed if it is to fulfil the high expectations raised.

1. with its emphasis on the "local community" there is a tendency to see this as a relatively homogeneous social group. In fact, those making use of resources within a given *terroir* are usually very diverse. Households within a given village or camp are very varied in their interests and their capacity to engage in land improvements of various sorts.

2. emphasis on the farm economy neglects the fact that most households pursue a highly diverse pattern of income-earning activities, of which farm production is only one. Migrants' earnings are often used not for improving the farm, but for investment in trade and in livestock holdings. Such investment is seen as essential as a means to protect incomes from risk.

3. there has tended to be an in-built bias in GT approaches towards sedentary farming populations, whose physical situation and appropriation of natural resources fits better the concept of a *terroir*.

However, such a bias will have damaging implications for more mobile production systems that can exploit more effectively the natural diversity found within the Sahel. Such damage may lead to further conflict.

Conclusions

Decision makers in government and donor agencies need to encourage policies which retain a degree of flexibility and mobility within rural production systems. Such flexibility is essential to reduce vulnerability to a variety of risks. It is challenging to see how this might be done within a context where better environmental management is seen as inextricably linked to establishing much firmer rights for some over their resources, since this will inevitably mean the exclusion of others. Exclusion runs the risk of aggravating tensions and increasing conflict between different resource users, and most particularly between farmers and herders.

The concern of governments and donor agencies for better environmental management must be set within a broader social and economic context. Local populations cannot be expected to invest much time and resources in natural resource management, unless it is in their interests. Their interests include not only farming, but also a range of income-earning activities, including trade and migration. An effective programme to promote 'gestion de terroir' will need to incorporate this broader economic context into the design of interventions at local, national and international levels.

References

David, R. (1992): The effects of male outmigration on women's management of the natural resource base in the Sahel. Preliminary reports. SOS Sahel, London.

Toulmin, C. (1992): Cattle, women, and wells: Managing household survival in the Sahel. Oxford

Les acacias gommières au Sahel: Exsudation gommière et production-perspectives

J. Vassal¹ et M. Dione²

1. Institut de la Carte Internationale de la Végétation,
Université Paul Sabatier, Toulouse, France.
2. Institut Sénégalais de Recherches Agricoles, Direction des
Recherches sur les Productions Forestières, Dakar, Sénégal.

Summary

Acacias are characteristic components of the sahelian scenery. The more important species exuding gum arabic, a product highly demanded in the international market, are *Acacia senegal* and *Acacia seyal*. Sudan exports around 80% of the gum currently marketed in the world. In this country, a particular mode of farming of A. senegal (the hashab bush fallow system) has become traditional. In other sahelian countries, gum production has declined all along the 20 past years, the causes of this regression being climatic (drought) but also socio-economic and political.

Among the actions which could help to improve gum yield in the Sahel, the authors emphazise more particularly 1/ the enlargement of the area of gum production (by the use of additional Acacia species) and 2/ the application of experimental research upon the influence of phenological rates and rhythms (defoliation), mode and periods of tapping as well as climatic rhythms on the amount of gum exudation in the dry season.

Introduction

Les Acacias sont des élèments caractéristiques du paysages au Sahel, domaine dans lequel ils jouent un rôle éminent sur le plan écologique et socio-économique. Ils sont en effet des agents anti-érosion car ils contribuent à fixer les sols grâce à un réseau racinaire dense et profond. Par leurs associations symbiotiques ils favorisent l'amélioration de ces sols en azote. Ils sont par ailleurs source de bois de feu et charbon de bois, de bois d'oeuvre, de fourrage aérien précieux en saison sèche, ainsi que de gomme dite »arabique«.

Les Acacias ont, semble-t-il, été utilisés des le Néolithique. Le décryptage des hiéroglyphes égyptiens permet de penser que les espèces *A. nilotica*, *A. seyal* et *A. tortilis* étaient exploitées aussi bien pour leur gomme (comme ingrédient alimentaire, produit anti-inflammatoire et diurétique, pour les peintures à l'eau, l'impression des étoffes, les bandelettes de momies...) que pour leur bois (construction, bateaux, mobilier, objets d'art ou de culte tels que la mythique Arche d'Alliance...). La gomme arabique est par ailleurs citée dans des formules alchimiques grecques (sous le nom d'Akakia).

Le but de cette note est 1/ de faire un bilan des modes d'exploitation des gommiers au Sahel et de l'évolution de la production au cours des 30 dernières années 2/ d'évoquer quelques aspects des recherches menées en vue d'un meilleur contrôle du rythme et des causes de l'exsudation.

Les acacias gommiers les plus importants au Sahel: *Acacia senegal* et *Acacia seyal*

Acacia senegal (L.) Willd. var. *senegal* (»verek« en Ouolof, '»Patouki« en Peuhl, »awarwar« en Maure, »Hashab« en arabe soudanais) fournit l'essentiel de la gomme arabique commercialisée dans le monde. Cette gomme a d'excellentes qualités: elle est dure, claire et a de bonnes caractéristiques sur le plan hydrosolubilité, pouvoir rotatoire spécifique et viscosité. Les produits les plus renommés sont traditionnellement ceux »du Fleuve« (Sénégal) et du Kordofan (Soudan).

L'arbre, de petite taille, est caractérisé par un port flabellé, des feuilles bipennées; les rameaux portent des aiguillons (»épines« non vascularisées) disposés par 3 à l'insertion des feuilles (le médian orienté vers le bas); les fleurs sont en longs épis blanc-jaunâtre; les gousses, larges et plates, renferment des graines arrondies.

L'espèce est distribuée, au Sahel, entre les isohyètes (100) 200-600 (800) mm dans une zone marquée, en moyenne, par 9 à 11 mois de sécheresse. Les températures moyennes mensuelles varient entre 20°C (pour le mois le plus froid) et 35°C (pour le mois le plus chaud). Les sols préférentiels sont sableux et profonds (souvent dunaires); les sols argileux sont généralement tolérés sous de plus forte pluviométries.

Acacia seyal Del. (»Sourour« en Ouolof, »Boulbi« en Peuhl, »Sadra Bed« en Maure, »Tahl« en arabe soudanais) fournit une gomme moins prisée car friable et souvent colorée (par la présence de tannins). C'est aujourd'hui un produit d'appoint important, notamment au Soudan, vu la régression de la production de gomme »senegal«.

L'arbre est de taille analogue à celle d'*A. senegal*. Les troncs sont rouge ou blanc-verdâtre, pulvérulents. Les rameaux portent de véritables épines (donc vascularisées), disposées par 2 (stipules modifiées). Dans la variété orientale *fistula* (»arbre siffleur« ou »wistle tree«) les épines creuses et renflées abritent des fourmis (myremécophilie). Les fleurs sont en têtes sphériques (glomérules); les gousses sont étranglées entre les graines, relativement étroites et falciformes.

L'espèce vit dans une aire géographique et climatique assez analogue à celle d'*A. senegal*. Elle admet des sols sableux ou argileux.

Gestion et production des gommiers — utilisations et commercialisation de la gomme arabique

Modes de gestion des gommeraies à *Acacia senegal*:

La gomme demeure un produit traditionnel de cueillette, notamment pour les pasteurs nomades (Peuhls, Maures). Elle exsude souvent sans saignée préalable; c'est ce que les soudanais appellent la gomme »wady«.

Dans plusieurs régions sahéliennes (Soudan, Tchad, Nigéria, Sénégal) les arbres sont généralement saignés. L'écorçage, souvent effectué à l'aide d'une hachette, consiste, à prélever, sur le tronc ou/et les branches, une bande d'écorce de 4-5 cm de large sur une longueur minimale de 40 à 60 cm. 2 instruments de saignée ont été créés par les soudanais et les sénégalais. Dans le premier cas, il s'agit d'une lame métallique analogue à un fer de hallebarde muni d'un crochet; dans le second cas, la lame tranchante est trapézoïdale. Ces deux types de pièces métalliques sont fixés à l'extrémité d'un manche de bois afin de favoriser le travail à distance. L'outil sénégalais est actionné *de bas en haut*; l'outil soudanais, après entaille de l'écorce, permet de tirer celle-ci *vers le bas* grâce au crochet latéral.

L'exploitation débute généralement lorsque l'arbre a 4 ou 5 ans. La »carre«, ne doit normalement porter que sur le quart de la circonférence de la fraction écorcée. La saignée est pratiquée au début de la saison sèche et dans le courant de celle-ci. La première récolte s'effectue 30 à 40 jours après écorçage, les autres tous les 10 à 15 jours en général. Dans l'Ouest du Sahel on distingue deux campagnes de récoltes: la grande campagne (en début de saison sèche) et la petite campagne (en mars, avril). Notons que les autres espèces de gommiers ne sont normalement pas saignées.

Au Soudan a été mis au point, dans la ceinture gommière, un type de gestion très productif connu sous le nom de »Hashab bush fallow system« fondé sur l'assolement (»shifting cultivation«) c'est-à-dire de jachère arbustive. Les jardins à gommiers (»gum gardens«) sont exploités durant 10 à 12 ans par les villageois (l'arbre produit dès l'âge de 4-5 ans). Lorsque les gommiers ont une productivité moindre, ils sont coupés. Sur la parcelle ainsi défrichée, qui a bénéficié d'un enrichissement du sol grâce aux symbioses racinaires, sont effectuées des cultures traditionnelles (mil, arachide, melon, sorgho, sésame). Les rejets d'Acacias sont régulièrement coupés. Cette parcelle est abandonnée après 4-5 ans lorsque le sol est épuisé. La reconstitution du verger est alors favorisée en laissant se développer les repousses d'Acacias et de jeunes individus issus de germinations. Ce système fonctionne ainsi »en mosaïque«, chaque parcelle illustrant une étape de ce mode d'exploitation. Notons qu'au Soudan est aussi pratiqué le semis direct, notamment au Kordofan: les Acacias croissent ainsi parallèlement aux cultures traditionnelles. Lorsque le sol est épuisé, seuls les gommiers sont exploités.

En ce qui concerne les productions moyennes annuelles par arbre au Soudan, celles-ci sont très variables et s'échelonnent de 100 g à 1 kg.

Dans les autres pays sahéliens, on peut signaler des tentatives de gestion sylvo-agricole des gommeraies entre les années 30 et 60. Les résultats n'ont guère été probants. Au Sénégal, signalons les résultats encourageants du programme sylvo-pastoral mis en place dans le cadre du »projet sénégaloallemand«. Dans ce même pays, les plantations villageoises (PROBOVIL) incluant des gommiers constituent une initiative prometteuse (voir Dione et Vassal, ce vol.).

Commercialisation de la gomme

Circuits de distribution et tonnages: La gomme est normalement centralisée par des grossistes et commercialisée par des sociétés privées agréées ou par des organismes d'Etat. Les comptoirs commerciaux de Sociétés européennes d'export-import, notamment françaises, ont souvent périclité au Sahel francophone, notamment au profit de commerçants libanais, marocains, mauritaniens...

Au Soudan, pays producteur essentiel, la gomme est centralisée sur les marchés locaux par les marchands, triée puis commercialisée par la Gum Trade Company (créée en 1970) qui a le monopole de ce marché. Celui-ci est ainsi »normalisé« par fixation d'un prix minimum sur les marchés d'enchères. On distingue au Soudan 1/ la gomme nettoyée (»cleaned gum«) sans écorce ni débris ou sable, mais avec encore un certain

% de poussière ou de gomme rouge, 2/ la gomme triée à la main (»hand picked selected gum«) avec beaux et gros morceaux de gomme claire. La gomme est acheminée vers Port Soudan ou l'entrepôt de la Gum Cie a une capacité de stockage de 60 000 t (réserve »tampon« de 20 000 t).

Le Soudan est le plus gros producteur et exportateur sahélien. Voici les moyennes annuelles de production depuis 1960 correspondant essentiellement à de la gomme »Hashab«:

1960-1969:	46 000 t
1970-1976:	35 000 t
1977-1981:	37 000 t
1982-1989:	28 000 t

Actuellement ce pays produit environ 25 000 t de gomme Hashab pour 8 000 t de gomme Tahl qui prend une part relativement importante du marché pour des utilisations industrielles autres que la confiserie (empesage des vêtements, confection de banco...).

Dans les autres pays sahéliens, le marché de la gomme est peu organisé, surtout depuis la dernière décennie. La qualité du produit est par ailleurs généralement médiocre car la gomme est souvent vendue mal triée voire non triée. En ce qui concerne les quantités, certains pays tels que la Mauritanie ont vu leur production s'effondrer à la suite des dégâts de la sécheresse des années 70. La production tchadienne a quasiment disparu pendant quelques années en raison des évènements politiques. Au total, les productions annuelles sont faibles et difficiles à estimer par pays compte tenu des exportations frauduleuses d'un pays à l'autre. Au Sénégal, après une légère augmentation en 1971 (Freudenberger 1988), la production de gomme »senegal« s'est ensuite stabilisée autour de 500 à 2 000 t selon l'année. Elle n'est aujourd'hui que de quelques centaines de tonnes par an. Au Mali et au Tchad on note de 200 à 300 t de gomme »senegal« par an. Le Tchad fait par ailleurs aujourd'hui un effort particulier pour commercialiser la gomme "seyal" (jusqu'à 5000 t annuellement). Enfin, au Nigeria, les productions annuelles de gomme »seyal/senegal« avoisinent 1 500 à 2 000 t[1].

Cours moyens de la gomme arabique: Les prix moyens varient actuellement entre 10 et 20 FF le kg. Au Sénégal, les prix de 1970 à 1987 ont fluctué entre 4 et 44 FF/kg (Freudenberger 1988). Aujourd'hui, la

---

1) *Les données récentes sur les tonnages et les prix ont été aimablement fournies par Mr Thévenet, CNI, Rouen, France.*

meilleure gomme sénégalaise se négocie autour de 21.000 FF la tonne. Les prix au Soudan sont légèrement inférieurs, soit environ 15 FF le kg.

Bref rappel des causes de la régression des gommeraies

La raréfaction des gommiers et la chute des rendements sont liées, pour une part, aux crises climatiques (faible pluviométrie) très sensibles depuis une vingtaine d'années. On constate ainsi que l'isohyète 100 mm s'est décalé vers le sud au point de toucher le fleuve Sénégal au Nord de St. Louis et de se rapprocher de la boucle du Niger au Mali (Rognon 1991). Ainsi, dans la Station expérimentale ISRA de M'Biddi (nord Sénégal) la moyenne des pluies annuelles était-elle de l'ordre de 400 mm de 1931 à 1960 (Giffard 1974) alors qu'elle avoisine aujourd'hui 300 mm. Les mortalités ont été très élevées dans certaines régions, notamment au Mali, Burkina Faso, Mauritanie (Trarza)... L'homme est aussi responsable de cette régression car il inflige diverses mutilations aux arbres pour assurer l'alimentation en fourrage du bétail, pour s'approvisionner en bois ou augmenter la production de gomme (saignées profondes, extensives et trop répétées; pratique du feu pour stimuler l'exsudation). Fragilisés par la sècheresse, les gommiers supportent très mal ces traitements. Il faut ajouter à cela les difficultés générales de régénération dues au piétinement et à l'ingestion par les troupeaux des jeunes plantules.

Ces différents facteurs ont ainsi conduit à une chute de la production gommière dans les différents pays. Ce recul a été de l'ordre de 10 000 t au Soudan entre 1970 et 1976.

Intérêt industriel de la gomme arabique

Rappelons que la gomme arabique est un hydrocolloide complexe à poids moléculaire très élevé. Il s'agit d'un polysaccharide de type arabinogalactane incluant une fraction azotée (Street & Anderson 1983, Fenyo & Vandevelde 1989). Les meilleures gommes sont inodores, sans saveur, claires et dures, fortement hydrosolubles, de faible viscosité et à pouvoir rotatoire *négatif*. C'est le cas de la gomme »senegal«: viscosité moyenne de 16 ml/g; rotation spécifique moyenne autour de -30°. La gomme »seyal« a une viscosité moyenne voisine de 12 ml/g mais un pouvoir rotatoire *positif* voisin de +50° (Anderson 1977).

La gomme arabique a de nombreuses applications industrielles dues à son pouvoir émulsifiant, stabilisant et épaississant. Elle est utilisée comme ingrédient ou additif en confiserie, dans les aliments diététiques, les crèmes et desserts ainsi que pour les boissons pulpées (action suspensoïde dans les sodas, mousse de bière...). Elle est aussi beaucoup employée en pharmacie (pastilles et dragées, sirops, crèmes, lotions...).

On l'exploite également dans des domaines comme la pyrotechnie, les peintures à l'eau, la protection des plaques offset, les colles... La demande est donc forte sur le marché international ceci malgré une concurrence partielle de produits de remplacement tels que les amidons modifiés, les gommes de graines, les extraits d'algues ou la gomme xanthane.

Sur le plan alimentaire, la directive CEE 74/329 du 18.06.1974 autorise la commercialisation de la gomme arabique sous le code E 414. Divers travaux ont été réalisés pour apprécier les réponses allergiques à la gomme »senegal« utilisée dans l'alimentation (Monneret-Vautrin 1983; Fournier 1983; Strobel & Ferguson 1986 cited by L. Brimer 1993 in press): les résultats obtenus sont assez contradictoires. L'innocuité paraît bien établie pour ce qui concerne les produits cosmétiques (Guillot *et al.* 1983). Des controverses existent quant à la digestibilité et les apports caloriques de la gomme »senegal«. Il semble aujourd'hui hasardeux d'établir la valeur calorique de cette gomme pour l'homme (Brimer, communication personnelle).

Amélioration de la production de gomme arabique

L' amélioration de la production en gomme arabique est une préoccupation permanente des organisations internationales, des forestiers et industriels depuis une vingtaine d'années. Plusieurs symposiums ou documents généraux sur le marché de la gomme arabique témoignent de l'importance de ce problème (rapports et colloques du CNUCED/GATT 1970 et 19878/79 — colloques de la Société Iranex, Marseille, 1973, 1976 — rapport CNUCED/GATT-UNSO 1983 — colloque de l'institut International d'Enseignement et de Recherches sur les Colloïdes Naturels, Marseille 1983 — colloque et compte rendu ISRA/DRPF-SYGGA III, St. Louis, Sénégal 1988/89). Des programmes de plantations expérimentales ou villageoises de gommiers ont été mis en place notamment au Soudan et au Sénégal (Dione et Vassal, ce vol.): ils ont permis l'amélioration des techniques agronomiques et de gestion des gommeraies, un premier processus de sélection, des essais de multiplication ainsi qu'une sensibilisation des populations au problème de la protection et de la régénération du potentiel sahélien en ligneux productifs. Parallèlement se sont développées des recherches interdisciplinaires portant sur l'amélioration des qualités physico-chimiques de la gomme »senegal«, les méthodes de multiplication *in vitro*, les différentes espèces de gommiers et la maîtrise des phénomènes de gommose. Ces deux derniers points seront plus spécialement traités ici ainsi que dans l'article Dione & Vassal (ce vol.).

Comment élargir la gamme des espèces gommières

— Parmi les Acacias du »groupe senegal« (subgen. Aculeiferum Vas.), 2 autres espèces gommières pourraient être plus particulièrement retenues.

Acacia laeta R. Br. ex Benth. produit une gomme dure et claire de bonne qualité (viscosité: proche de 21 ml/g; pouvoir rotatoire spécifique: -42° — Anderson 1977), souvent confondue avec celle d'*A. senegal*. Les 2 espèces sont en effet très proches systématiquement mais *A. laeta* a des aiguillons généralement par 2 et un nombre plus réduit de folioles de plus grande taille. Elle est distribuée dans la partie Est du Sahel jusqu'à la latitude 4° Ouest et bénéficie d'un climat analogue à celui d'*A. senegal* mais supporte des sols souvent rocheux à argilo-calcaires plus arides. C'est donc une espèce légèrement plus xérophile.

Acacia polyacantha Willd. subsp. *campylacantha* (Hochst. ex A. Rich.) Brenan exsude une gomme qui a également des qualités proches de celles d'*A. senegal* (viscosité: 16 ml/g environ; pouvoir rotatoire spécifique: -12° — Anderson 1977) mais demeure peu exploitée. L'arbre a des caractéristiques assez nettement distinctes: aiguillons robustes, par deux — nombreuses paires de pennes et de folioles — longs épis. L'espèce se distribue globalement entre les isohyètes 300 et 1200 mm dans les savanes souvent inondées. Cette distribution illustre les possibilités d'extension méridionale de la zone gommière.

— Parmi les Acacias proches d'*Acacia seyal* (subgen. Acacia) nous citerons plus particulièrement l'espèce *A. ehrenbergiana* Hayne (= *A. flava* (Forssk.) Schweinf.) dont la gomme, dure et claire, a un pouvoir rotatoire spécifique négatif (proche de -8°, Anderson et Bridgeman 1984) exceptionnel dans ce groupe. L'arbre, souvent confondu avec *A. seyal*, a un tronc rosâtre non pulvérulent (écorce se détachant par plaques); les feuilles sont plus courtes que les épines stipulaires; les glomérules de fleurs sont jaune clair. L'espèce est distribuée au nord de l'isohyète 300 mm jusqu'au delà de l'isohyète 100 mm d'où son intérêt pour l'extension septentrionale de l'aire gommière. Très xérophile, elle traverse le Sahara et se retrouve çà et là au sud de l'Afrique du Nord. Elle tolère des sols souvent squelettiques.

Parmi les autres espèces gommieres de ce groupe, nous mentionnerons: *Acacia tortilis* (Forssk.) Hayne, dont la sous-espèce *raddiana*, très xérophile, est largement répartie de la zone nord-saharienne au Sahel;

Acacia nilotica (L.) Willd. ex Del. dont les différentes sous-espèces colonisent les sols argileux sahéliens entre les isohyètes 200 à 800 mm;

Acacia sieberana DC. qui affectionne les sols limoneux et a une distribution plus méridionale (jusqu'aux régions méridionales préforestières).

Notons que les gommes exsudées sont de qualité moindre car souvent colorées et friables. La gomme Babul produite par la variété *indica* est traditionnellement utilisée en Inde (antihémorragique, apprêt des tissus...).

Quelques aspects actuels des recherches sur les modalités d'induction de la gommose:

Influence des saignées sur l'induction de gommose (Mouret 1987; Vassal 1992; Vassal et Mouret 1992): La gomme résulte d'une destruction cellulaire, génératrice de poches »lysigènes« apparaissant prioritairement dans le phloème interne. Ces lacunes augmentent de volume par accroissement tangentiel et centrifuge. Certains vaisseaux sont oblitérés par la gomme. Celle-ci semble provenir des cellules de parenchyme ligneux voisin particulièrement riche en amidon. Les réserves amylacées semblent bien constituer le matériau saccharidique de base nécessaire à la biosynthèse de la gomme (Joseleau et Ullmann 1985, 1990).

Au niveau des blessures, tous les tissus sont transformés en gomme. Les poches gommeuses libériennes ont une taille peu à peu décroissante en s'éloignant verticalement et tangentiellement des blessures puis disparaissent. Ceci montre le *rôle inducteur des saignées*. Néanmoins, ce facteur est nécessaire mais non suffisant car tous les arbres blessés n'exsudent pas de la gomme. Notons par ailleurs que seule une saignée superficielle (ne dépassant pas l'écorce) sera efficace étant donné l'origine libérienne de la gomme.

Influence du climat sur le volume d'exsudation et sur l'induction gommeuse (Vassal et al. 1992): Si l'on considère le poids moyen de gomme exsudée par arbre, on note que la production est étroitement corrélée à la pluviométrie de l'hivernage précédant la production (Sène 1988; Dione 1989): à une pluviométrie élevée correspond une bonne récolte. Il apparaît que, sur sol sableux, la pluviométrie optimale est globalement comprise entre 300 et 500 mm.

Les pics de production gommière observés en 1989-1990 à la station expérimentale de Mbiddi, au Nord Sénégal, se situent en décembre. Ils succèdent à une chute brutale du degré hygrométrique, dès l'arrêt des pluies, c'est-à-dire en octobre-novembre. Les arbres sont alors soumis à un *stress hydrique* marqué qui joue vraisemblablement un rôle très important dans l'induction de gommose (Vassal 1992). Cette période octobre-novembre s'avère ainsi la plus favorable pour les saignées. Toutefois, si la pluviométrie d'hivernage est nettement inférieure à 300 mm, les saignées seront globalement peu productives et lesantes. Elles devront être évitées dans la mesure où les sols ne sont pas en mesure de conserver un stock hydrique suffisant (Dione et Vassal, ce vol.).

Relations entre état phénologique et production gommière (Vassal et al. 1992; Dione & Vassal, ce vol.): Durant la saison sèche, les arbres se défeuillent asynchroniquement selon leur situation dans la toposéquence dunaire (Dione et Vassal, ce vol.). En cumulant les résultats obtenus dans 7 placeaux de la station forestière sénégalaise de Mbiddi (280 arbres — saignées d'octobre/novembre — observations 1989-90) on met en évidence une relation entre état phénologique et production gommière. En effet, si l'on constitue 4 classes de production (0 = pas de production ; 1 = production < moyenne; 2 = production comprise entre 1 et 2 fois la valeur moyenne; 3 = production supérieure à 2 fois la moyenne), on constate que la classe 3 correspond à des lots d'arbres fortement et précocément défeuillés (pic moyen de défoliation de 70% en janvier). La production moyenne par sujet est dans ce cas maximale en décembre et correspond à 350 g environ. Inversement, des arbres peu et tardivement défeuillés (40% de défoliation en avril) ne produisent pas de gomme. Les classes 1 et 2 ont un comportement intermédiaire: le pic de production moyenne/arbre de décembre est inférieur à 100 g.

Les saignées pratiquées sur des arbres insuffisamment défeuillés seront donc peu ou non productives. Des écorçages tardifs, synchrones d'un degré estimé suffisant de défoliation, ne seront pas pour autant productifs (Dione et Vassal, ce vol.). Les saignées les plus inductrices de gomme paraissent donc devoir être conjuguées, sur des sujets suffisamment défeuillés (70% environ), avec la brusque chute d'hygrométrie du début de saison sèche responsable d'un net changement de régime hydrique de l'arbre.

Conclusion

Les Acacias demeurent un important espoir pour le Sahel dans le contexte actuel de désertification et d'appauvrissement économique. La diversité de leurs utilisations permet d'envisager leur emploi dans différentes actions de reforestation à finalité sylvo-agricole ou sylvo-pastorale.

La forte demande en gomme arabique sur le marché international plaide en faveur de solutions d'aménagement impliquant non seulement l'espèce *Acacia senegal* mais aussi d'autres Acacias qui, mieux valorisés, permettraient l'extension géographique de l'aire gommière. L'amélioration de la production en gomme arabique pose encore différents problèmes liés au contexte social voire politique des pays concernés. Elle suppose notamment une protection efficace des peuplements productifs, une rationalisation des modes de commercialisation et de gestion (par exemple sur la base du modèle soudanais), une information appropriée sur les méthodes et périodes de saignées, tenant en particulier compte de la pluviométrie et de l'état physiologique de l'arbre (exprimé par son rythme de défoliation). Les saignées devront être éventuellement évitées de façon à préserver les arbres après un hivernage déficitaire. Enfin, la recherche fondamentale doit être poursuivie afin de mieux évaluer les variations de qualité physico-chimique des exsudats et de cerner les processus d'induction physiologique de la gommose et de biosynthèse de la gomme en vue d'une meilleure maîtrise du processus d'exsudation.

SELECTION BIBLIOGRAPHIQUE

Anderson, D.M.W. (1977) — Chemotaxonomic aspects of the chemistry of Acacia gum exudates. Kew Bull., 32 (3): 529-536.

Anderson, D.M.W., Bridgeman, M.M.E. & De Pinto, G. (1984) — Acacia gum exudates from species of the series Gummiferae. Phytochemistry, 23 (3): 575-577.

Brimer, L. — sous presse — The chemistry of the Acacias.

Cnuced/Gatt (1972) — La commercialisation des principales Gommes Hydrosolubles, 159 pp., Genève.

Cnuced/Gatt (1978) — Le marché de la gomme arabique: production, commercialisation, utilisation, 181 pp., Genève.

Dione, M. (1989) — Quelques résultats sylvicoles préliminaires concernant les deux phénotypes d'*Acacia senegal*. 3ème Symposium sur le Gommier et la Gomme Arabique, St Louis, Sénégal. (SYGGA 3): 105 -109. Publ. ISRA, Dakar.

Fenyo, J.C. & vandevelde, M.C. (1985) — Macromolecular Distribution of *Acacia senegal* Gum (Gum Arabic) by Size-Exclusion Chromatography. Carbohydrate Polymers, 5: 21, 51 -273.

Fournier, R. (1983) — Toxicologie générale et phénomènes allergiques liés aux hydrocolloides avec référence particulière à la gomme arabique. In Acquisitions récentes dans les domaine des hydrocolloides végétaux naturels: 85-99. P.U. Aix Marseille.

Freudenberger, M. (1988) — Contradictions of gum arabic afforestation projects: observations from the Linguere Department of northern Senegal. Bull Int. Group Study Mimosoideae, 16: 87-122.

Giffard, P.L. (1974) — L'arbre dans le paysage sénégalais, 431 pp. CTFT, Dakar.

Guillot, J.P. et al. (1983) — Evaluation de l'innocuité de gommes et mucilages végétaux ou de certains de leurs dérivés semi-synthétiques utilisés dans les formulations cosmétiques. In Acquisitions récentes dans les domaines des hydrocolloides végétaux naturels: 115-124. P. U. Aix-Marseille.

Iranex — (1973 et 1976) — Gommes et colloïdes végétaux naturels hydrosolubles. 3ème et 4ème Symposium, 201 pp. et 256 pp., Marseille.

Joseleau, J.P. & Ullmann, G. (1985) — A relation between starch metabolism and the synthesis of gum arabic. Bull. Int. Group Study Mimosoideae, 13: 46-54.

Joseleau, J.P. & Ullmann, G. (1990) — Biochemical evidence for the site of formation of gum arabic in *Acacia senegal*. Phytochemistry, 29: 3401-3405.

Monneret, D.A. & El Hamoui, El K. (1983) — Etude expérimentale chez le lapin de la réponse immunitaire à IgM, IgG et IgE à la gomme arabique, par voie digestive, en comparaison avec les voies sous-cutanée et intra-péritonéale. In Acquisitions récentes dans le domaines des hydrocolloides végétaux naturels: 101-114. P.U. Aix-Marseille.

Mouret, M. (1987) — Les Acacias gommiers — Essais expérimentaux — Recherches histologiques sur la gommose. Thèse Univ. P. Sabatier, Toulouse, 234 pp.

Rochebrune, A.T. de (1898) — Toxicologie africaine, 2 vol., 500 pp.

Seif El Din, A.G. (1975) — The future of gum arabic in Sudan. Sudan International 1 (12-13): 24-27.

Sene, A. (1988) — Recherches sur la productivité gommière d'*Acacia senegal* dans le nord-Ferlo (Sénégal). Thèse Univ. P. Sabatier, Toulouse, 243 pp.

Street, C.A. & Anderson, D.M.W. (1983) — Refinement of structures previously proposed for gum arabic and other *Acacia* Gum exudates. Talanta, 30 (11): 887 893.

Sygga III (1989) — Troisième Symposium sous-régional sur le gommier et la gomme arabique. 302 pp. Publ. ISRA/DRPF, Dakar.

Vassal, J. (1992 — sous presse) — Etat des connaissances sur l'induction de gommose chez *Acacia senegal*. In Physiologie des arbres et arbustes en zones arides et semi-arides, 5 pp. Publ. Groupe d'Etude de l'Arbre, Paris.

Vassal, J. & Mouret, M. (1992 — sous presse) — Etapes histologiques du processus de gommose chez *Acacia senegal*. In Physiologie des arbres et arbustes en zones arides et semi-arides, 6 pp. Publ. Groupe d'Etude de l'Arbre, Paris.

Vassal, J., Sall, P., Dione, M., Fenyo, J.C., Vandevelde, M.C., Servantduvallet, S., & Chappuis, A. (1992) — Modélisation du comportement de populations artificielles d'Acacias gommiers (*Acacia senegal*) dans le Ferlo sénégalais. Compte rendu de fin du programme MRT 88 L 0465, 75 pp.

Sécurité alimentaire et stratégies paysannes: La dynamique des banques de céréales dans le nord du plateau central du Burkina Faso

Ernest Yonli
University of Ouagadougou
Burkina Faso

Introduction

Depuis le début de la décennie 70, le Burkina Faso (comme les autres pays du Sahel) traverse une crise alimentaire du fait de la sécheresse et de la faible productivité de l'agriculture céréalière. Pour la période 1970-1983, le bilan céréalier du Burkina fait apparaître un déficite annuel moyen de 3% de la production nationale par rapport aux besoins (cf. Lecaillon et Morrison 1985).

Dans la région centrale semi-aride du pays (communément appelée plateau central), les rendements du sorgho et du mil montrent nettement une tendance à la baisse due à la régression des terres fertiles et à la forte variabilité pluviométrique.

Les faibles performances des systèmes de production traditionnels en vigueur s'accompagnent d'une dégradation des terres arables et de l'éco-système en général. Dans le même temps, la pression démographique contribue à accroître la demande alimentaire tandis que l'émigration des jeunes ruraux fait grossir le nombre de personnes à charge par actif agricole.

Face à une telle précarité dans l'approvisionnement alimentaire des ménages notamment ruraux, des initiatives nouvelles ont vu le jour dans le but d'accroître les disponibilités céréalières tout en facilitant par des actions appropriées, l'accès à la nourriture pour tous les différents groupes de population. Parmi ces initiatives qui visent la reconstitution de la société, de l'économie rurale et de l'agro-écologie, l'expérience des banques de céréales semble être une des plus remarquables.

La banque de céréales peut être définie comme une organisation paysanne assurant le stockage, l'achat et la vente de céréales en vue de garantir la sécurité alimentaire au nivau local. Chaque banque céréalière est dirigée par un comité de gestion élu.

La première banque de cérals a été créée en 1974 par une organisation non-gouvernementale (ONG) dénommée FONADES. Avant la fin de la décennie 70 on en était à 66 banques de céréales pour l'ensemble du pays. C'est à partir de l'année 1979/1980 que les premières banques céréalières initiées par des projets gouvernementaux voient le jour.

En effet, face à la réponse positive des populations rurales aux créations de banques céréalières, l'Etat s'est vu contraint de s'associer aux ONG pour assurer le développement de ces structures socio-économiques orientées vers la sécurité alimentaire au niveau des villages.

Sous la houlette du Fonds de l'Eau et de l'Equipement Rural (F.E.E.R.), les projets nationaux ont connu une croissance rapide. De 263 en 1980/1982, les banques céréalières mises en place sont passées de 478 en 1982/1983, puis à 1177 en 1985/1986 sur l'ensemble du territoire national (cf. Ledoux 1986). Le Plan Populaire de Développement (P.P.D.) initié en 1984/1985 a contribué largement à cette croissance des banques céréalières.

Le dernier inventaire national réalisé en 1989 par le FEER fait état de 1490 banques de céréales dont 550 (37%) dans les 5 provinces du Nord-Plateau central.

Avec une capacité moyenne de stockage de 30 tonnes par banque céréalière, la capacité totale de stockage des banques de céréales équivaut à près de 50% celle de l'Office National de Céréales (OFNACER) soit environ 45.000 tonnes.

Typologie des banques de céréales

La distinction entre les différentes banques de céréales se fait souvent en fonction de la situation alimentaire des zones d'implantation. Ainsi au Burkina Faso, on peut retenir essentiellement trois zones qui sont respectivement, les régions structurellement déficitaires en matière de production céréalières, celles que l'on définit comme étant des régions d'équilibre (instable) et enfin celles qui connaissent une production excédentaire.

Les zones structurellement déficitaires
C'est dans ces régions que les problèmes d'approvisionnement alimentaire se posent avec le plus d'acuité et ceci pour plusieurs raisons:

- la production céréalière y couvre rarement les besoins et les paysans ont besoin d'acheter des céréales dès le début de la saison sèche et tout le long de la période de soudure;
- les années de sécheresse se succèdant les unes au autres, les réserves locales de céréales sont quasi-inexistantes;
- l'enclavement dans lequel se trouve ces régions surtout en saison des pluies, fait que les approvisionnements externes sont coûteux et sont par conséquent irréguliers.

Dans ce type de région comme la zone sahélienne du Burkina Faso, les banques de céréales jouent le rôle de boutiques villageoises de céréales puisqu'elles doivent être en mesure de vendre des céréales tout le long de l'année. Pour de telles régions (cas du Sahel burkinabè) où les revenus alternatifs (élevage) ne manquent pas, les banques céréalières remplissent des fonctions remarquables de sécurité alimentaire en augmentant les disponibilités céréalières sur les marchés locaux surtout dans les zones inaccessibles en hivernage. Par ailleurs, les banques céréalières connaissant des coûts de stockage relativement bas (souvent inférieurs au différentiel saisonnier des prix) arrivent à approvisionner les populations à des prix favorables tout en garantissant leur marge commerciale.

Les zones à équilibre précaire
Ce sont des régions qui alternent bonnes et mauvaises récoltes d'une année à l'autre. A la différence du cas précédent, la précarité de l'équilibre alimentaire n'empêche pas de vendre une partie de la production pour racheter plus tard pendant la soudure à des prix nettement supérieurs. En fait, ce phénomène que Gergely *et al.* (1990) appellent "surcommercialisation" est bien connu au plateau central du Burkina Faso et dans la plupart des pays du Sahel. En général la surcommercialisation (vente de la récolte au-delà du surplus) est plus accentuée dans les régions où les revenus alternatifs sont faibles ce qui contraint des paysans à céder une grande partie de leurs récoltes afin de satisfaire aux besoins monétaires immédiats. Dans ces conditions, même dans une année excédentaire, ces régions connaissent un approvisionnement alimentaire irrégulier du fait que les céréales vendues après la récolte vont en grande partie dans les centres urbains. Par conséquent l'offre céréalière locale se trouve fortement réduite surtout pendant la soudure.

Ce sont ces caractéristiques propres aux zones à equilibre précaire qui font dire à la plupart des auteurs que ces régions sont les mieux indiquées pour la mise en place des banques de céréales. C'est d'ailleurs ce que confirme l'expérience du Burkina Faso où 862 des 1490 banques céréalières recensées en 1989 soit 58% se trouvent dans de telles régions.

Les zones excédentaires

Bien qu'initialement conçues pour les deux types de régions que nous venons de voir, on constate que les banques de céréales ont également été mises en oeuvre dans les zones de surplus comme les régions Ouest et Sud-Ouest du Burkina. Une des questions que l'on se pose dans ces conditions est de savoir quel rôle pourraient jouer les banques céréalières qui y sont installées.

Il y a d'abord le fait que dans ces régions dites excédentaires, on rencontre souvent des exploitations qui manquent de vivres et de moyens financiers suffisants pour couvrir tous les besoins alimentaires du ménage une année durant. Ce qui signifie qu'une offre céréalière globalement abondante peut rencontrer à certaines périodes de l'année une demande individuelle peu solvable, au niveau local même à des prix jugés abordables. Il en résulte souvent des difficultés énormes pour écouler le surplus de production à l'intérieur comme à l'extérieur de ces régions surtout lorsque la campagne agricole est nettement excédentaire. On s'aperçoit alors que de telles régions ont besoin de structures de régulation intersaisonnière et interannuelle des prix. En effet, un des contrastes les plus marqués de la question céréalière au Sahel, c'est souvent l'existence de surplus importants dans certaines régions excédentaires d'un pays alors même que d'autres régions se trouvent dans une situation de quasi-famine. Ce phénomène inhérent au comportement des acteurs du commerce céréalier s'est plus ou moins aggravé depuis la création des offices publics de commercialisation, les commerçants ayant désormais tendance à orienter leurs flux vers les zones où la demande solvable est permanente en l'occurence les centres urbains ou alors vers les zones où les coûts d'opportunité des transferts permettent de réaliser des marges commerciales substantielles.

Dans le même temps, les offices publics connaissent des coûts d'exploitation prohibitifs qui les empêchent de disposer de ressources financières suffisantes permettant de réaliser une régulation des marchés à l'échelle nationale au moyen de stocks régionaux d'intervention. Ainsi, face à la spéculation des commerçants privés et à la défaillance de l'action publique, les banques de céréales peuvent créer un réseau de valorisation externe des surplus céréaliers dans ces régions déficitaires.

Dans les régions excédentaires, l'importance des banques céréalières réside dans la nécesité de garantir la sécurité alimentaire des ménages en difficultés tout en permettant à la grande majorité des ménages qui sont excédentaires d'écouler leurs surplus à un prix rémunérateur. C'est pourquoi les banques céréalières de ces régions doivent travailler à créer un espace de commercialisation beaucoup plus régional ou national que local, en développant des transactions importantes avec les banques de céréales des régions déficitaires. Il s'agit de parvenir par de telles opérations d'échange, d'ouvrir des circuits et des flux commerciaux à même de relever le prix des céréales dans les zones de surplus et de l'infléchir dans les régions déficitaires. A terme, le prix d'équilibre sur le marché sera fonction de l'ampleur des flux maitrisés par les banques de céréales et ceux contrôlés par les autres acteurs du marché céréalier.

L'instauration d'une situation de concurrence à laquelle participent tous les acteurs devant conduire à une auto-régulation du marché ayant des effets positifs au plan micro et macro-économique. Ainsi les banques de céréales, au moyen d'un stockage rationel peuvent permettre une valorisation externe des céréales de la région en commercialisant toute l'année avec les demandeurs des autres régions. Les paysants organisés autour de la banque céréalière de leur village trouvent là une bonne occasion d'écouler leur surplus à des prix qu'ils n'obtiendraient pas au marché local. De même, comme le note Gergely *et al.* (1990), "outre l'intérêt pour le village, on peut faire remarquer que le fait de pouvoir différer les ventes dans le temps a un intérêt macro-économique de régulation du marché en permettant une stabilisation des prix".

Fonctions et situation actuelle des banques de céréales

Originellement conçues pour servir de palliatif au manque de vivres entre deux récoltes au niveau des villages, l'analyse et l'expérience révèlent aujourd'hui que cet objectif primaire des banques céréalières s'accompagne de plusieurs objectifs satellites. Il est de plus en plus question de régulation des marchés, de stabilisation des prix et des revenus des producteurs à côté de l'objectif originel de sécurité alimentaire au niveau des villages.

Cette multiplication des objectifs des banques de céréales voulue par les différents promoteurs et imposée par la problématique céréalière actuelle, exigent que l'on se concentre de plus en plus sur deux volets quand on parle des banques céréalières: sécurité alimentaire au niveau local et régulation du marché céréalier.

C'est à toutes ces deux dimensions que se rapportent les différentes fonctions des banques de céréales. Parmi ces fonctions, trois nous paraissent primordiales.

La fonction de stocage

La constitution de stocks de réserve ou de commercialisation (la prééminence de l'une sur l'autre étant fonction de la zone d'implantation) est une fonction essentielle des banques de céréales. Cette double fonctionnalité au niveau du stockage tient d'une part au rôle que doit jouer toute banque de céréales et d'autre part au comportement des producteurs par rapport au marché.

1. La première fonction de stockage est la suivante: peu après la récolte, la banque céréalière achète des céréales aux paysans qui ont besoin de liquidités pour acheter des biens durables et payer leurs dettes. Dans la période dite de soudure, la banque céréalière revend ses stocks aux paysans. Tenant compte du fait que les prix de revente de la banque de céréales ne sont pas généralement éloignés de ceux auxquels elle a acheté les céréales aux paysans juste après la récolte, on peut dire qu'il s'agit là d'une "épargne en nature" pour les producteurs.

   Dans les villages où les banques céréalières n'existent pas, ces paysans (vendant à la récolte pour racheter plus tard) dépendent en grande partie des commerçants privés qui, tout en achetant les céréales à bas prix à la récolte (offre abondante) les revendent plus tard (soudure) à des prix prohibitifs pour une partie importante des producteurs. Il apparaît clairement que l'existence d'une banque céréalière achetant, stockant et revendant à des prix accessibles constitue un débouché alternatif sécurisant pour les paysans obligés de "brader" leurs céréales à la récolte.

2. La deuxième fonction en matière de stockage se rapporte au stock de sécurité retenu à la fin de l'année pour pouvoir pallier à un éventuel échec de la récolte l'année suivant. Le maintien de ce stock de sécurité relève de la responsabilité de la banque de céréales. En effet, depuis la disparition des silots collectifs de la période coloniale et l'absence ou la faible représentativité des stocks de sécurité de l'OFNACER au niveau des villages, les banques de céréales tendent à combler ce besoin de réserve collective pluriannuelle. Ainsi, le paysan individuel associé à une banque de céréales qui fonctionne de façon satisfaisante peut se permettre se réduire volontairement son propre stock de sécurité.

   Dans un tel cas de figure, la vente d'une partie de ses propres réserves procure au paysan des revenus monétaires supplémentaires qui peuvent être investis soit dans l'exploitation agricole, soit dans dans une autre activité productive non-agricole.

La fonction commerciale

Jusque là nous n'avons parlé que des échanges de céréales qui se passaient entre la banque de céréales et les producteurs. En réalité celle-ci a des rapports commerciaux avec les autres acteurs du marché céréalier que sont les commerçants privés et l'Office National des Céréales (OFNACER).

Nous avons déjà fait remarquer que les paysans dépendaient de moins en moins des commerçants privés du fait de l'existence des banques de céréales. Ces dernières servent aussi de relais entre l'OFNACER et les consommateurs ruraux. Ainsi lorsque les prix du marché sont assez élevés, la banque céréalière a la possibilité d'acheter des céréales auprès de l'OFNACER au prix officiel qui reste constant pendant toute l'année. La capacité de groupage de la banque céréalière lui permet de transférer des quantités importantes de vivres au village à des périodes où les paysans ne peuvent trouver des céréales sur le marché libre à des prix avantageux.

Historiquement perçue comme une tâche secondaire, la fonction commerciale des banques de cérales prend de plus en plus de l'importance dans l'optique de la régulation des marchés et de l'amélioration des revenus des producteurs. Il semble de plus en plus évident qu'une bonne maîtrise de leur fonction commerciale permettra aux banques céréalières de réduire d'une part les effets de la surcommercialisation que subissent les paysans dans les zones à équilibre précaire et d'autre part de valoriser au mieux les surplus commercialisables dans les zones excédentaires. C'est ce qui fait dire à certains auteurs que l'amélioration de la fonction commerciale des banques de céréales peut constituer les bases d'un mouvement coopératif commercial excédentaires, tout en participant de manière concurrentielle au marché céréalier.

La fonction crédit

En matière de crédit, deux aspects sont à distinguer au niveau des banques de céréales: l'octroi des crédits aux banques de céréales par les ONG ou les projets nationaux pour la constitution d'un fonds de roulement et les crédits distribués par les banques céréalières aux paysans.

1. Jusqu'à une période récente, l'octroi de crédit en nature aux paysans par les banques de céréales était une opération courante. En effet le rôle social des banques de céréales semblait être un des éléments

moteurs à la base de leur création. Lors d'une étude effectuée en 1989 par le FEER sur un échantillon de 32 banques céréalières du pays, 62,5% ont déclaré qu'elles faisaient du crédit aux paysans en difficultés.

Les critères applicables en matière de vente à crédit varient d'une banque de céréales à l'autre avec des taux allant de 120 à 150%. Cependant, la pratique de la vente à crédit pose d'énormes problèmes aux banques céréalières à cause de la faiblesse du recouvrement. Lorsque deux années de mauvaises récoltes se succèdent, les paysans sont incapables de rembourser leurs dettes à la banque de céréales et celle-ci se retrouve sans ressources pour poursuivre ses activités. L'enquête du FEER de 1989 révèle que 66% des banques céréalières de l'échantillon connaissent des non-remboursements qui menaçaient la survie des banques de céréales concernées.

Quand on sait que les taux d'impayés des banques céréalières elles-mêmes par rapport à leurs sources de financement atteignent 40 à 60%, on s'apperçoit que la gestion du crédit constitue un des goulots d'étranglement majeurs dans le développement des banques de céréales.

2. On rencontre plusieurs modes de financement dans la création et la promotion des activités des banques de céréales. En règle générale toutes les sources de financement (ONG, projets nationaux...) fournissent des fonds non remboursables pour la construction du bâtiment, la formule du crédit étant seulement appliquée pour la mise en place du fonds de roulement. Trois types de crédits sont couramment utilisés:

- le crédit à moyen terme (3 à 5 ans) d'un montant qui varie généralement entre 500.000 FCFA et 2.000.000 FCFA avec des taux d'intérêt situés entre 7 et 10% l'an;
- le crédit de campagne dont les montants sont fonction des besoins exprimés par chaque banque de céréales, besoins qui dépendent le plus souvent de l'issue de la récolte céréalière au début de la période de collecte. Les taux d'intérêt sont du même ordre que dans le cas précédent;
- le crédit-épargne qui est pratiqué dans les zones où l'organisation des caisses d'épargne et de crédit ont souvent précédé la construction des banques de céréales. Ici, le montant accordé à chaque banque de céréales varie en fonction des sommes déposées sous forme d'épargne par les paysans associés. Les crédits octroyés pour les opérations des banques de céréales excédents rarement 12 mois avec des pénalités de retard par mois après ce délai.

Les deux premiers types de crédit sont ceux pratiqués par la majorité des bailleurs de fonds avec plusieurs variantes. Le troisième cas est surtout le fait d'une ONG nationale, l'Association pour le Développement de la Région de Kaya (A.D.R.K.) qui pratique depuis plusieurs années une riche expérience en matière d'organisation et d'animation du monde rural.

Au-delà des différences dans la forme et le volume des crédits distribués, ce sont la gestion et les effets induits des fonds injectés qui permettent de mesurer l'impact des banques de céréales dans le développement de l'économie rurale.

Problématique du financement des activités des banques de céreéales

Toutes les études récentes sur les banques de céréales reviennent constamment sur deux constatations:

- le concept de banques de céréales a connu une évolution qui confère aujourd'hui à ces structures paysannes un double rôle: sécurité alimentaire et régulation des marchés;
- la viabilité des banques de céréales est désormais une question centrale de la problématique céréalière au Sahel dans un environnement économique marqué par une libéralisation progressive des marchés céréaliers de la région.

De ces deux constatations, on peut dégager plusieurs facteurs influençant la dynamique des banques de céréales et la mesure dans laquelle celles-ci peuvent remplir leur rôle actuel et potentiel. Parmi ces facteurs on retiendra:

- le mode de financement interne et externe des activités d'achat, de stockage et de vente des banques de céréales;
- les conditions et les dispositifs nécessaires à une meilleure participation des banques de céréales au marché dans un cadre intégralement concurrentiel;
- les stratégies permettant d'accroître l'efficacité économique des banques céréalières (rentabilité des activités et amélioration des revenus des producteurs);
- la capacité des banques céréalières à s'intégrer dans les circuits traditionnels d'approvisionnement et désapprovisionnement nationaux et trans-frontaliers.

Dans les pages qui suivent nous aborderons les points relatifs au premier aspect.

La mise en place des capitaux de base
La construction du bâtiment et le fonds de roulement initial constituent ce que l'on appelle les investissement de base.

1 — En règle générale, les promoteurs fournissent des fonds nécessaires à trois types de dépenses dans le volet *réalisation du local*:

- les matériaux de construction (ciment, tôles, bois et fer...);
- la rémunération de la main d'oeuvre spécialisée (maçon);
- aide alimentaire à la main d'oeuvre d'appoint.

Qu'il s'agisse des promoteurs privés (ONG) ou publics (projets nationaux), ce volet de dépenses est de plus en plus couvert par des subventions non remboursables.

En réalité, c'est l'expérience des échecs multiples qui a dissuadé les promoteurs d'octroyer les fonds de construction à crédit. On sait aujourd'hui par exemple que sur les 1500 banques de céréales inventoriées en 1989, 1200 ont effectivement démarré leurs activités dont 800 seulement étaient en fonctionnement avec un tonnage stocké ne dépassant pas 7000 tonnes. Ainsi, c'est pres de la moitié des capitaux investis qui l'ont été à fonds perdus puisques personne ne sait comment et quand ces installations pourraient être utilisées.

2 — Quant au *fonds de roulement*, sa mise en place se fait souvent en nature (céréales) ou en espèces, mais dans tous les cas sous forme de crédit pour la plupart des projets nationaux.

Le montant idéal du fonds de roulement nécessaire pour un fonctionnement efficient d'une banque de céréales est un sujet controversé pour la plupart des spécialistes. En effet, sur la base d'une population donnée, de l'ampleur prévue du déficit céréalier dans ce village et de la norme de consommation individuelle par mois, quel doit être le niveau du stock de sécurité de la banque de céreales? C'est de cette réponse que dépend le volume de fonds nécessaire à la constitution du stock de réserve de la banque céréalière.

Pour une région comme le Yatenga (Nord-Plateau central) par exemple qui doit faire face tous les ans à un déficit de sa production céréalière, on peut adopter les normes suivantes pour un village de 1000 habitants:

Durée prévue du déficit: 3 mois
Population cible: 1000 personnes
Norme FAO de consommation/personne/mois: 16 kg
Tonnage utile: 1000 x 3 x 16 = 48 tonnes
Prix moyen — sac de 100 kg à la récolte: 6000 FCFA
Enveloppe financière utile: 2.880.000 FCFA

Une autre démarche consiterait à considérer une partie de la population soit environ 30% qui ferait face à un manque de vivres pendant 3 mois (exemple correspondant aux régions d'équilibre instable). Les autres données restant inchangées, on obtiendrait:

tonnage utile: 1000 x 3 x 0,3 x 14 = 14,4 tonnes.
Env. financ. utile: 864.000 FCFA.

Les 2 exemples sont empruntés respectivement à Ledoux et Acopam dans de Klerk (1988).

Ces deux exemples tendent à fournir des indications sur l'importance des moyens financiers nécessaires à la constitution du stock de sécurité de la banque céréalière. Dans le fond, la détermination du "niveau souhaitable" du stock de sécurité fait appel à plusieurs autres critères comme la probabilité d'un manque de vivres dans les années à venir, les modifications dans la demande alimentaire ou le caractère incertain du niveau des prix céréaliers. Plusieurs types d'analyse peuvent être utilisés pour estimer ces variables mais le degré de précision dépend des données disponibles et de la connaissance de leur méthode de collecte et d'estimation. Par exemple, l'étendue des risques de pénuries alimentaires et l'ampleur d'un déficit céréalier dans l'année qui suit la période de référence ont fait l'objet d'analyse dans c. Schweigman *et al.* (1988) et Snijders *et al.* (1988).

D'une manière générale, on s'aperçoit que la viabilité des banques de céréales dépend de plusieurs facteurs que la simple disponibilité des fonds ne suffit pas à occulter tant chacun de ces facteurs a une incidence sur l'environnement économique des banques céréalières à plus ou moins long terme. Il est toutefois certain que la capacité des banques de céréales à générer des ressources nouvelles pour le remboursement des emprunts et la reproductibilité des opérations d'achat, de stockage et de vente à court terme, est une condition de premier plan pour leur survie.

Les capacités d'auto-financement

Les aptitudes des banques céréalières à constituer des fonds propres dépendent des frais supportés pour leurs activités et de la rémunération de leurs activités. Pour être viable, une banque céréalière devrait réaliser 20 à 40% de marge bénéficiaire par an par rapport au prix d'achat des céréales. Comme les marges bénéficiaires sont étroitement liées à la gestion économique, une banque de céréales qui utilise mal son fonds de roulement (mauvais recouvrement des crédits par exemple) ou qui organise mal ses opérations peut connaître des pertes insurmontables.

En réalité, les différentes études de cas montrent une grande vulnérabilité financière de la plupart des banques de céréales. En dehors des banques céréalières des zones excédentaires où la capacité de différer les ventes permet de réaliser les ventes à meilleur prix, les marges bénéficiaires obtenues en règle générale suffisent juste à rembourser les fonds de roulement. C'est ce que confirme l'exemple ci-dessous à partir des estimations de N. Gergely *et al.* (1990).

Ainsi on constate par exemple que pour un fonds de roulement de 45 FCFA pour 1 kg de céréales à rembourser en 9 FCFA/an sur cinq ans, seule la banque céréalière de la colonne (3) p. 205 peut rembourser tout en réalisant une accumulation d'une partie des recettes. A partir de ces estimations les auteurs du rapport révèlent les constations suivantes:

- une banque en condition moyenne, qui doit rembourser son fonds de roulement n'a pas la capacité d'autofinancer son développement;
- des délais de remboursement inférieurs à cinq ans risquent de se traduire par un appauvrissement de la banque;
- ce type de banque supporte difficilement un intérêt sur le fonds de roulement prêté.

Il convient de garder à l'esprit que ces remarques ne suggèrent nullement un renforcement des subventions non remboursables. Tout dépend de l'environnement économique de la banque et notamment de la situation de la production céréalière, de la formation des prix et des opportunités de revenus pour les ménages des producteurs.

Mode d'organisation et de rentabilisation des ressources financières

Aujourd'hui, l'idée de supprimer les offices céréaliers publics, dans le cadre des programmes de restructuration économique fait penser de plus en plus aux banques de céréales pour prendre le relais. On s'attend à ce que ces dernières jouent un rôle au niveau micro (disponibilité et

Zone d'implantation	Zone déficitaire FCFA/kg	Zone équilibrée FCFA/kg	Zone exédentaire FCFA/kg
Eléments de coût/bénéfice			
Marge brute	16 1	13	20
Frais sur achats	2,50	-	-
Frais moyens de la banque	4,50	4,50	4,50
Marge nette	9,00	8,50	15, 50
Frais supplémentaires	(1,50)	(1,50)	(1,50)

accessibilité aux céréales) et macro (adaptation de l'offre marchande à la demande solvable). Cependant l'analyse financière montre que dans la situation actuelle, les banques de céréales ne sont pas en mesure de remplir ces fonctions.

Dans le domaine du financement des activités des banques de céréales, plusieurs questions demandent à être étudiées ou approfondies. Les questions prioritaires semblent être les suivantes:

- quels sont les coûts des activités préalables à la mise en place d'une banque de céréales (identification des villages, évaluation des besoins, compétences requises...);
- quelle est la hauteur de participation financière du village et sous quelle forme (cotisation, épargne collective...) doit-elle être acquise;
- quelles sont les possibilités de financement interne (caisse d'épargne/crédit, banques commerciales) et externe;
- les formules de mise en place des fonds (subventions, crédits) sont-elles compatibles avec les capacités réelles du village bénéficiaire;
- l'environnement économique du village (revenus alternatifs, marché important, voies de communication) est-il propice pour rentabiliser les activités de la banque de céréales;
- quel est le coût de l'encadrement nécessaire au suivi des opérations et à la valorisation de l'expertise villageoise.

Les réponses à toutes ces questions ne relèvent pas seulement de mesures opérationelles immédiates. La recherche peut être mise à contribution notamment dans la validation de plusieurs hypothèses qui permettent de mieux situer le rôle actuel et potentiel des banques de céréales dans le cadre d'un développement durable.

Les axes d'investigations de la recherche en cours

La recherche que nous menons vise deux objectifs:

1. Identifier le dégré d'influence actuelle et potentielle des banques céréalières sur la sécurité alimentaire au niveau local.

2. Développer un cadre d'analyse pertinent pour la compréhension du comportement des agents économiques au niveau rural, notamment dans leur position vis-a-vis du marché. L'étude des interactions entre les acteurs du marché céréalier aura pour point d'ancrage la banque de céréales. Ces interactions peuvent se résumer schématiquement de la manière suivante:

En discutant les rôles des différents acteurs, il faut faire une distinction entre la situation actuelle et la situation potentielle. La situation actuelle peut différer d'un village à l'autre, par exemple un point de vente de l'OFNACER peut être présent ou absent, le rôle des ONG peut être dominant ou marginal, la banque de céréales peut être très organisée ou non, le marché privé peut être dominé par des grands commerçants ou par les petits commerçants etc. Dans cette étude on analyse un rôle potentiel des banques de céréales sur la base des rôles existants de l'OFNACER et du marché privé.

Le rôle des ONG sera analysé en ce qui concerne leur contribution potentielle au développement des banques de céréales, en particulier par la fourniture des crédits ou de l'aide alimentaire. Pour éviter tout malentendu, il convient de noter que la production céréalière comprend ici le sorgho ainsi que le mil et le maïs. Une distinction est faite entre les décisions relatives à la production et celles qui portent sur l'offre sur le marché. Cependant, ces décisions peuvent être étroitement liées les unes aux autres sur les superficies à emblaver, les choix des cultures et variétés, de la date de semis, de la méthode agricole. Ce sont des décisions qui sont déterminées par la disponibilité des facteurs de production-terre, main d'oeuvre, capital, par la consommation prévisible et par la présence d'un surplus de la récolte de l'année précédente. Ces eléments-là ont fait l'objet d'autres études dans le cadre de notre programme de recherche CEDRES/AGRISK. Nous nous limitons ici aux décisions relatives à l'offre céréalière au marché, c'est-à-dire la vente d'une partie de la production et l'achat de céréales. La décision de vendre comporte deux éléments différents: le moment de la vente et la quantité destinée à la vente.

Le commerce des céréales se fait à différents niveaux: entre la banque

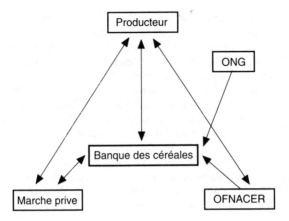

N.B. Les relations correspondant aux pointillés feront l'objet d'autres recherches.

---

de céréales et le producteur, entre la banque de céréales et les commerçants privés et l'Office National des Céréales (OFNACER, qui est l'organisme pour la vente et l'achat de céréales). Les thèmes de recherche sont les suivants:

- stratégies de vente et d'achat des producteurs;
- facteurs déterminants de ces stratégies;
- fixation des prix de vente et d'achat réalisés entre banques de céréales et des producteurs;
- stratégies de vente et d'achat de la banque de céréales;
- formation des prix au marché privé.

Nous avons déjà fait remarquer que les paysans dépendent de moins en moins des commerçants privés, grâce aux banques de céréales, et qu'ils y réalisent en outre des prix "plus favorables". De ce fait, ils vendront et achèteront quasiment toujours leurs céréales à la banques de céréales. La fixation des prix "plus favorables" constitue l'un des principaux thèmes de recherche. La stratégie commerciale de la banque de céréales occupe une place centrale dans le projet. La recherche est axée sur les questions suivantes: quelle est la stratégie optimale pour la banque de céréales en ce qui concerne la vente et l'achat de céréales sur le marché privé ou auprès de l'OFNACER, compte tenu des conditions secondaires suivantes: elle doit acheter ces céréales aux paysans juste après la récolte, elle doit les revendre aux paysans en période de manque, elle dispose d'un stock de sécurité; elle obtient des crédits auprès des banques ou des ONG (Organisation Non-Gouvernementale).

La stratégie optimale dépend dans une large mesure du niveau de la production céréalière – dans une année de production déficitaire, la stratégie commerciale des producteurs et des banques de céréales sera tout à fait différente que dans une année de production excédentaire –, ainsi que des prix du marché privé et ceux de l'OFNACER. La formation des prix est un des thèmes centraux de la recherche. L'on espère que la présence des banques de céréales achetant après la récolte des céréales aux paysans, mènera, sur le marché privé, à une hausse des prix après la récolte et à une baisse des prix pendant la soudure. Il s'agit là d'un aspect qui recevra une attention particulière dans la recherche.

L'étude des interrelations sera effectuée à l'aide d'un modèle mathématique de programmation linéaire et de simulation.

REFERENCES BIBLIOGRAPHIQUE

de Klerk, T. (1988) – Document de base – Projetes banques de céréales, CON, Wageningen

De Lardemelle, L. (1991) – Les banques de céréales peuvent-elles et ivent-elles satisfaire tous les besoines des producteurs de céréales au sahel?, Ouagadougou

FAO (1990) – L'ajustement structurel ela commercialisation des produits agricoles, Rome

F.E.E.R. (1989) – Inventaire des banques de céréales au Burkina Faso, Ouagadougou

F.E.E.R. (1989) – Enquêtes Moulins et Banques de céréales, document final, Ouagadougou

Gergerly et al. (1990) – Evaluation des banques de céréales au Sahel, rapport de synthèse, F.A.O., Rome

Lecaillon, J. et Morrison, C. (1985) – Politiques économiques et performances agricoles: le cas du Burkina Faso, 1960-1983, OCDE, Paris

Ledoux, G. (1986) – Inventaire et Evaluation des banques de céréales au Burkina Faso,

Ouedraogo, M. (1990) – Reflexion sur l'évolution des banques de céréales, F.E.E.R., Ouagadougou

Schweigman, C. (1988) – Observations quantitaves sur les risques dans l'approvisionement alimentaire sur le plateau Mossi, R.U.G/Université de Ouagadougou

Snijders, T. (1988) – L'analyse statique de données agricoles du Plateau Mossi, R.U.G/Université de Ouagadougou

Yonli, E. (1988) – Marché et prix dans l'approvisionnement du plateau Mossi en sorgho et mil, R.U.G/Université de Ouagadougou

A note on pest management in the Sahel

Ole Zethner
Danagro Adviser A/S.
Copenhagen
Denmark

Pests

Pests are defined as organisms harmful to man, his crops and livestock. Pests include animals *e.g.* insects, mites, nematodes, birds and rodents, disease-causing agents *e.g.* fungi, bacteria and viruses, and weeds. This very short outline deals only with pests affecting agricultural crops, exemplified mainly by a few pests of millet in the Sahel.

Pests are a severe constraint for Sahelian farmers trying to manage their agricultural resources. During recent decades a number of factors have increased losses inflicted by pests. Droughts during the early 1970's and 1980's have increased the importance of certain pests such as the Millet Spike Borer (*Heliocheilus albipunctella*), which was not a pest at all before the droughts. Reduced fallow and rotation has increased the survival rate of certain insects, fungi and parasitic weeds from one year to the next. The progressive degradation of soils facilitates parasitism of cereals by Witchweed (*Striga hermonthica*). Continuous cutting and burning of trees and scrubs reduce the survival of some natural enemies of insect pests, which depend on flowers of this natural vegetation for sustenance. Some pests of exotic crops (*e.g.* cassava) have been introduced unintentionally, causing havoc to the crops.

Losses

The magnitude of pre-harvest crop losses caused by pests in Sahel averages around 40%, but varies greatly depending on the crop, year, location etc. Losses caused by weeds are particularly important, as they occur each year. Post-harvest losses may also be considerable, averaging 10-20%.

Given that farmers anticipate losses of up to 50% due to attacks by pests, they are driven to cultivate double the area.

Control Methods

Weeding and other forms of manual control (*e.g.* picking/burning of pests; removal/burning of fungus diseased plants; bird scaring) is part of farmers' sound management activities. Especially weedings are extremely time-consuming (2-3 times during the 3-4 month cropping season) and require efforts by men, women and older children. Lack of labour during such peak periods (due to schooling, sickness, etc.), is one of the main constraints affecting agricultural yields in Sahel.

Rotation is still widely practiced, and does reduce the losses caused by certain pests. So does intercropping of crops or crops and trees, in particular if one crop or tree species is nitrogen fixating. Such intercropping may constitute a major tool for improving soils, but has yet to be introduced by the majority of farmers.

Chemical control of pests is rarely used in the Sahel, and almost exclusively in crops cultivated for sale (cotton, some rice) or when locusts or grasshoppers occasionally threaten to destroy all crops. In subsistence crops we must foresee more chemical control to be used for pests which are capable of totally destroying a crop (*e.g.* blister beetles (*Psalydolytta sp.*) and armyworms, both frequent pests of millet). Increased use of herbicides may also be expected due to the lack of labour at times of weeding.

Biological control with natural enemies of un-intentionally introduced exotic pests (so-called "classical biological control") has proven to be very efficiant in the case of *Cassava Mealybug*, and in some other exotic crops, *e.g.* mango. Biological control of indigenous pests of indigenous crops is, however, far more difficult as this may require time consuming, constant rearing and releases of the natural enemies.

The best potential for pest control in the Sahel is found in the field of breeding pest-resistant varieties of crops. Thus, the international agricultural research institutes (*e.g.* IITA in Nigeria, ICRISAT in Niger) have succeeded/are succeeding in creating varieties of maize resistant to the Maize Streak Virus, and sorghum varieties with some resistance to *Striga hermonthica* among other accomplishments. Bottlenecks for extension of such varieties are found in the national agricultural research systems (NARS) and the very weak extension services found practically all over Sahel.

Monitoring and scouting for pests is rarely carried out in the region. Such activities should determine whether pest populations are high enough to merit intervention by the farmers (economic threshold level). Much education and training is required for such activities. Monitoring forms the basis for Integrated Pest Management (IPM), whereby one means an approach to combine two or more methods to control pests, and at the same time reduce the use of pesticides to an absolute minimum.

Future

The main constraints for improved pest prevention and control in the Sahel, are the lack of well trained human resources, and low levels of investment in agriculture. At farm level, the lack of labour for weeding during peak periods should be compensated by limited and well planned used of herbicides. This necessitates a willingness by farmers to invest some of their surplus from cash crops in growing subsistence crops.

Governments must seriously invest more money and interest in improving the conditions for agricultural research workers and extension staff workers. Both parties must be urged and facilitated to work closely together with the farmers, and receive greater training in IPM, and in how to communicate with both male and female farmers.

Summaries of participants projects

Andersen, Kirsten Ewers
Keywords — Forestry (social), land and tree tenure.
Abstract — Relationship between local organisation and government with respect to ressource management.

Bolwig, Simon
Main activities — Preparing fieldwork in Burkina Faso 1993.

Boussoufa, Abdelouahab
Main activities — Have been working in Sahel contries (Niger, Mali, Burkina Faso) since 1983.

Brøgger-Jensen, Steffen
Title — Study on Sahelian bio-diversity by means of satellite image analysis and ornithological surveys.
Keywords — Sahel, habitat, satellite imagery, ornithological surveys, habitat selection, diversity.
Abstract — The aim of the project is to develop a method for mapping and monitoring of biological diversity in the Sahel zone, permitting implementation of strategies for the conservation and monitoring of bio-diversity. The Sahelian biotopes hold a number of endemic biological assets and constitute the main wintering ground for a significant number of Palearctic migratory bird species. The relations between the distribution of bird species and communities and the habitat types and land-use patterns will be elucidated by means of satellite data analysis and standardized ornithological survey methods. On the basis of the habitat selection patterns revealed in the analysis, a framework will be established for the use of bird species and bird communities as biological indicators to set priorities for management of biodiversity in large geographical areas. While carrying out ornithological surveys, this approach should at the same time ensure a further understanding of patterns and processes in Sahelian ecosystems. Census areas have been placed in Senegal, where ground surveys for satellite image analysis and botanical surveys have been conducted, contributing with essential descriptive and analytical information on the environment. The project is carried out in collaboration with Centre de Suivi Ecologique, Dakar, Services des Parc Nationeaux, Dakar, Inst. of Geography and Inst. of Population Biology, both University of Copenhagen.

Bøgh, Eva
Title — Modelling water-use and plant production in the Sahel.
Keywords — Water-use, millet, surface mapping, modelling, GIS, remote sensing.
Abstract — HAPEX-Sahel is an extensive soil-plant-atmosphere experiment taking place over representative surface-types in Niger. The programme is aimed at modelling surface processes on micro- and large-scale basis (remote sensing). Within this range I'm involved in modelling of water-use and biomass produktion on millet-fields. Furthermore, I take part in the process of integrating data in a Geographical Information System.

Carus, Hanne
Title — Natural resource management planning, Niger.
Keywords — Land-use planning, resource management, community participation and organisation.

Abstract — As a basis for advising on better management of the natural resources in an area with a fragile environment in Eastern Niger, a comprehensive study of a smaller region is being undertaken. The study comprises: existing organisation of land-use, mapping of natural landscapes and land use by satellite images, water resources, range land resources, agricultural production systems, animal husbandry, firewood situation. The study shall suggest strategies for the use of the natural resources in a sustainable manner in close dialogue with the different communities living in the area.
Main activities of institution — Consultancies outside Scandinavia within the fields of water supply, rural development and environment.

Christensen, Per Christian

Keywords — sustainable land-use, Natural forest/resource management, Peoples participation.

Abstract — Have worked for 3 ½ years as forestry-expert with a the FAO in Burkina Faso. Have worked with management of natural forests and sustainable land use. Have participated in evaluation missions in Niger for The World Bank, UNSO and DANIDA.Have as team leader gained considerable practical experience in working with the local population concerning management of natural resources — especially forests; Socio-economic studies; Various different approaches to Establishment of forest-cooperatives; Aerial survey; Photo-interpretation; cartography; Training of farmers in forest techniques (exploitation, planting, sowing, fireguards); On-the-job training of local technicians; Inventory planning and execution; Preparation of volume tables Research/experimentation concerning silviculture and forest/bush-fires.
Have on evaluation missions worked with household energy, privatisation, erosion control, integrated land-use, nursery management, fuelwood policy, taxation regulation.

Degnbol, Tove

Title — How can donors support the establishment of an enabling environment for local natural resource management?

Keywords — Environmental planning, role of the state, institutional constraints, Mali.

Abstract — With the national programme to combat desertification in Mal,as the case, the research project focuses on the institutional problems related to national environmental planning. The role of the state in the establishment of an enabling environment for local ressource management is discussed, and institutional constraints for a further decentralisation are identified.

Ellehøj, Peter

Keywords — Development Economics, Monetary Economics, International Political Economy.

Abstract — Economic advisor for the UNDP in Senegal 1989-1992 research associate, institute of economics 1989.
Published several articles on international economic coordination and other international economic issues. ODA reporting systems.

Ellemann, Lis

Title — The Maasai's use of and interaction with the natural vegetation.

Keywords — Ethnobiology

Abstract — The purpose of my Ph.D.-study is to describe the significance of plants for the Maasai and the interaction, between them and the natural vegetation. The ethnobotanical research is carried out in collaboration with anthropologist Nina Johnsen, University of Copenhagen and covers all categories of plants used by the Maasai and their animals. It includes the Maasai's selection and use of pasture for their herds as well as their use of plants in traditional medicine and in their health care for human and cattle. Information given by the Maasai about their management of pasture will be compared with the data obtain with vegetation studys to describe their knowledge in a natural scientific context.

Engberg-Pedersen, Lars
Title — Inside Village Councils: Natural Resource Management in Burkina Faso.
Keywords — Village politics, National resource management, governing the commons, decentralisation policies.
Abstract — The purpose of the research project is to study the capacity of local organisations to formulate and implement policies. The results and the causes of these policy processes are analysed. Moreover, the point is "to get inside" local organizations and investigate decision-making processes within these organisations. The management of natural resources by village councils in Burkina Faso is taken as a case. Theoretically, the discussions relate to institutional perspectives on organizations, the management of common pool resources, and decentralization policies.

Fries, Ingrid
Keywords — Schools, environmental education, Burkina Faso.
Main activities — Chairman of UN association in Upplands Väsby.

Houlberg, Rikke
Title — Traditional Open Well Rehabilitation, Sudan.
Keywords — Mapping, diagnosing, and design of the need for well rehabilitation.
Abstract — The Sudanese Red Crecent/Danish Red Cross project is an integrated rural development project operation in the Derudeb district.
I. Krüger Consult AS is involved in groundwater resource development, which is the main activity of the project.
The aim of the project was 1) to map all traditional open wells in the district, 2) to indicate the resource fullness of the individual well, 3) to develop a serie of well rehabilitation designs, 4) to define the proposed type of well rehabilitation for each well, 5) to set up a training course for artisans and supervisors, and 6) to implement a training course.
Main activities of institution — Country services outside Scandinavia within the fields of water supply, rural development and environment.

Jacobsen, Carl Christian
Main activities — Newly appointed project coordinator for rural water supply and environmental protection project in Zinder and Diffa, Niger.

Johansen, Henrik Brade
Main activities — Home-office management of several projects in various Sahel-countries.
Main activities of institution — Consultancies in Africa mainly within the field of rural and small-towns water supply; environmental protection and rural development.

Jensen, Flemming Pagh
Title — Study on Sahelian bio-diversity by means of satellite image analysis and ornithological surveys.
Keywords — Sahel, habitat, satellite imagery, ornithological surveys, habitat selection, diversity.
Abstract — The aim of the project is to develop a method for mapping and monitoring of biological diversity in the Sahel zone, permitting implementation of strategies for the conservation and monitoring of bio-diversity. The Sahelian biotopes hold a number of endemic biological assets and constitute the main wintering ground for a significant number of Palearctic migratory bird species. The relations between the distribution of bird species and communities and the habitat types and land-use patterns will be elucidated by means of satellite data analysis and standardized ornithological survey methods. On the basis of the habitat selection patterns revealed in the analysis, a framework will be established for the use of bird species and bird communities as biological indicators to set priorities for management of biodiversity in large geographical areas. While carrying out ornithological

surveys, this approach should at the same time ensure a further understanding of patterns and processes in Sahelian ecosystems. Census areas have been placed in Senegal, where ground surveys for satellite image analysis and botanical surveys have been conducted, contributing with essential descriptive and analytical information on the environment. The project is carried out in collaboration with Centre de Suivi Ecologique, Dakar, Services des Parc Nationeaux, Dakar, Inst. of Geography and Inst. of Population Biology, both University of Copenhagen.

Juul, Kristine

Title — The effects of drought related migration on tenure and resource management in semi-arid lands — the oase of Senegal.
Keywords — Pastoral migration, resource management, tenure systems.

Jørgensen, Karl Aage

Keywords — Hydrogeology, rural and urban water supply, water resource evaluation. Countries: Niger, Burkina Faso, Mali, Guinea.
Main activities — Projects in the Sahel regions since 1982:
Niger 1982-90: Consultancies on Rural and Urban water supplies, water resource management, in both sedimentary basins (Iullminden, Tchad, Koramas) and Basement (Damagaram, Afr, Liptako)
Burkina Faso 1984-91: Urban water supplies, feasibility studies and boreholes in 14 towns.
Mali 1986: Urban water supply, Bamako, desk study.
Guinea 1986-91: Urban water supplies, boreholes and feasibility studies for 7 towns in total.

Koch-Nielsen, Holger

Main activities — Development advisor (private consultant). Book: "The right independent development".

Larsson, Helena

Title — Linear regressions for canopy cover estimation in Acácia woodlands using Landsat TM, MSS and SPOT HRV XS data.
Keywords — Regressions, canopy cover, Acacia wood.
Abstract — The aim of the study was to establish remote sensing models for estimation of canopy cover in Acacia woodlands. The models were established using Landsat TM and MSS data and SPOT HRV XS data and based on field data from eastern Sudan. The models were derived using the Reduced Major Axis (RMA) method, Correlation coefficients between NDVI and canopy cover are for Landsat TM 0.552, for Landsat MSS 0.698 and for SPOT HRV XS 0.718. The confidence intervals of predicted canopy cover are also presented.

Larsen, Karl Erik (Calle) Schou

Title — Zerograzing, Feasibility study on farming systems at the Kilimanjaro mountain, Tanzania, with special attention to the small scale dairy sector.
Keywords — Zero grazing, farm systems, hole farm analyse, dairy, sustainable productions systems, Chagga.
Abstract — M. Sc. thesis made as a feasibility study on the farmin systems of Chagga peasants at the Kilimanjaro mountain, Tanzania. The task was to invenstigate what are the main reasons for an insufficient use of the dairy stock. An important aspect of the study was to analyse, how vunerable the farming system was to change in production metods. Both concerning the lifefoundation of the peasant families as well as as the stability of the ecosystem. Some 17 families was interviewed and had a total of 100 head of cattle, it concerned relatively large stocks on 4-5 head of cattle, the mainpart was crossbreed. The study confirmed that existing cattle production potential was not being utilized completely, which primarily was due to three things. 1. Reproduction patterns. 2. Low feeding intensity. 3. Insufficient knowledge about intensive milk production. Of major constrains from the external

society it is important to pinpointhe obligation to grow coffee on a certain amount on the farm. This limit the farmers possibilities of adjusting their production to the market conditions. It was found that the peasants have not received any real guidance in feed planning. They have only been told what was good to feed with, but not anything about how, when or how much they should feed. Only a release of land from coffee growing can give a pronounced increase in feeding capacity and milk production. The farmers lack of knowledge, is primarily regarded to be due to three conditions: poor training, poor advisory service and poor exchange of experiences between the farmers. All three conditions are estimated to be difficult to change on short term basis. The overall conclusions is – 'If milk production is to be improved the main stress should be laid on training of the advisory service staff.'

Lawesson, Jonas E.
Title — Studies of flora, vegetaion and gradients in West Africa.
Keywords — Sahel, Sudanian, Sudano-Guinean, vegetation, classification, ordination, Senegal.
Abstract — Ecological studies are carried out in Senegal, West Africa. Flora and vegetation structure and phytogeography are studied in about 80 sites located in national parks, classified reserves or sylvopastoral and game reserves covering the Sahelian regional transition zone, the Sudanian regional centre of endemism and the Guinea-Congolian/Sudania regional transition zone. The northern and central part of Senegal with generally open woody vegetation is sampled with strip transects, while the southern area with denser formations is studied by means of quadrats. The vegetation analysis is carried out with hierarchical divisive classification. Important gradients are investigated with canonical ordination. The vegetation of the study sites has been grouped into physiognomic formation classes: semidesert, grassland, wooded grassland, thicket, shrubland, bushland, woodland, dry forest, gallery forest, and further divided into 41 generalized vegetation types. Only few vegetational changes have occurred in the northern part of Senegal during the last 50 years, whereas Sudanian transition woodland has decreased and now is found only in protected sites in southern Sudanian phytochorion. Most of the vegetation types of the Guinea-Congolian/Sudania regional transition zone seem to be unchanged from earlier. Soconday Combretum woodland seems to be more abundant than previously reported. Niche relationships in canonical space of most of the woody species included, are studied by means of analyses of the weighted abundances and standard deviation along the principal axes. Tolerance, N_2 diversity and density are found to be generally in accordance with contemporary models. It is intended to expand the analyses to additional methods of non-hierachical classification, and furthermore include data from other Sahelian countries, in order to determine the homogenity/inhomogenity of Sahelian vegetation types and physiognomy.

Lefebre, Alain
Title — Gender relations and economic transformations in Hausa and Mossi villages.
Keywords — Gender identity, men's study, Burkina Faso, Niger, economic changes in rural areas.
Abstract — My actual research concerns the relations between men's perception of gender relations with the women's possibilities to improve their socio-economic status in two patriarchal societies of West Africa, the Hausa and Mossi in Niger and Burkina Faso respectively. The study is an attempt to reach a better knowledge of gender relations by looking at them from the men's side. I argue that even though anthropological studies of women have brought many evidences of women's manoeuvrability in social, economic and sexual matters, their power is nevertheless restricted to the specific female domain in societies with a strong patriarchal ideology. The economic transformations in the rural areas throughout this century have not been accompanied by a concomitant change in the peoples's system of value. According to the rationale of gender relations, Hausa and Mossi men will not support women-oriented development projects, which aim at giving women a greater economic independence, if they perceive them as a threat to their power and control.

Leth-Nissen, Søren
Title — ALCOM (Aquaculture for local community developement).
Keywords — Aquaculture, extension, natural resources management, small water bodies, institutional strengthening.
Abstract — The two projects that ALCOM runs in eastern province, Zambia, deals with extension in fish farming and management and enhancement of production of small water-bodies. The overall theme is increased production and management of the natural resources through community participation. A special emphasis is put on women and youth. ALCOM has developed a special approach on how to reach small-scale rural farmers through extension service. Fish farming is a new activity in the eastern province and it has taken more than five years to develop, test and implement this approach. Now the results are starting to show. Fish farming is booming. Institutional strengthening is sought achieved through collaboration with already existing governmental and non-governmental institutions with good results.

Lillebæk, Jens
Title — Village water supplies based on solar energy; five years experience of management at community level.
Keywords — Rural development, Niger, water supply, community management and empowerment, solar energy, technology transfer, operation and maintenance systems.
Abstract — Four village water supply systems, serving more than 12,000 people, have been in operation since the beginning of 1988 in east Niger. Experiences are being studied and used in the planning and organisation of new community managed water supplies, e.i.: 1. Development in macro-political and organizational framework (recipient country as well as donor) has been of major importance for the results obtained. 2. At the village level, problems encountered are often related to conflicts in management methods used by the traditional leadership and the "modern" management recommended or imposed by the project. Possibilities and consequences of bypassing traditional leadership have to be considered carefully. 3. Water is valued in the Sahel region, and a cost-efficient symbiosis with traditional water supplies can be observed: The improved water supply is used for drinking water whereas the cheaper, traditional water supplies continue to be used for other needs. 4. Local, private installation and maintenance capacity is being built up. A very low repair frequency on the solar technology used seems to be the most important obstacle for a maintenance system.
In general, the experience gained in the community managed water supplies has been positive. Community management can be a cheap and efficient organization form in rural areas, basically because it is highly motivating for the people involved. This way of organizing water supply projects in the Sahel region may represent an important development potentiel: Community empowerment related to water supplies can create a platform for other development initiatives.
Main activities of institution — Consultancies outside Scandinavia within the fields of water supply, rural development and environement.

Lykke, Anne Mette
Title — Sustainable Use of Natural Vegetation in the Sine Saloum Region in Senegal.
Keywords — Senegal, vegetation, savanna, conservation.
Abstract — The aim of my Ph.D. project is to analyse various aspects of the different vegetation types in the Delta du Saloum National Park, and on the basis of this to seek an understanding of the kind and degree of human impact possible without causing irreversible degradation of the vegetation.
The National Park covers various vegetation types; woodland, wooded grassland, gallery forest, mangrove and other saline vegetation types. On the basis of a vegetation analysis, I seek an understanding of the vegetation structure and composition and relate it to the way it is used by the local people, especially the impact of fire will be analysed. The work is carried out in cooperation with the Service of the National Parks in Senegal and with the University of Dakar, Senegal.

Madsen, Jesper
Keywords — Shelterbelt, sand dune fixation, agroforestry.
Abstract — 1978-79 and 82-83: Shelterbelt consultant.
1980-81: Zaire, Head of Forest Service, Agrifor (private company).
1984-85: Senegal, Associate expert, Probovil (FAO project).
1986-90: Supervisor for shelterbelts consultants.
1987: Sudan, sand dune fixation along the Nile (DANIDA project).
1988: Somalia, Forester, sand dune fixation (UNSO project).
1990-: Head of Shelterbelt Division.

Markussen, Birgitte
Title — Development Support Communication.
Keywords — Educational video, production, training.
Abstract — Based on several fieldworks in Latinamerica in relation to FAO Development Support Communication projects, ways of monitoring the individual and the social effects of training as well as video production is being elaborated.
Have worked as short term educational video consultant in Northern Nigeria for Danagro Adviser A/S in 1991 and 1992, doing training in educational video production, and worked out precedents for different categories of video productions as well as strategies for large-scale dessimination of training programmes according to the local culture. Among the themes I have worked with in Northern Nigeria are: tree nurseries, tree planting, wood stoves, self help, and communal development.

Meyer, Marlene
Title — Change in Agricultural Land-use In Northern Ghana in relation to Environmental and Socio-economic Factors.
Keywords — Land-Use, remote-sensing, semi-arid farming systems, landscape ecology.
Abstract — On the basis of historical aerial photos, historical land-use maps and recent SPOT images, the development in farming systems and agricultural land-use and landscape in Northern Ghana is analysed over a thirty years period. The study is performed on village, district and regional level.

Nicolaisen, Ida
Title — The Carlsberg Foundation's Nomad Research Project.
Keywords — Cultural and social studies.
Abstract — As editor of the Carlsberg Foundation's Nomad Research Project and engaged in anthropological studies among pastoral nomads and hunting gathering peoples of the Sahel, I shall present a brief outline of the above mentioned research project. My own part in this is a) to prepare a second edition and write up a second volume of Johannes Nicolaisen's book: Ecology and Culture of the Pastoral Tuareg; b) write up field material from the nomadic Haddad of Tchad.

Nielsen, Ivan
Title — Ongoing botanical research in Senegal carried out by the Department of systematic botany, AAU.
Keywords — Vegetations studies, floristic inventories, documentation centres, Senegal, Dacar.

Noppen, Dolf
Main activities — Project planning, appraisal and review.
Abstract — Most recent mission for DANIDA was a project formulation in Niger: Water and Resource Management.
Oksen, Peter
Title — Natural Resource Management in the village Karagou-Mandaram, south-western

region of Diffa Department, Niger.

Keywords — Land-use, farming-systems, bas-fonds, cuvettes, agricultural development, land- tenure, remote sensing.

Abstract — At village level a description and analysis of the exploitation-system is made. The exploitation-system consists of 3 primary strategies based on each a landscape-type. The landscape-types or natural resources available to the village are delimited and on this basis the objectives and strategies of the peasants are analyzed and the major production constraints identified.

The study is based on three months field work in the village and Landsat satellite images will be used in the analysis of natural resources.

Olesen, Grethe Ahlmann
Main activities — Field work in Somalia 1989. Agropastoralists' use and abuse of the somali environment.

Olsen, Lise Malling
Keywords — Development issues, including women in development.
Abstract — Education and vocational training; Training needs; Gender aspects in French-speaking West africa.

Poulsen, Gunnar
Title — Freelance consultant, operating mainly in Africa.
Keywords — Sustainable production systems/Socio-economic, demographic factors.
Abstract — My main concern during recent years has been to assist smallholders in developing countries to cover basic necessities by the exploitation of natural resources, without placing in jeopardy those physical and biological elements of the resource base which are indispensable for their long-term survival. In this same context I am firmly convinced that technical/agronomic solutions alone, hardly ever will solve problems but that assistance, in order to be meaningful, must get to grips with the whole range of socio-economic factors as well as culturally-induced patterns of behaviour which underlie people's decision-making and prospects for innovative action. I am also deeply concerned about the predicament: How shall we go about attempting to raise the sustainable productivity of farmland sufficiently rapidly to prevent the otherwise unavoidable destruction of still remaining, important forest ecosystems, as a consequence of expansion of farmland. Together with improved family planning, I see such action as the only means available for saving many remaining forests with what they include of flora and fauna, importance as water catchments and homeland values for ethnic groups.

Rasmussen, Christa Nedergaard
Keywords — environment, education, rural areas, children, youth.
Abstract — Environmental Education projects for children and young people inside and outside the school systems.

A second 3 year phase has just been prepared for Senegal together with the Senegalese Red Cross and Enda Tiers Monde. The project area is the Thies and St. Louis regions.

In Burkina Faso, the project is already in the second phase — implemented by the Burkinian Red Cross in cooperation with the Naam groups in Yatenga and Soum. In Sudan, the project implementation has been very slow. The project is implemented in the Ed Duiem Region by the Sudanese Red Crescent in Cooperation with the Institute of Environmental Studies at the Khartoum University and the Barkt-Er-Ruda Teaching Centre.

An inter-regional seminar on Environmental Education for Children and Youth is planned for 1993. The idea is to contribute to the creation of a west african network for environmental education experiences. A long term goal is to let members of the local project teams in Burkina Faso and Senegal be external, short term experts helping to identify and implement a similar project in Mali (1994). Also supervising some small gardening projects in Senegal and a sewing centre in Burkina Faso.

Reenberg, Anette

Title — 1) Monitoring land-use and production sustainability in Northern Burkina Faso (research grant from DANIDA/RUF).

2) Natural resource mapping and the monitoring potential of satellite images (Dep. Diffa, Niger) (cooperation with Krüger Consult).

Keywords — land-use, landscape types, land degradation, agricultural systems, monitoring changes, remote sensing.

Abstract — (activity 2 only — 1 is the continuation of activities presented at the 1992-workshop).

The objectives of the study have been defined by the TOR delimiting an integrated work including in addition components dealing with hydrogeology, agrostology, wood resources and socio-economic issues. The present sub-component (L'etude cartographique des resources naturelle) has the following aim: — to present a mapping of the natural environment in the region mainly based on satellite images, — to evaluate the potential and limitations for the utilization of satellite based and other possible information in environmental monitoring, and — to suggest a system suitable for the future monitoring of environmental resources. This includes a general presentation of the landscape types (unités de paysage), characterized by geomorphology, vegetation, land-use etc. Furthermore, sand encroachment is evaluated with respect to local variations as well as development trends, and changes in land-use strategies are investigated. Some of the themes are demonstrated for selected test areas only, as the aim of the work is — on a limited budget — to provide a general mapping of the natural in the study region and an evaluation of the potential utility of satellite images for a future and more detailed resource monitoring.

Schaumburg-Müller, Henrik

Keywords — Structural adjustment policies.
Main activities — Member of DANIDA´s research council.

Sihm, Poul A.

Keywords — Pastoral Development, Natural resource Management, Rural Development in the Sahel in East- and West Africa.
Main activities — Dairy Development in the Middle East (FAO) 1964-67.
Animal Health and Production Development Aghanistan 1967-73.
Development Economics 1-year diploma at Oxford University.
World Bank as Project Officer Pastoral Development 1974-91.
Retired from the World Bank November 1991.
Started own consulting firm, 1992.

Tarp, Elsebeth

Keywords — Planning, Monitoring of DANIDA financed activities.
Abstract — Involved in DANIDA activities in Bukina Faso (natural resource management).

Thioune, Ousmane

Title — Environmental Education in the Sahel — An Analysis of the Environmental Education Techniques Suitable for use in rural areas in Senegal.
Keywords — education, environment, Sahel, rural, techniques, conservation.
Abstract — Research: A description of the environmental awareness raising initiatives in rural areas in Senegal (governmental and non-governmental organisations). A description of how the senegalese rural people understand and conceptualize the environment, how they realize and identify causes and effects of the environmental problems.

It is acknowledged that in order to properly communicate environmental information, there is the need to employ the most suitable techniques, whose use should be adequate to the relevant target group. Based on this need, this project is aimed at identifying and testing a number of environmental education strategies suitable for use in rural areas in a developing country, namely Senegal, with a view to promoting the country's economic, social and political reality, the present proposal is expected to offer realistic suggestions of means to promote environmental education in areas which do not normally benefit from awareness-raising strategies.

Project: Preparation of an environmental education plan for rural areas in Senegal. Actually, a first draft of a project formulation is being submitted to environment project funds.

Zethner, Ole
Title — Integrated land management in Sahel.
Keywords — Forestry, Agro-forestry, Integrated pest management.
Abstract — Planning, Identification, Evaluation of forestry/agro-forestry, soil conservation activities in Sahel/Sudan areas. Assisted DANIDA with sector planning for tropical/sub-tropical forestry. Worked on integrated pest management of basic food crops in regional CILLS project (1983-88) (Insect pests, diseases, weeds). Presently writing a chapter on integrated pest management in Africa as part of forth-coming UNEP publication.

Institutions and private firms

THE ROYAL VETERINARY AND AGRICULTURAL UNIVERSITY
Danish Centre for Tropical Agriculture & Environment

The "Danish Centre for Tropical Agriculture and Environment" (DCTAE), is an inter-disciplinary coordinating department created to meet the need for professional international service from The Royal Veterinary and Agricultural University (KVL), Copenhagen. The centre started July 1, 1992 on request from KVL's scientific staff. DCTAE is financed through overheads from the KVL's Third World engagements. The centre is lead by a board with seven members, on behalf of a Centre Council. All members of the centre are council members.

DCTAE main activities:
* Study programs for individual or groups at Ph.D., M.Sc. and Diploma level.
* Research and development.
* Management contracts.
* International consultancies.
* Render KVL's resource base available for international agencies and private companies.
KVL Tropical Resource Base comprises:
* More than 130 scientists with research and working experience in tropical agriculture.
* An average of 100 Ph.D., M.Sc. & Diploma Students per year, from the third world.
* Staff from related sectoral research institutes.
* 3,000 students, in seven different disciplines, many with experience from the tropics.

KVL's areas of expertise concerning the Sahel:
1988-1991 Agricultural development strategies in the Sahel — An examination of the cereals marketing in Burkino Faso. Project leader: M. Speirs.
1993 DCTAE will most likely make a mission for the World Bank in the eastern part of Sahel (Ethiopia, Sudan and Djibouti (and Kenya and Uganda)). The mission will take place in the spring 1993. The aim of the mission is: Preparation of a Framework for Action on Agriculture Research in the East African region. The Fram-

ework for Action shall be designed for the East African National Agricultural Research Systems (NARSs), specifically with regard to: The food crops sector — Livestock production — Cash/export crops — Natural resource management and environmental protection (including agro-forestry). The missions task will also be to examine the quality and impact of NARS scientists' work and the effectiveness of multi-country and regional information network and to identify and recommend programs for research coordination and knowledge exchange. The Mission is lead by DCTAE.

I. Krüger Consult AS (KCO)

KCO activities in the Sahel
1. Water and rural development, Niger KCO is undertaking a major Danida Rural Development project in south-western Niger (Zinder and Diffa- departments). The project has the following components:

- Water supply by handpump to several hundred minor villages incl. establishment of village-based operation and maintenance and local repair and spare-part distribution.
- Solar-driven water supply to approx. 25 major villages, establishment of village committes responsible for operation, maintenance and money-collection to pay for repairs and spare-parts. Establishing a spare-part distribution system.
- Environmental protection activities such as tree planting, fencing to stop sand-erosion, bush-fire protection and -training.
- Promotion of gardening activities in "cuvettes", producing salad, tomatoes, onions, peppers and other vegetables for the markets in nearby towns.
- A broad study of a part of the Diffa-department (Goudoumaria) has just been finalized, dealing with a wide array of issues: cartography, hydrology, agrostology, animal husbandry, land-rights, wood-resources, as well as comprehensive village-case studies. The study shall form the basis for an integrated natural resource management project.

2. Regional solar energy programme, PRS, Western sahel KCO is undertaking an EEC-financed regional solar-energy study (Programme Regional Solaire) in the 5 western Sahel-countries: Senegal, Mauritania, Gambia, Cap Verte, Guinea-Bissau.
   The study will give the basis for deciding where some 300 solar-energy installations shall be installed in the 5 countries.
   A first phase of the project is already under implementation: In the five countries mentioned as well as in Chad, Niger, Mali and Burkina, several hundred solar-energy units have already been or are under installation for water-pumping, refrigeration, community electrification.
   As a separate project, KCO is undertaking an advisory function in Niger as regards the implementation of the first phase.

3. Water supply, Sudan KCO is undertaking a project for Danish Red Cross, mapping and improving traditional wells and training local communities in management of water and wells in Red Sea Hills district, Sudan. The project is community based and takes a participatory approach.

University of Aarhus, Moesgård, Denmark.
Department of Ethnography and Social Anthropology

The research at the Department of Ethnography and Social Anthropology in Aarhus is carried out as individual projects, which are co-ordinated into inter-cultural subjects such as: nationalism, identity, ethnic minorities, and development issues.

In the following the main research projects taking place in Sahel or in neighbouring areas will be presented, briefly:

- A Ph.D. project has just been completed by Inge Wittrup about the Mandinka culture in Gambia. The project concentrates on the relationship between the sexes, and especially on the women's development; including how periodic droughts influence the agricultural production of the women.
- Ingeborg Higashidani is finishing a Ph.D. (Magisterkonferens) on involuntary migration in Somalia. Her work is based on field work in refugee camps in Somalia. One of her main conclusions concerns the change of the relationship between the sexes during their lives as refugees. A change which is causing problems when the authorities still approach the refugees according to the traditional pattern of the sexes.
- Another Ph.D. (Magisterkonferens) project is going on in Somalia, concerning the notion of development in relation to the present situation in Somalia as well as in Ethiopia. This project is carried out by Grethe Ahlmann Olesen.
- The Ph.D. (Magisterkonferens) project of Birgitte Rasmussen deals with non-formal education and training programmes in rural development. The project focuses on how training material can be related to the local context, and how dissemination of training material can be accomplished with the crucial participation of the local population. The project is based on work performed in Peru, Mexico, as well as in Northern Nigeria.
- Christiane Oware Knudsen is doing research funded by Danida, on female circumcision in Ghana. The purpose of the research is an attempt to study female circumcision from a cultural perspective, in order to see whether or not such a practice has a place in a development process. The project involves an analysis of the equality of men and women, which was highlighted, internationally, during the United Nations Decade for Women from 1976 to 1985.
- The department has for some years been lacking a lecturer or a senior lecturer with a specialization in the Sahelian region. But starting from 1993, a lecturer has been appointed to work at the Department of Ethnography and Social Anthropology for four years with a regional specialization in West Africa which should strengthen the research in this area. The lecturer, Bjarke Paarup-Laursen, has been working with: cultural analysis, ritual studies, and recently with medical anthropology, focusing on the perception of diseases and the decisive factors involved with the choice of treatment in Northern Nigeria. His present appointment focuses on man's social and cultural organization in relationship to nature.

SAHEL WORKSHOP • 4-6 January, 1993
Sandbjerg Manor, Sønderborg, Denmark

PROGRAMME

MONDAY 4 January

Introduction by the Organisers
Leon Brimer

Population and Social Conflict
Chair: Christa N. Rasmussen

Environmental Problems and Political Security: the Horn of Africa.
Lecturer: Bryan Spooner, IUCN, England.

The Tuareg Conflict in Mali.
Lecturer: Gunvor Berge, Centre for Development and Environment, Oslo University, Norway.

Implications of Social Change on Household Strategies in the Sahel.
Lecturer: Camilla Toulmin, IIED, London, England.

Danish Activities in the Sahel
Chair: Christa N. Rasmussen / Claudia Heim

Presentation of Ongoing Projects and Programmes.
By representatives of research institutions, private companies, DANIDA and NGO's.

TUESDAY 5 January

Management of Natural Resources
Chair: Marlene Meyer / Lars Krogh

Impact of Non-African Meat Imports on Cattle Trade Between West African Countries.
Lecturer: Henri Josserand, Club du Sahel, Paris, France.

Food Crops and Food Security on a Regional Perspective.
Lecturer: Ernest Yonli, (CEDRES), University of Ouagadougou, Burkina Faso.

Cash Crops - the Example of Gum Arabic - and the French-Senegalese Research and Development Cooperation.
Lecturers: Jacques Vassal, Université Paul Sabatier, Toulouse, France and Mamadou Dione, DRPF/ISRA, Dakar, Senegal.
Management of Natural Forests in the West African Sahel Area.
Lecturer: Jöran Friis, International Rural Developement Centre, Uppsala University, Sweden.

Workshops

***Workshop A:* Constraints for Sustainable Management of Natural Resources — Local Perspective.**
Discussion leader: Leon Brimer.

Lecturers:
Lars Engberg Pedersen, Danish Business School: *The Role of Local Institutions. Programme de Gestion du Territoire, Burkina Faso.*
Ernest Yonli, CEDRES, Burkina Faso: *Cereal Banks in the Northern and Central Burkina Faso.*
Kristine Juul, Roskilde University Centre: *Social Conflict over Gum Extraction in Senegal.*

and others.

***Workshop B:* Constraints for Sustainable Management of Natural Resources — National and Regional Perspective.**
Discussion leader: Annette Reenberg.

Lecturers:
Mike Speirs, Danagro Adviser.: *Is Self-sufficiency of Individual Countries a Reasonable Solution to the Food Crisis in the Sahel?*
Per Christensen, Head Forester: *Sustainable Land-use with Reference to Natural Forests-Research, Management and People's Participation.*
Peter Ellehøj, Danida (formerly UNDP, Dakar): *The Problems of The CFA Monetarian Union.*
M. Salih, Nordic Africa Institute, Uppsala: *Pastoralism as an Underestimated Aspect of Sahelian Production Systems.*

and others.

***Workshop C:* Population and Social Conflicts.**
Discussion leader: Holger Koch Nielsen.

Lecturers:
Jerry Ndamba, Blair Research Laboratory, Zimbabwe: *The Impact of Demografic Changes on the Interrelations Between Health, Water and Environment — Bilharziosis as an Example.*
Alain Lefebvre, Anthropologist: *Changing Gender Relations Caused by Migration (Niger and Burkina Faso).*

and others.

WEDNESDAY 6 January

Panel Discussion
Chair: Tove Degnbol

The Danish Resource Base – Problems, Visions and Scope for Improved Cooperation.

Panel:
- Hans Jørgen Lundberg represents Danida.
- Thyge Christensen represents NGOs.
- Tove Degnbol represents research institutions.
- Jean-Pierre Zafyriadis represents private companies.

Evaluation
Chair: Marlene Meyer

Curicula of the invited Speakers

Gunvor Berge, mag. art. Born in 1954, she studied social antropology at the University of Oslo, where she graduated in 1985. Since 1987, she has been tied to the Norwegian Ministry of Foreign Affairs' research program in Mali, as well as working on a Ph.D.-thesis funded by the Norwegian Research Council, focusing on the Tuareg society in Northern Mali. Her place of work is the Centre for Environment and Development at the University of Oslo.

Mamadou Dione, B.Sc., M.Sc., Ph.D. Born in 1952, he studied Natural Sciences at Université Cheikh A. Diop de Dakar (Senegal), and Forestery at Université Laval, Faculté de Foresterie et Géodésie, Québec (Canada). He gained his Ph.D. from Université P. Sabatier de Toulouse (France). He has worked on problems concerning agroforestry in general and the production of gum arabic in particular since 1984. He is now head of the 'Station des Recherche Forestriere de M'Biddi' (Sénégal), thus being in charge of several programmes under the organisation ISRA – Direction des Recherches sur les Productions Forestieres.

Jöran Fries, born in 1929, has studied forestry at the Royal College of Forestry, now a faculty of the Swedish University of Agricultural Sciences in Uppsala, Sweden. After two years of work in Swedish forests he returned to the University, where he graduated as Dr. of Forrestry and was appointed Professor. After 20 years of research in forestry growth and yield he joined the International Rural Development Centre of the University, where he has mainly been dealing with projects in the Sahelian West Africa and in Tunisia. He has recently started a research project in Burkina Faso on the management of natural forests.

Henri Josserand, B.A., M.A., Ph.D. Born in 1948, he studied economics and political science at the University of Liberia, received a M.A. from the University of Toledo, Ohio, and a Ph.D. in natural resource management and economics from the University of Michigan, while working at the University of Michigan, Center for Research on Economic Development. Has spent about fifteen years doing research and policy analysis/advice in developing countries, especially west Africa, before joining the Paris-based OECD to work as staff economist at the Club du Sahel. Has worked mostly on the economics of production and marketing in traditional primary sector areas (livestock and fisheries), and in agricultural policy.

Jerikias Ndamba, B.Sc., Ph.D. Born in 1958, he studied biology at the University of Glasgow, U.K., where he graduated as B. Sc. (Hons) 1983. From 1984-1990 he worked as a Medical Research Officer at the Blair Research Laboratory, Zimbabwe. He joined the Royal Danish School of Pharmacy, Copenhagen 1990 as a Ph.D. student, completing his Ph.D. 1993, with the thesis 'Agronomic practices that influence the yield, molluscicide potency and phytochemistry of the berries of *Phytolacca dodecandra*, a plant molluscicide'. From 1990, he has been Senior Medical Research Officer at the Blair Research Institute (Zimbabwe), acting as the Head of the Schistosomiasis Section.

Bryan Spooner, B.Sc., M.Sc. Born in 1952, he studied Agriculture and Agrarian Development Overseas at Wye College, University of London and gained his M.Sc. in 1975. Self-trained in sociology and impact assessment he has spent 19 years working as an independent consultant in environment and development. He has worked in Africa, the Middle East, Asia and South-east Asia with NGO's consultancy companies and the UN aid agencies. In 1991 his research for the World Conservation Union (WCN) led to the publication "Fighting for Survival. Insecurity, People and the Environment in the Horn of Africa."

Camilla Toulmin, D.Phil. Born in 1954, she directs the Drylands Programme at the International Institute for Environment and Development, London. This programme combines research, information, training and activities in support of the NGO community in Africa. Having studied economics at university, Camilla has worked paricularly on agricultural and livestock production systems in the semi-arid regions of Africa, and spent two years carrying out fieldwork amongst the Bambara of central Mali, described in "Cattle, Women and Wells; Managing Household Survival in the Sahel", Oxford 1992. Currently, she is a member of the International Panel of Experts, constituted to support the negotiation of a global convention to combat desertification, due to be completed by June 1994.

Jaques Vassal, Dr. Born in 1993, he is Professor of Botany at the University Paul Sabatiér, International Institute for Vegetation Mapping, Toulouse, France. As taxonomist he published a new system of classification of the genus Acacia (Doctorat d'Etat 1972). He has developed research on Mimosoideae and created the International Group for the Study of Mimosoideae, which he managed from 1973 to

1992 (7 international meetings — annual Bulletins). From 1988 to 1992 he directed a pluridisciplinary research programme to improve gum productivity of Sahelian Acacias (joint project France/Senegal).

Ernest Yonli, Researcher at the "Centre d'Etudes, de Documentation et de Recherche Ecopnomique et Sociale" (CEDRES), University of Ouagadougou, Burkina Faso, was born in 1956 and graduated in 1984 at University of Paris, where he studied economics. He is now working on a doctoral thesis dealing with cereals banks and agricultural development policy in Burkina Faso for several years, in collaboration with the systems, marketing and food security issues in Burkina Faso, and has also worked as a consultant for the Dutch aid programme. His present research focuses on the organization of cereals banks in the northern provinces of the country, and his work forms part of a joint research programme between a number of institutes in Burkina Faso, Ghana and the Netherlands.

Address List*

Andersen, Kirsten Ewers, Rambøll & Hannemann, Bredevej 2, 2830 Virum

Berge, Gunvor, Center of Development and Environment, University of Oslo, P.B. 1106, 0166 Oslo 3, Norway

Bolwig, Simon, Institute of Geography, University of Copenhagen, Øster Voldgade 10, 1350 Copenhagen K.

Boussoufa, A., Rambøll, Hannemann og Højlund, Jernbanevej 65, 5210 Odense NV

Bovin, Mette, Strandgade 49 B, 3000 Helsingør

Brimer, Leon, Inst. of Pharmacology and Toxicology, Royal Veterinary and Agricultural University, Bülowsvej 13, 1870 Frederiksberg C

Brøgger-Jensen, Steffen, Ornis Consult, Vesterbrogade 140, 1620 Copenhagen V

Bøgh, Eva, 'Hapex -Sahel", Institute of Geography, University of Copenhagen, Henrik Ibesensvej 49, st.tv., 1813 Frederiksberg C

Carus, Hanne, I. Krüger Consult A/S, Gladsaxevej 363, 2860 Søborg

Christensen, Per Christian, Head Fortester, Højskolevej 29, 8680 Ry

Christensen, Thyge, Ass. d'Amitié Danemark - Burkina Faso, Overdrevet 21, 8382 Hinnerup

Degnbol, Tove, Institute of Geography, Roskilde University Center, P.B. 260, 4000 Roskilde

Dione, Mamadou, Institut Sénégalais de Recherches Agricoles, Direktion des Recherches sur les Production Forestières, BP 2312, Dakar, Senegal

Ellehøj, Peter, DANIDA, Asiatisk Plads 2, 1448 CopenhagenK

Ellemann, Lis, Institute of Botany, University of Århus, Nordlandsvej 68, 8240 Risskov

Fries, Ingrid, Backvägen 7, 194 40 Upplands Väsby, Sweden

Fries, Jöran, IRDC, Swedish University of Agricultural Sciences, P.B. 7005, 75007 Uppsala, Sweden

Heim, Claudia, Thorshavnsgade 10, 2.tv., 2300 København S

Houlberg, Rikke, I. Krüger Consult A/S, Gladsaxevej 363, 2860 Søborg

Jacobsen, Carl Christian, I. Krüger Consult A/S, Gladsaxevej 363, 2860 Søborg

Jensen, Flemming Pagh, Ornis Consult, Vesterbrogade 140, 1620 Copenhagen V

Johansen, Henrik Brade, I. Krüger Consult A/S, Gladsaxevej 363, 2860 Søborg

Josserand, Henri, Club Du Sahel, 39 Bd Sujet, 75775 Paris, France

Juul, Kristine, International Development Studies, Roskilde University Center, P. B. 260, 4000 Roskilde

Jørgensen, Agnete, Institute of Botany, University of Århus, Nordlandsvej 68, 8240 Risskov

Jørgensen, Karl Aage, Rambøl & Hanneman, Jernbanevej 65, 5210 Odense NV

Koch-Nielsen, Holger, Development Advisor, Højskolevej 17, Vallekilde, 4534 Hørve

Krogh, Lars, Institute of Geography, University of Copenhagen, Øster Voldgade 10, 1350 Copenhagen K

Larsen, Carl Erik Schou, Center for Tropisk Jordbrug, Rolighedsvej 23, 1958 Frederiksberg C

Larsson, Helena, Dept. of Physical Geography, University of Lund, Solvegatan 13, 223 62 Lund, Sweden

Lawesson, Jonas Erik, Institute of Botany, University of Århus, Nordlandsvej 68, 8240 Risskov

Lefebvre, Alain, Tagensvej 88, 2. tv., 2200 Copenhagen N.

Leth-Nissen, Søren, FAO, c/o Provincial Fish Culture, P.O. Box 510738, Chipata, Zambia

Lillebæk, Jens, I. Krüger A/S, Gladsaxevej 363, 2860 Søborg

Lundberg, Hans Jørgen, DANIDA, Asiatisk Plads 2, 1448 Copenhagen K

Lykke, Anne Mette, Institute of Botany, University of Århus, Nordlandsvej 68, 8240 Risskov

Madsen, Jesper, Danish Land Development Service, Hedeselskabet, P.B. 110, 8800 Viborg

Marcussen, Henrik Secher, Institute of Geography, Roskilde University Centre, P. B. 260, 4000 Roskilde

Markussen, Birgitte, University of Århus, Dept. of Soc. Anthropology, Moesgård, 8270 Højbjerg

Meyer, Marlene, Institute of Geography, University of Copenhagen, Øster Voldgade 10, 1350 Copenhagen K

Michelsen, Jette, DANIDA, Asiatisk Plads 2, 1448 Copenhagen K

Ndamba, Jerikias, Dansk Bilharziose Laboratorium, Jægersborg allé 1D, 2920 Charlottenlund; *present address*: Blair Research Laboratory, Josia Tongogara Avenue, PO Box 8105, Cau Seway, Harare, Zimbabwe

Nicholaisen, Ida, Institute of Anthropology, University of Copenhagen, Frederiksholms kanal 4, 1220 Copenhagen K

Nielsen, Ivan, Institute of Botany, University of Århus, Nordlandsvej 68, 8240 Risskov

Noppen, Dolf, Nordic Consulting Group, Jaris Nosevej 9, 2670 Greve

Oksen, Peter, Institute of Geography, University of Copenhagen, Øster Voldgade 10, 1350 Copenhagen K

Olesen, Grethe Ahlmann, Knudrisgade 37, 8000 Århus

Olsen, Lise Malling, Women and Development, KULU, Dr. Margrethesvej 11, 4. sal, 8200 Århus N

Pedersen, Lars Engberg, Center of Development Studies, Gammel Kongevej 5, 1610 Copenhagen V

Poulsen, Gunnar, Forestry and Landuse Consultant, Egevænget 1, Gadevang, 3400 Hillerød

Rasmussen, Christa Nedergaard, Danish Red Cross, Dag Hammerskjölds Allé 28, 2100 Copenhagen Ø, Denmark

Reenberg, Annette, Institute of Geography, University of Copenhagen, Øster Voldgade10, 1350 Copenhagen K

Salih, Mohammed, Nordic Africa Studies, P.B. 1703, 75147 Uppsala, Sweden

Schaumburg-Müller, Henrik, Copenhagen Business School, Dalgas Have 15, 2000 Frederiksberg

Sihm, Poul A., PIA Consult, Døvlingvej 2, 6933 Kibæk

Speirs, Mike, Danagro Adviser, Granskoven 8, 2600 Glostrup

Spooner, Bryan, Pendaner Hampton Lane, Near Brook Ashford, Kent TN 25 5PN, England

Strømgaard, Peter, DANIDA, Asiatisk Plads 2, 1448 Copenhagen K

Tarp, Elsebeth, DANIDA, Asiatisk Plads 2, 1448 Copenhagen K

Thioune, Ousmane (ENDA- Dakar), Pt.: Research Unit on Environmental Education and Development, Dep. of Env. Science, University of Bradford, Bradford, West Yorkshire BD7 1DP, England, U.K.

Toulmin, Camilla (IIED), International Inst. of Environment & Development, 3 Endsleigh Street, London WC1 H0DD, U.K.

Vassal, Jacques, Institut de la Carte International de la Végétation, Université Paul Sabatier, 39 Allées J. Guesde, 31 062 Toulouse cedex, France

West, Flemming, DANIDA, Asiatisk Plads 2, 1448 Copenhagen K

Yonli, Ernest, CEDRES, University of Ouagadougou, B. P. 7164, Ouagadougou 03, Burkina Faso

Zafiryadis, Jean-Pierre, I. Krüger Consult A/S, Gladsaxevej 363, 2860 Søborg

Zethner, Ole, Danagro Adviser, Granskoven 8, 2600 Glostrup

* When nothing else is indicated, the address is in Denmark.